Macromedia® Contribute™ For Dumm

Cheat Sheet

P9-AOW-133

WITHDRAWN

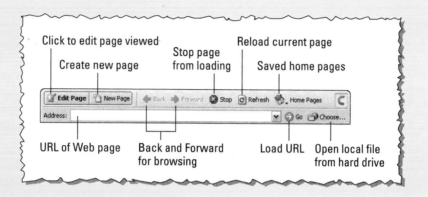

Click to edit page viewed

Create new page

Stop page from loading

Reload current page

Saved home pages

URL of Web page

Back and Forward for browsing

Load URL

Open local file from hard drive

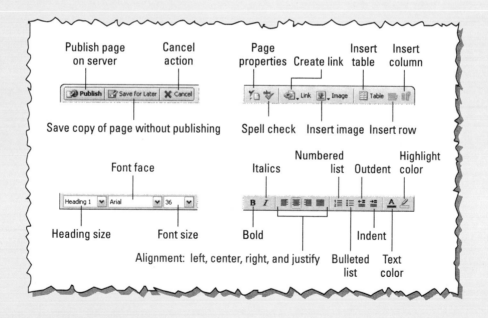

Publish page on server

Cancel action

Page properties

Create link

Insert table

Insert column

Save copy of page without publishing

Spell check

Insert image

Insert row

Font face

Italics

Numbered list

Outdent

Highlight color

Heading size

Font size

Bold

Indent

Alignment: left, center, right, and justify

Bulleted list

Text color

For Dummies: Bestselling Book Series for Beginners

Macromedia® Contribute™ For Dummies®

Cheat Sheet

Set colors   Page title   Locate background image

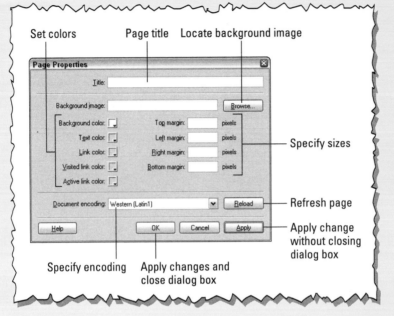

Specify sizes

Refresh page

Apply change without closing dialog box

Specify encoding   Apply changes and close dialog box

Alter image size   Reset actual image size

Locate image file

Specify alignment

Specify image border

Apply changes without closing dialog box

Add spacing around image   Alternative text   Apply changes and close dialog box

Copyright © 2003 Wiley Publishing, Inc.
All rights reserved.
Item 3751-2.
For more information about Wiley Publishing,
call 1-800-762-2974.

For Dummies: Bestselling Book Series for Beginners

Macromedia®
Contribute™
FOR
DUMMIES®

by Janine Warner and Frank Vera

WILEY

Wiley Publishing, Inc.

APR 7 2004

Macromedia® Contribute™ For Dummies®

Published by
Wiley Publishing, Inc.
909 Third Avenue
New York, NY 10022

www.wiley.com

Copyright © 2003 by Wiley Publishing, Inc., Indianapolis, Indiana

Published by Wiley Publishing, Inc., Indianapolis, Indiana

Published simultaneously in Canada

For general information on our other products and services or to obtain technical support, please contact our Customer Care Department within the U.S. at 800-762-2974, outside the U.S. at 317-572-3993, or fax 317-572-4002.

Wiley also publishes its books in a variety of electronic formats. Some content that appears in print may not be available in electronic books.

Library of Congress Control Number:

ISBN: 0-7645-3751-2

Manufactured in the United States of America

10 9 8 7 6 5 4 3 2 1

1B/SQ/QS/QT/IN

WILEY is a trademark of Wiley Publishing, Inc.

About the Authors

Janine Warner is an author, newspaper columnist, and university instructor.

Her many books about the Internet include *Contribute For Dummies, Dreamweaver MX For Dummies,* and *50 Fast Dreamweaver Techniques*. She also teaches a Dreamweaver course at The University of Southern California in the Annenberg School for Communications.

A frequent speaker at industry events in the US and abroad, Janine's syndicated newspaper column, *Beyond The Net,* appears in print and online, including in *The Miami Herald*.

Janine draws on many years of Internet experience and has managed a wide range of Web projects. From 1994 to 1998, she ran Visiontec Communications, a Web design company that served such diverse clients as Levi Strauss & Company, Airtouch International, and ConnectMedia.

From 1998 to 2000, she worked for The Miami Herald, first as their Online Managing Editor, and later as Director of New Media, managing a team of designers, programmers, journalists, and sales and marketing staff. She also served as Director of Latin American Operations for CNET Networks, an international technology media company.

An award-winning former reporter, Janine earned a degree in journalism and Spanish from the University of Massachusetts, Amherst, and worked for several years in Northern California as a reporter and editor. She speaks fluent Spanish and some Portuguese. To learn more, visit www.janinewarner.com.

Frank Vera is a Web development consultant who specializes in programming solutions for dynamic Web sites.

With more than seven years programming experience on the Web, Vera specializes in high-end Web site development using HTML, XML, Vignette StoryServer and Syndication Server, PHP, Tcl, C++, Visual Basic, Java, Perl, ASP, Oracle, and MySQL. He also has extensive experience with Web design programs, including Macromedia Dreamweaver, and Microsoft FrontPage.

From 2000 to 2002, Vera worked for ZDNet Latin America, first as Publishing Operations Manager, and later as Director of Technology, where he managed technical operations, wrote documentation on proprietary systems, and conducted training programs for staff in the US and Latin America. Prior to that, he served as System Administrator for PP Corp. in Miami, Florida.

Vera studied Computer Animation at the Art Institute of Fort Lauderdale and is a Microsoft Certified Systems Engineer.

Dedication

We dedicate this book to everyone who wants to "contribute" to the wonderful world of the Web.

Authors' Acknowledgments

Janine Warner: I used to try to thank everyone I could think of in my books — former teachers, mentors, friends — but I always felt I was forgetting someone (please forgive me if you're one of those wonderful people).

These days, I feel that I have been graced by so many wonderfully supportive people that I can't possibly thank them all — no publisher will give me enough pages for that. So I'll focus these acknowledgements on the people who made *this* book possible.

First, let me thank my wonderful coauthor for helping me deliver this manuscript on time and for adding his experience as a Web site administrator to ensure readers get everything they need out of this book. Frank, your attention to detail, diligence about deadlines, and casual wit and charm helped me get through this book with a lot less stress.

Special thanks to my fabulous editor, Andrea Boucher, who always manages to give my books special attention, even with all the other demands on her time. Andrea, your sense of humor, gentle reminders, and high standards are always appreciated.

Thanks to my well-traveled acquisitions editor, Bob Woerner, who I finally had the pleasure of meeting in SF this past year. Without you, this book would never have happened. Thanks for having faith in me, for pushing to make this happen, and for supporting the project every step of the way.

Finally, I must always thank my four fabulous parents, Malinda, Janice, Helen, and Robin, and to that list I add the newest member of my family. Thank you, Daniel, for enriching my life and for understanding when I had to disappear every once in a while to finish this book.

Frank Vera: I have to start with saying that I am very grateful to Janine for asking me to help her with this book. In the few years that we've known each other, you have been a welcome addition to my life. Your encouraging words and optimism have, at times, pushed me along when nothing else would (even though you didn't know it at the time). Janine, thank you for being my friend and for being the only person you know how to be: you.

My family has always been an awesome source of support and drive in my life. My parents, Elsa and Francisco Vera: Thank you for bringing me into this world. Without your love and example, I never could have accomplished anything in my life. My little sister, Dr. Dinorah Vera, MD: Dee, you are without question the best example of how to reach for the stars and actually get there. Your persistence, and maybe downright stubbornness, has always impressed me. I measure my success, or sometimes my lack thereof, by comparing to myself you. Thanks, Dee. To my older sisters and their husbands, Susy and Sergio Morales and Magda and Peter Portilla: Thank you for listening to my mindless ramblings and guiding me when I needed it. To my nephews and their wives, Danny Portilla, Sandy and Fabian Portilla, and Gracie and Gaby Alvarez: Thanks for putting up with my oh-so-exciting discussions about computers, but especially to my nephews' wives: Thanks for letting me for take so much of your husbands' time with silly things.

I want to thank a couple of my professors, Richard Orr, and Trudy McNair: Without your support and patience, I never could have worked on this book. The editor of this book, Andrea Boucher: Thanks for all of the hard work, attention to detail, and for helping me with technical difficulties along with Ronald Terry.

Finally, I want to thank friends and people who have influenced me along the way: Ivonne Berkowitz (we've never met, but I borrowed this idea from you), Generosa Gonzales (Tia), Norys Hernandez, Thomas Santanta, Adriana Peña, William James King II, Drew Guilliland, Carlos Alejo, Sheila Mayoral, Christi Ackerson, Debby Wuhl, Craig Paterson, Warren Van Der Woude, Farrell and Jan Ackerman, Francisco Rivera, Miguel Peralta, Tatiana and Bernardo DeAraujo, Manuel Alonso (Senior and Junior), Peter Schmidhoffer, Justo Sardiñas, Dave Marcotte, Robinson Mejia, Rene Ruiz, and countless others. Thank you for being a part of my life and helping to make me who I am.

Publisher's Acknowledgments

We're proud of this book; please send us your comments through our online registration form located at www.dummies.com/register/.

Some of the people who helped bring this book to market include the following:

Acquisitions, Editorial, and Media Development

Project Editor: Andrea C. Boucher

Acquisitions Editor: Bob Woerner

Technical Editor: Danilo Celic

Editorial Manager: Carol Sheehan

Media Development Manager: Laura VanWinkle

Media Development Supervisor: Richard Graves

Editorial Assistant: Amanda Foxworth

Cartoons: Rich Tennant
(www.the5thwave.com)

Production

Project Coordinator: Kristie Rees

Layout and Graphics: Seth Conley, Sean Decker, Tiffany Muth, Jeremey Unger

Proofreaders: Laura Albert, David Faust, John Greenough, TECHBOOKS Production Services

Indexer: TECHBOOKS Production Services

Publishing and Editorial for Technology Dummies

    Richard Swadley, Vice President and Executive Group Publisher

    Andy Cummings, Vice President and Publisher

    Mary C. Corder, Editorial Director

Publishing for Consumer Dummies

    Diane Graves Steele, Vice President and Publisher

    Joyce Pepple, Acquisitions Director

Composition Services

    Gerry Fahey, Vice President of Production Services

    Debbie Stailey, Director of Composition Services

Contents at a Glance

Table of Contents

Introduction

All the Web designers I know seem to be constantly racing against tight deadlines and always wishing they had more time to develop their sites even further. Whether you're an experienced Web designer or you are completely new to this Internet thing, you probably don't have time to wade through another thick book. That's why I love writing books in the *For Dummies* series — because they're not really for Dummies, they're for people who need to go from zero to up and running in a matter of hours, not weeks, even if they don't know anything about the topic before they buy the book.

About This Book

Macromedia Contribute For Dummies is designed to introduce you to all of the advantages of this program without making your head hurt. Macromedia designed Contribute to be easy to use; I designed *Macromedia Contribute For Dummies* to ease you into painlessly using Contribute so you can focus on the tasks at hand — keeping your Web site up to date and looking good, even when the Webmaster is out to lunch or on vacation. (If you're the Webmaster, you find what you need in these pages, too.)

You'll quickly discover how Contribute combines a powerful Web design tool with an easy-to-use interface to make Web design easy for anyone. With *Macromedia Contribute For Dummies*, you don't have to worry about all the technical details, like the cryptic HTML programming language. Instead, you're introduced to a program that's as easy to use as any Word processor, and you find out how to do all the important things — from adding text, images and tables to your pages to setting links and publishing your work on a Web server.

If you're a professional Web designer, this book introduces you to the newest member of Macromedia's professional Web design toolkit. You discover the power of this new companion program and how to set up your Web site so that others can update pages without your help. That means you won't have to bother with all of the minor requests and tedious changes that can fill your days and leave you little time for the more complex development work that only you can do.

Best of all, Macromedia designed Contribute in a way that makes it possible to control what can be changed and what can't by other people. That means that when a designer finishes developing a site in Dreamweaver, Contribute's updating features can be limited to only certain pages or certain parts of pages where regularly changes need to be made. That way, a Web designer can give clients or other staff members the ability to update a site without messing up the code or changing any of the key design elements by accident.

Note: Contribute was not designed to build a Web site from scratch. By that, I mean if you want to create a new Web site on your own, this isn't the program for you. Contribute is designed for people who want to edit or add pages to an *existing* Web site. If you need to develop an entire Web project, you need a more advanced program, such as Macromedia Dreamweaver. If your site was built with Dreamweaver, you'll find Contribute an ideal companion program designed to help you work on the site without needing to know all the complex features of Dreamweaver. Even if your site was built with another program, such as Microsoft FrontPage or Adobe GoLive, you can use Contribute to work on it, but you won't be able to use some of the more advanced features. Find more about working with other programs in Chapter 6.

How to Read This Book

I designed *Macromedia Contribute For Dummies* to make your life easier as you work with this Web program. You don't have to read this book cover to cover and memorize every word (although I'd be flattered, and worried about your social life, if you did). Instead, each section of the book stands alone, giving you easy answers to particular questions and step-by-step instructions for specific tasks so you can do what you need to do today — not after completing the equivalent of a college course.

Want to find out how to change the background color on a page, create a nested table, build HTML frames, or get into the really cool stuff like style sheets and layers? Then jump right in and go directly to the section that most interests you. Oh, and don't worry about keeping all these steps in your head. You don't have to memorize anything. The next time you need to do one of these tasks, just go back and review that section. Feel free to make notes in the margins and dog-ear the pages, too — I promise the book won't complain!

What Not to Read

Don't read anything in this book that doesn't interest you (and don't take it to the beach with you, unless you really want to). Some of the material here is for people just starting out in Web design; other parts cover really advanced features you may not need to know.

The first parts are designed for "contributors" to a Web site. Read these sections if you're new to Web design and someone just gave you the program to help update or add new content to the Web site. This book and most of the contents are designed to show you the basics of Web design and how to use Contribute to edit or add information to a Web site. If you fall into this category, let me reassure you that you probably don't have to read Part IV because that section is designed for the more technical types who will be administering your Web site. Part IV explains how to set up the site for new users, control who has access, and generally take care of all that behind the scenes stuff. Think of Part IV as the mechanic's guide and the rest of the book as instructions for driving. You don't have to worry about what's under the hood to make this thing work; you just have to learn where the steering wheel is and how to get it in gear.

If you are the mechanic (okay, maybe so you don't really get your fingernail's dirty, but you know what I mean), Part IV quickly shows you how to set permissions and get this new program integrated into your site. Rest assured, Macromedia made it easy so even if you've never had to control permissions before, you should be able to figure it out, especially if you follow the step-by-step exercises in Chapters 12, 13, and 14.

If you're a designer, the person who has the talent and experience to create pages in a program like Dreamweaver, then you'll want to stick with Dreamweaver. Contribute is a companion program with a very limited feature set. But I still wanted to make sure you'd get something out of this book, so glancing through the basics will help prepare you to answer the inevitable questions from your team members (the interface in Contribute is quite different from Dreamweaver, even though it works in much the same way). You also find guides to templates and Cascading Style Sheets (CSS) in Chapters 9 and 10. I include those, even though they apply more to Dreamweaver than Contribute, because they are the features in Dreamweaver that are most valuable if your team using Contribute, and I wanted to make sure that anyone using Macromedia's newest program also knows how to get the most out of Dreamweaver.

No matter who you are or what your previous experience is, I recommend you pick and choose the information that best fits what you want to do. Don't feel that you have to read everything to get the most out of this book. Use it as the reference that I intended it to be. You're reading this book because you need to know how to get your project up and running — so focus on the parts of this book you need now. I'm sure you don't have time for anything else!

Foolish Assumptions

When Macromedia developed Dreamweaver, it set out to make a professional Web development program and identified the target audience as anyone who spends more than 20 hours a week doing Web design. Fortunately for the rest of us, they designed Contribute to be super easy to use, even if you've never done Web design before.

Macromedia doesn't assume you're a professional Web developer and neither do I. In keeping with the philosophy behind the *For Dummies* series, this book is an easy-to-use guide designed for readers with a wide range of experience. It helps if you're interested in Web design and want to create a Web site, but that desire is all that I expect from you. In the chapters that follow, I show you all the steps you need to work on Web pages, and in the glossary in the back of the book, I give you all the vocabulary you need to understand the process.

Conventions Used in This Book

Keeping things consistent makes them easier to understand. In this book, those consistent elements are *conventions*. Notice how the word *conventions* is in italics? That's a convention I use frequently. I put new terms in italics and then define them so that you know what they mean.

When I type URLs (Web addresses) or e-mail addresses within regular paragraph text, they look like this: `www.janinewarner.com`. Sometimes, however, I set URLs off on their own lines, like this:

```
www.janinewarner.com
```

Yes, that's my personal site, and I'm not afraid to give you my e-mail address in this book. I've gotten lots of e-mail from readers over the various versions of this book and I always try to answer your unique questions as best I can, even if English isn't your first language.

I set off URLs so you can easily spot them on a page if you want to type them into your browser to visit a site. I also assume that your Web browser doesn't require the introductory `http://` for Web addresses so I leave that part out, but if you use an older browser, remember to type this before the address.

Even though Contribute makes knowing HTML code virtually unnecessary, you may have to occasionally wade into HTML waters. So I set off HTML code in the same monospaced type as URLs:

```
<A HREF="http://www.janinewarner.com">Janine's Web Site</A>
```

(That's the HTML code that makes a URL a link to a Web page.)

When I introduce you to a set of features, such as options in a dialog box, I set these items apart with bullets so that you can tell that they're all related. When I want you to follow instructions, I use numbered steps to walk you through the process.

How This Book Is Organized

To ease you through the learning curve associated with any new program, I organized *Macromedia Contribute For Dummies* to be a complete reference. You can read it cover to cover (if you want), but you may find it more helpful to jump to the section most relevant to what you want to do at that particular moment. Each chapter walks you through the features of Contribute step by step, providing tips and helping you understand the vocabulary of Web design.

The following sections provide a breakdown of the parts of the book and what you'll find in each one so you can jump right to the section you want. You'll also find a comprehensive table of contents and a great index to help you find your way to just the information you need — when you need it.

Part I: Hitting the Web Running

This part introduces you to Contribute and covers getting started with the basics. Chapter 1 is designed to help you appreciate what you can do with Contribute and how it's different from Dreamweaver. You also find some important background about the Internet and Web design in general. I include this because I know most people who use Contribute are still very new to working on the Web. If all this seems too basic for you, or you're anxious to get started, then dive right into Chapter 2 and you find a handy reference to toolbars and menu options, along with how to set preferences and get started with this great little program. In Chapter 3, you find out how to edit existing pages, add new content, and format text so you can start adding information to your Web site.

Part II: "Contributing" to Your Web Site

Links are what make the Web go 'round, connecting one page to another and making it possible to display images and other elements on a Web page. In Chapter 4, you find out everything you need to know to link from one page to another, to link to a different Web site, and to create e-mail links. In Chapter 5, you discover how easy it is to add graphics to your pages, how to insert background images, and even find a few tips about where to get images you can use on your site — whether you're a graphics guru or not. Chapter 6 covers how to work on Web pages that are created in a program other than Dreamweaver. If your Web site was designed in Dreamweaver, you can skip this chapter, but if you're working on Web pages that were created in another program, such as Microsoft FrontPage or Adobe GoLive, this chapter helps you work around some of the unique challenges you'll face as you interact with pages created in those and other programs.

Part III: Looking Good (Even if You're Not a Designer)

In Chapter 7, you see how tables can be used on a Web page to create complex designs, something quite different from the way you generally use tables in a spreadsheet program and far more important than most new designers appreciate. In Chapter 8, you find all you need to know about working on a site that is designed with frames. Frames are one of the more complex features of the Web because one page is really made up of multiple pages, making it more difficult to edit sites designed in frames.

In Chapter 9, you get an overview of Cascading Style Sheets — how they work and how they can save you time. You find out how to apply CSS in Contribute, but you also get a list of style definition options available in Dreamweaver and see how to create and apply your first styles in both Contribute and Dreamweaver. I include both because this feature is so important in Contribute, but you can use CSS only in limited ways in Contribute — you have to use Dreamweaver if you want to actually create new style sheets.

In Chapter 10, you discover how important templates are for keeping design consistent and controlling what elements on a page can be changed and what elements are protected. Again, I cover everything you can do in Contribute, plus include some information about what's possible in Dreamweaver so that you have what you need to make the most of this feature.

Last, but certainly not least, in Chapter 11 of Part III, you find out how to publish your edited pages on the live Web site. This is the exciting part, where you get to see your work come to life, but it's also the part you have to be most careful of because this is where your work becomes public and visible to anyone looking at your Web site.

Part IV: The Administrator's Guide to Setting Up Contribute

This part is for Webmasters, IT staff, and individuals who want to administer their own sites and use Contribute to update them. If your job is only to edit and add new pages, you don't have to worry about all the techy stuff in this chapter. You don't need to know how to administer Contribute in order to use it to update a Web site.

Although this section is more technical than the first part of the book, you don't have to be a programmer or really techy to figure this out, especially with the easy to follow step-by-step exercises included here. In Chapter 12, you find out about setting up and managing new users and Contribute connections.

In Chapter 13, you discover how to control permissions and who can publish or make changes to the site. In Chapter 14, you find more about managing this collaborative environment and troubleshooting.

Part V: The Part of Tens

In the Part of Tens, you get ten time-saving tips for using Contribute, ten tips for managing and working within a Web design team, and ten great Web design tips that help ensure your pages look always look great, even if you're just getting started on the Web. You also find ten great Web sites that provide excellent examples of what's possible on the Web with Contribute and Dreamweaver.

Part VI: Appendixes

In the appendixes, I include a comprehensive glossary because one of the biggest obstacles to working on the Web is just understanding all the vocabulary. If you read something or hear something from one of the techs that you don't understand, look it up in this handy reference. You also get an appendix filled with great Web sites designed with Dreamweaver and Contribute.

Icons Used in This Book

This icon signals technical stuff that you may find informative and interesting but isn't essential for using Contribute. Feel free to skip over this stuff.

This icon indicates a tip or technique that can save you time and money — and a headache — later.

This icon reminds you of an important concept or procedure that you'll want to store away in your memory banks for future use.

This icon points you toward valuable resources on the World Wide Web.

Danger, Will Robinson! This icon warns you of any potential pitfalls — and gives you the all-important information on how to avoid them.

This icon tunes you into information in other *For Dummies* books that you may find useful.

Where to Go from Here

Turn to Chapter 1 to dive in and get started understanding the Web. You find a great overview of Web design and some important background to help you get off on the right side of the keyboard. Chapter 2 provides an overview of Contribute and gives you a good sense of all the things you can do with this program. If you're anxious to start editing your first pages, or you're on a tight deadline, jump into Chapter 3, which is designed to show you how to add some text or images to a page and get it up on your Web site right away. If you're responsible for setting up Contribute, administering permissions, and all that other really techy stuff, skip ahead to Chapter 12, full of information to make you look like a pro. Whatever you need, you should be able to use the table of contents or the index in the back to find the right chapter or page for the specific trick or technique you need. Jump right in to the section you need and don't miss a beat as you work to make those impossible Web design deadlines. Most of all, don't forget to have fun!

Part I
Hitting the Web Running

The 5th Wave   By Rich Tennant

THE GLACIER MOVEMENT PROJECT UPDATE THEIR WEB SITE

Camera ready? Wait a minute, hold it. Ready? Wait for the action... steady... steady... not yet... eeeasy. Hold it. Okay, stay focused. Ready? Not yet... steeeady... eeeasy...

In this part . . .

*I*f you're new to contributing to a Web site, Part I gets you caught up quickly. You get an introduction to working on the Web, a comprehensive guide to the features of Macromedia Contribute, and a tour of the toolbars, menus, and panels that make Contribute so easy to use.

Chapter 1

Hitting the Web Running

In This Chapter

▶ Comparing Contribute to Dreamweaver

▶ Understanding the evolution of the Web

▶ Understanding the design limits

▶ Targeting your market with a good design

*T*he Web has evolved from novelty to wild west to finally becoming a core business function that more and more people need to be able to "Contribute" to. As Web sites have become more complex, companies, universities, and nonprofit organizations have discovered that these Web sites take a lot of time and resources to maintain. Many are also realizing that the technical staff can't handle all the minor changes, let alone the major content updates demanded by the various departments, management, and staff. But hiring outside consultants, or training everyone on staff to make changes with a program as complex as Dreamweaver, is cost-prohibitive and time-consuming.

Enter Macromedia Contribute, a program designed to meet the challenge of Web site updating and maintenance by providing an incredibly easy to use interface that is fully-integrated with Dreamweaver, yet still priced competitively enough that you can afford to let many people in the office have their own copies.

If you're brand new to working on the Internet, take a deep breath and don't worry. This book is designed to ease you into a program that is designed to be super simple to use. What better way to get started on the Web? And, I promise, I'll hold your hand the entire time.

Comparing Dreamweaver and Contribute

I have always loved Dreamweaver (see in Figure 1-1) because it enables me to work faster and more efficiently than any other tool I've worked with for creating Web sites — and I've tried them all. In addition to this book, I wrote *Dreamweaver MX For Dummies,* which is designed to help you get the most out of Macromedia's comprehensive Web design program.

When I heard that Macromedia was coming out with a companion program designed to make it easy for people who've never worked on the Web before to help update Web sites, I knew it would also be a valuable tool.

If you're reading this book, you should appreciate that more and more people are being asked to help out with the company Web site. Few small companies can afford to keep enough full-time Web developers on staff to do all the Web site development themselves and it's expensive to hire outside consultants to make simple updates.

That's where Contribute comes in (see Figure 1-2). It serves as a companion to Dreamweaver and is a tool that can be shared with almost anyone in a company, not just the "technical" staff.

Contribute has all the power you need to edit existing pages, insert images, and even add new pages. Yet Macromedia's careful integration with Dreamweaver makes it possible for a Webmaster to "lock" any part of a page, preventing "contributors" from inadvertently causing problems (which means that you can't do too much damage, even if you're not sure what you're doing). This also means that the techs can sleep better knowing no one will create more work for them when they're supposed to be saving them time.

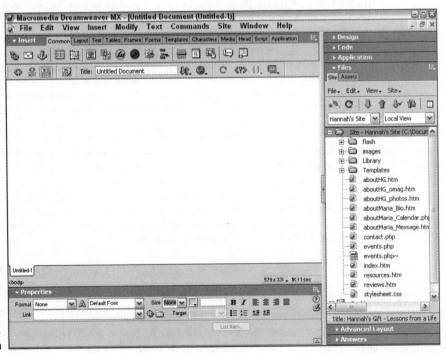

Figure 1-1:
Macromedia
Dream-
weaver MX.

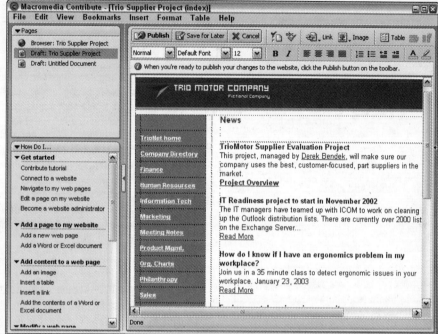

Figure 1-2:
Macromedia
Contribute,
the perfect
partner to
Dream-
weaver.

Contribute can even be used to update pages on the most advanced sites where advanced interactive programming and databases are used. But again, the most delicate and complicated sections of the pages are automatically locked, so Contribute users can update content without breaking links or altering the programming code that makes a dynamic site function.

Contribute includes support for some of the most powerful and time-saving features of Dreamweaver, such as templates (which are ideally suited to sites maintained by Contribute users). You can also use advanced HTML features, such as Cascading Style Sheets, which can be set up in Dreamweaver and then applied in Contribute to ensure uniform style across a page or entire site.

In keeping with Macromedia's open program development, Contribute can be used to update any Web site, even if it was created with Microsoft FrontPage, Adobe GoLive, or by a geeky programmer who still prefers to do all of the HTML coding manually in a simple text editor. (See Chapter 6 for more on working with these kinds of sites.)

What the heck are they talking about?

"We're gonna FTP the HTML, and they'll code in the ASP for the SQL DB. Okay?"

If you ever find yourself in a meeting, twiddling your pen and wishing you had access to subtitles while someone spouts technobabble like this, don't panic. You may be surprised to find out that even the techies don't always understand each other. And although you may have no idea what all of those acronyms mean, if you have good business sense and management experience, you're still probably better qualified than most programmers to manage your Web project.

Techie: This term is used loosely to refer to anyone who works with technology, including programmers, database specialists, and sometimes even designers who are technically savvy.

Reassure yourself with what you do know, and know how important you are. For starters, you probably know your alphabet, so you can at least identify the letters in all of those strange acronyms. Whether you just know a few other acronyms yourself, you undoubtedly know a few acronyms these techies don't know (PTA, CIA, MTV — even if they're not related to the Internet, the acronyms you already know count for something). Resist showing off with your own special vocabulary — no one likes a showoff. Instead, approach the task of studying these new terms with the confidence that you've gained from all the undoubtedly more difficult lessons you've had to learn to get into this situation in the first place.

You picked up this book, and that's a good start. My guess is that you feel you have to read it — or at least skim it — before you get to work in the morning. Fear not. This book, like all *For Dummies* books, is supremely skimmable. Bone up tonight, be prepared to say a few smart things in the morning, and then get back here and read the details.

Creating the Web

One of my favorite aspects of the World Wide Web is that it wasn't created by some marketing genius or advertising agency. No one with an MBA thought up this great business model and then set out to make millions by building a worldwide billboard. No, the Web was created by a group of geeky scientists in Switzerland who just wanted to share their technical diagrams with other geeks.

Prior to the Web, most of the information on the Internet was text, and it wasn't even formatted (no fancy fonts, colored text, or even bold and italics). But in the early 1990s, the Web changed all that, making it possible to display images and later sound, animation, and video. It was a breakthrough so radical that even its creators couldn't have predicted its impact.

Designing in an imperfect world

One difficult concept for many people to grasp is that on the Web, you don't
have total control over the design of your pages. People think they have
control just like they do when they're working with the printed page. In print,
you can choose cool fonts and set margins and leading (the space between
lines) to the exact distances you want. The Web doesn't work that way.
I know some graphic designers who became unhappy because they were
forced to work on the Web. One told me she felt handcuffed; another said he
was kicking and screaming all the way. Why do they hate it? Because they
can't use all the big, fancy graphics they want because of the *bandwidth
problem*. And they can't completely control the placement of every element
on the page.

The Web's greatest feature is also its greatest limitation. The Web was
designed to display information in a way that any computer on the planet can
view. That kind of versatility is great because it reaches large and diverse
audiences. But at the same time, it limits your design because it has to work
on so many different kinds of computers. Some of computers have large
monitors; others have small ones. Some monitors are black and white; others
are color. Some computers are loaded with cool fonts; most have only the
dozen or so they came with. Differences between Macintosh and Windows —
and many other systems you may never even heard of, such as UNIX and
Linux — also must be reckoned with. To make matters worse, browsers
that are used to view Web pages are also different. They support different
features, and even on the same computer, a page can look different when
viewed on different (older, for example) versions of a Web browser.

What do all of those differences mean for Web design? Web pages need to be
designed with versatility because they must adapt to achieve an optimum
presentation on each computer. Your best hope is designing a page that looks
great at the high end (a fast new computer with the latest browser) and yet
still appears passable at the low end (a laptop with a black and white display
and an older version of AOL software). In the following section, you discover
a bit about the history of how the Web became so complicated and a few
tricks to help compensate for it

Understanding the limits of HTML

To fully appreciate the design limitations of the Web, you must return to its
humble beginnings. Long, long ago (in the mid-1990s), the World Wide Web
was created by a group of systems programmers who wanted to share their
work with each other more easily. Unfortunately for the graphic designers
who've jumped on this technological bandwagon, these programmers didn't

care about fancy fonts and complex page designs. They merely wanted to be able to hyperlink their information. So, the first version of HyperText Markup Language (HTML) used to create Web pages was a simple set of formatting tags designed to provide basic formatting that worked on a wide variety of systems.

This simple formatting was accomplished in a number of ways; for example, by allowing only one image format — the Graphics Interchange Format (GIF) — and by using a default font that was likely to be on everyone's computer, typically Times font. (The JPEG image format was added later.) Then the programmers made font sizes relative rather than exact. Instead of setting text to an exact point size, they set up relative sizes. For example, the text of a Heading 1 HTML tag appears larger on-screen than the text of a Heading 2 tag, which is larger on-screen than the text of a Heading 3 tag, and so on. However, exactly how much larger depends on the browser and platform on which the headings are viewed. Designers back then couldn't specify the size of Heading 1, but they were assured that it would be bigger than Headings 2 and 3. That worked fine when the Web still was a dirt road traveled by academics.

No one could have predicted the phenomenal growth of the Web, but any graphic designer can tell you that artists and ad agencies were never going to settle for the first version of HTML. Then came the browser wars. The first browser was called Mosaic, and your tax dollars went a long way toward making it happen. But a student who worked on that project, Mark Andreeson had the foresight to realize that when the Web reached the broader audience, Mosaic's limited abilities to display formatted text and graphics would be a real letdown. When Mark was approached by Jim Clarke to make a commercial version of the browser, the NCSA (National Center for Supercomputing Applications) insisted that they call it something else. That something else became Netscape, and it was the most popular browser on the Web before Microsoft's Internet Explorer came into being. Today Mark is a multimillionaire, and the Web is a much prettier place.

But not all has been cheery fonts and other fancy features, and Netscape wasn't the only player in this process. In their effort to make the Web a more beautiful place, the creators of Navigator added their own features to HTML, but not everyone else adopted their innovations. America Online (AOL), for example, created its own browser, and AOL took a long time to catch on to Netscape Navigator's new design capabilities, but finally gave up and made Netscape available to its members. Yet for people who still use the old browsers provided by AOL, pages on the Web can look quite different than they do for those who use the latest version of Netscape Navigator or Internet Explorer.

The real competition has been between Netscape and Microsoft. Not to be outdone by anyone, Microsoft decided to create its own HTML features, even though they wouldn't be displayed in Navigator. The two companies now race to keep up with each other, and a good designer has to work hard to make sure Web pages look good to both audiences. If you want to reach the broadest audience, bear in mind that nearly a hundred different browsers are in use, including multilingual ones. Okay, you don't have to worry about all of them. Enough similarities exist so that you'll be safe if you design for the more common ones (Netscape Navigator and Microsoft Internet Explorer), but make sure you test in older versions of these browsers and not just the new one your designer is using.

Browsers are becoming more versatile by the second, and, considering that the two more popular browsers are free (or nearly free), you may nevertheless be surprised that you have to worry about people visiting your Web site with old versions of browsers. Although it may be hard to imagine, many people still are using that first version of Netscape Navigator, even though Netscape has gone through multiple upgrades since then. Why don't people upgrade? Some are reluctant to "fix what ain't broke." Then there's the fear that learning to use the new browser takes time, along with the general fear of downloading anything (or lacking the simple knowledge about how to do it). Still others fear that downloading software from the Internet causes their computers to contract viruses. And that's just among home users. Corporations tend to be slow to upgrade because they don't want to spend money retraining their employees more often than is necessary and, besides, upgrading an entire network is a big task.

What saves designers who want to use the latest features and still reach this diverse audience is that if a browser doesn't understand a new feature, it generally ignores it. That means that if you're careful about what you do, the worst thing that will happen is not all of your viewers will get to see all the coolest tricks on your site. What you must ensure is that all of your viewers can read the content and understand the meaning of the site, even if they don't hear the background sound or see the animation. The best way to ensure that your pages are okay is to test them while using a variety of browsers on a variety of platforms.

What's Hot and What's Not

Whether you want to look hot or cool, retro or ultramodern, you want to achieve your style without going broke. How can you look like a million bucks on a budget?

First, you become clear about the goals that you have for your Web site and who your audience is. Looking cool doesn't mean the same thing to everyone, so you want your site to target the people you most want to attract. What keeps the interest of four-year-olds is not the same as what holds the attention of baby boomers (well, not most of them, at least).

Always keep your audience in mind as you design your site. If you're running the Disney site, you need hot graphics, video, sound, and animations. But if you run the *Microprocessor Report* and your audience is a bunch of busy engineers who just want to get some information in a hurry, you need to make sure they don't have to wait long for graphics to download.

Many people on the Web today suffer from the *more-is-always-better syndrome.* But like most syndromes, it isn't healthy. The best Web sites often are the simplest, combining a few well-designed images to achieve an overall look that fits the image the company wants to portray. Likewise, simple often means easier to navigate. If you overwhelm your viewers with too many images and animations, you're likely to lose them.

A great design can make the smallest mom-and-pop shop look like it's made it to the top of its market. Following a few rules of good design enables you to make your business look more professional and your Web site easier to navigate. So before you get too far into working on your own Web site, take some time to look at what other people have done online. Yes, that's right, I have just given you my official blessing to spend a lot of time surfing the Web, even if your boss thinks that it's a waste of time. It isn't a waste of time — it's research, and if you're the boss, taking some time to do this kind of homework is even more important.

Ideally, you should look at a variety of Web sites, not just ones that are similar to your own. If you work in a bank, don't just look at other bank sites for ideas — look at travel agents and amusement park sites, check out movie sites, and scan through your home town newspaper online. If you're a parent, consider including your children in this effort — you may get some great advice. If you're managing a business and you're under 35, consider including your parents or grandparents to get the perspective of someone who's lived a little.

You find more interface and design tips in Chapter 17.

Chapter 2

Introducing Contribute

● ●

In This Chapter

▶ Installing and setting up the program

▶ Looking over the workspace

▶ Connecting to a Web site

▶ Specifying preferences

● ●

*B*efore you dive into the meat of this cool new program, let me reassure you right up front: Macromedia Contribute was designed to make it easy for anyone to work on the Web, even if you've never done any Web development before. Even if you're new to computers and have barely used the Internet, you can be up and running with this program and "contributing" to your Web site before you know it.

We can all use a little help getting started with something new, but that's what you have this book for, and I don't expect you to know anything about the program already. In fact, the first thing you find in this chapter are instructions for installing Contribute. If you've already done that part (or someone else has done that for you), jump ahead to the section on "Getting to Know the Workspace" and you can start finding out all the great things this program can do. If you're on deadline and need to know how to add something to your site fast, jump ahead to Chapter 3, but don't forget to come back here to get an overview of all the cool things you can do with this program.

Contribute is designed for people who want to edit or add pages to an *existing* Web site. If you need to develop an entire Web project, you're better off using a more advanced program, such as Macromedia Dreamweaver. Contribute is an ideal companion to Dreamweaver because it's designed to help you work on a Web site without needing to know all the complex features of Dreamweaver.

Installing and Launching Contribute

Before you can use any program, you have to install it. Well, *someone* has to install it. If you work at a big company, nonprofit, or university, it's quite likely that someone else (usually someone from the tech support department) will install this program for you. If not and you are faced with the challenge of installing this program on your own, here's where you start. If Contribute appears in the list of programs on your computer already, start the program and skip ahead to the next section, "Getting to Know the Workspace."

If you don't already have a copy of Contribute, you can download a free, fully-functional 30-day trial version or purchase a licensed version directly from Macromedia's Web site. Visit www.macromedia.com and follow the links to Contribute to find out more.

Always make sure that you have closed all the programs on your computer before you install a new program. That means that before you install a new program like Contribute, you should shut down any programs you have running, such as e-mail or word processing. When all the other programs are closed, you can start the install process by double-clicking the install icon.

If you have a copy of Contribute on a CD-ROM and want to install it on your computer, insert the CD into your CD drive. The main screen of the CD should automatically open. Look for a .exe file or a file that says "Install" and double-click to launch the installation wizard. If you have a copy of the program that was downloaded over the Internet or copied to your hard drive, open the folder that contains the downloaded file and double-click the install icon or .exe file to launch the installation wizard.

The install wizard walks you through the process of installing the program — you simply select the Next button on each screen to advance through all the options and automatically install the program on your hard drive. Unless you know that you want to do something special when you install Contribute, choose all the features they recommend and simply follow the general instructions.

At the end, check the box that says Launch Contribute to automatically start the program after it's installed. When Contribute starts, it automatically looks for access to the Internet. If your computer is not connected to the Internet, or is having trouble connecting, Contribute prompts you with two options: Work Offline or Try to Connect Anyway. If you choose the second option, Contribute keeps trying to establish a connection for you. For more information on establishing a connection to your Web site, see Chapter 3.

You can use Contribute without being connected to the Internet. To do so, choose Work Offline when the program launches. If you want to go offline while you are working, choose File➪Work Offline and you can switch back and forth. Be aware, however, that if you use Contribute without being connected to the Internet, you can work only on new pages you create or existing pages that you already have copied to your computer. Similarly, you will not be able to publish your work until you are connected to the Internet and you have reestablished Contribute's connection to your site.

When the program launches successfully, the first screen to open is the Welcome screen shown in Figure 2-1. In the future, you can start Contribute by double-clicking the icon that is installed on your hard drive or by selecting Start➪Programs➪Macromedia➪Macromedia Contribute.

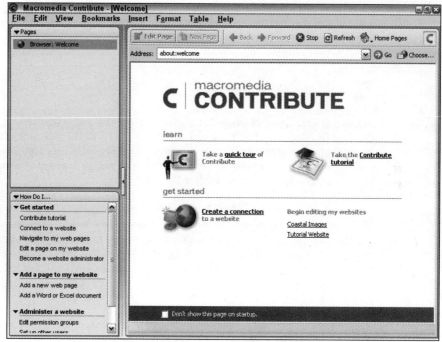

Figure 2-1: The first time you launch Contribute, you're greeted by the Welcome screen.

Getting to Know the Workspace

To help you fully appreciate Contribute's range of abilities, the following sections include a tour of the workspace and detailed descriptions of each of the buttons and menu items in the program.

If you're anxious to get started editing your first pages (or you're on a really tight deadline and need to get to work right now) jump ahead to Chapter 3 to find out how to get to work right away editing text on pages and adding simple images and links.

If you want to get a good overview before you jump in, keep reading. And if you do skip ahead because you just have to put this program to work right away, make sure you come back to this chapter when you have a little more time. Taking a few minutes to go over the range of options in this program will help make sure you're not missing anything in your rush to get your work online.

The Pages panel

In the top-left region of Contribute's workspace is a panel labeled Pages (see Figure 2-2). This panel is designed to keep track of all the pages you're working on so that you can manage your work as you make edits to existing pages, create new pages, and ultimately publish those pages to the live server where your work becomes part of the live Web site.

As you work on each page (whether it is a new page or an existing one), the file name is automatically added to this panel. To switch from one page to another, simply click the file name, and the page automatically opens in the main area of the Contribute workspace. In Figure 2-2, you can see three pages listed. The one selected on the left, Desert Scenes, is displayed in the main work area on the right.

The "How Do I" panel

In the left area of the Contribute workspace, just under the Pages panel, is a built-in help section (see Figure 2-2). This panel is designed to make it easy to find quick instructions about the main features of the program, from connecting to a Web site to adding images and even managing the administrative functions. If you like having this information handy, you can keep it open as shown in Figure 2-2, but most people who use this program

find that they want more work space for editing and developing pages.
To close the How Do I panel, click the arrow next to How Do I, and the panel
collapses, leaving more room for the Pages panel to expand down. To create
more space in the main work area, close both the Pages and How Do I panels
by clicking the small arrow box in the middle of the screen. When these
panels are closed, you have more room to work on your pages, as you see in
Figure 2-3. To view the panels again, simply click again on the small arrow
now at the far left in the middle of work area (visible in Figure 2-3).

Finding Contribute's many menu options

At the top of the screen, the Contribute menu bar provides easy access to all
the main features of the program. If you've used a word processing program
before, you'll find many of the same kinds of options — such as New Page,
Save, and Print — but you'll also find many options you've probably never seen
before, such as Publish, Preview in Browser, and Roll Back to Previous Version.
The following sections provide descriptions of these options and more.

Figure 2-2:
The Pages
panel keeps
track of
pages you
are working
on and
makes it
easy to
switch from
one page to
another.

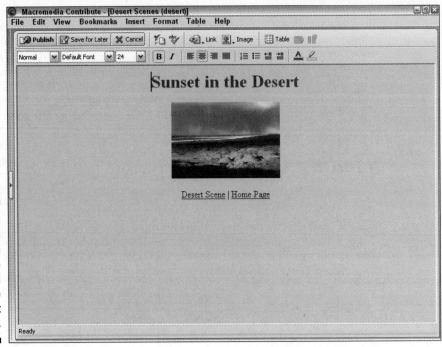

Figure 2-3:
Use the
small arrow
button on
the side of
the Pages
and Help
panels to
close the
panels and
create more
room to edit
your pages.

The File menu

Under the File menu, shown in Figure 2-4, you find the New Page option, which enables you to create a completely new page in your Web site. When you select this option, the New Page dialog box opens. To create a blank new page, choose Blank Web Page. You'll also find a variety of template options built into the program (use these to quickly create preformatted pages for calendars, resumes, photo albums, and more). In addition, you can use templates created specifically for your Web site to create new pages. You can't create templates in Contribute — you or someone else will need to use Dreamweaver to create templates — but you can create new pages using templates in Contribute. (Find more information on how to use templates in Contribute in Chapter 2 and how to create them in Dreamweaver in Chapter 10.)

The Edit Page option, under the File menu, is active only if you are browsing a page on the server that you have not yet started to work on. When you choose Edit Page, Contribute automatically downloads the page, saves a copy on your hard drive, and opens it in Edit mode. (Check out Chapter 3 for more information about downloading and editing existing pages.)

The Publish and Publish as New Page features are to be used when you're done with your editing work and ready to add your edited page to the live server. Be careful with this feature as it makes changes to the live site. Many Contribute users prefer to use the Save or Save for Later options and test their work before they publish the changes. Saving your pages regularly is always a good idea so you don't lose work if your system crashes or the power goes out. Using the Save option, under the File menu, saves a local copy but does not put it on the live server. The Save for Later option saves the page and closes it, and the Cancel Draft option deletes the version on your computer and leaves the page on the server unchanged.

The next three items clustered together under the File menu are Preview in Browser, E-mail Review, and Export. Let's look at those one at a time.

✔ **Preview in a Browser** enables you to view the page you are working on in a dedicated Web browser, such as Internet Explorer, instead of just looking at it through the browser in Contribute.

✔ **E-mail Review** is designed to facilitate your sharing your work with other members of your team before it goes live on the site. When you select this option, a copy of your page is saved on the server at a special address, which is then included in an e-mail message that you can send to request someone to look over your work. (You find more information about the E-mail Review feature in Chapter 11.)

✔ **Export** enables you to export your work in Contribute to a separate file, which you can save anywhere on your computer or on the network.

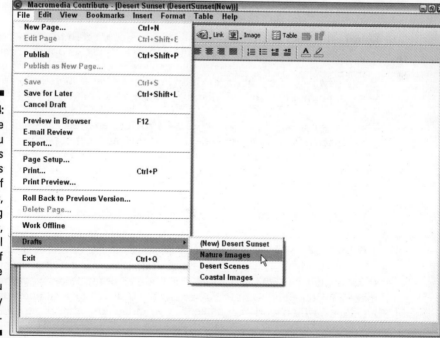

Figure 2-4:
The File menu provides easy access to a range of options, including Drafts, where you'll find a list of all the pages you are actively working on.

Page Setup, Print, and Print Preview work much like their equivalents in a word processing program and are designed to ensure you can create the best-looking version of your page if you want to print it.

By far, the most face-saving feature of this program is Roll Back to Previous Version, also available under the File menu. This feature enables you to "undo" any page you publish by replacing the new page with a saved version of the previous one. Essentially, if you hit the Publish button and then realize you've made a terrible mistake and it's on the live Web site, this feature lets you quickly put things back the way they were. (Find more about the Roll Back feature in Chapter 11.)

The Delete Page option works differently depending on how the site administrator has set up access to the server for Contribute users. (You find more information on how to control this feature in Chapter 13, which is designed for Contribute administrators.) As a user, you should know that the Delete Page option may or may not enable you to delete pages on the server. If you are not sure, be very careful of this feature because you can delete a page off the live server while you are viewing it if you choose the Delete Page option. If the site administrator has limited your ability to delete files from the server, then the delete key works only to delete pages that you have on your computer and is designed not to function for pages on the server. Depending on how your system is enabled, this option may be grayed-out and unavailable.

Contribute is designed to work while you are connected to the Internet, but you do have the option to Work Offline by selecting this option from the File menu. Be aware, however, that while you are working offline, you can only create new pages or edit pages that you already have on your computer and you can not publish your work until you are back online.

The Drafts option, shown in Figure 2-4, provides easy access to all the pages you are actively working on and contains the same list of pages you find in the Pages panel described earlier in this chapter. When you select Drafts, an arrow to the right reveals the pages available; select the page you want to work on to open it in the main work area.

The last feature listed in the File Menu, the Exit option, closes the program.

The Edit menu

The Edit menu, shown in Figure 2-5, contains many features that you may find familiar, such as Undo and Redo, which are great for quick fixes when you make a mistake and want to go back a step or two. You also find Cut, Copy, and Paste, which work much like they would in any other program.

The Paste Text Only option may be new to you. This option enables you to copy and past text from one area of your site to another without including formatting. When you copy a headline, for example, and then paste it somewhere else on your page, it should include all the formatting that you used to make it stand out as a headline. If you prefer that the text not have the headline formatting, choose Paste Text Only and it will be inserted as plain text.

You also find the Select All option, which enables you to select all elements on a page at once, and the Find option, which works much like the Find feature in a word processing program, enabling you to search for a word or phrase in a document.

The Preferences settings are also under the Edit menu. Before you start working with a new program, it's always a good idea to go through all the Preferences options to ensure that the program is set up the best way for you. You find specific instructions about how to specify preferences in the "Specifying Common Preferences" section later in this chapter.

Another feature that may be new to you is the My Connections option, which opens the My Connections dialog box where you can create, edit, rename, or remove connections to Web sites. Similarly, the Administer Web sites option provides easy access to those sites so you can switch from one to another if you have configured Contribute to work with more than one site. If you're working on only one site, you may never use this option.

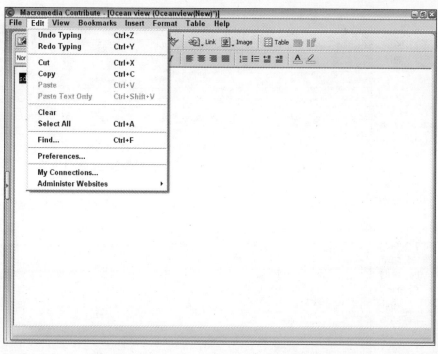

Figure 2-5:
The Edit menu contains many features you'll find familiar as well as some new ones, such as My Connections and Administer Web sites.

The View menu

The View menu (see Figure 2-6) provides access to the Sidebar, the area on the left of the workspace where the Pages and How Do I panels are stored. Select Sidebar to open the panels; select it again to close them.

The Browser option shifts the program into browse mode (as opposed to edit mode) so that you can *browse,* or navigate, around a Web site to test your work and find the pages you want to edit.

The Back, Forward, Stop, and Refresh options all work much like they do on a Web browser, such as Internet Explorer or Netscape. Back takes you to the previous page viewed, Forward takes you to the next page, Stop interrupts the downloading process when you are loading a page, and Refresh reloads the page, which is important if you want to see changes.

The Home Pages option provides quick access to the main page of the sites you have access to listed by site name, and Recently Published Pages provides a list of the most recent files that you have published to your server, listed by page title. With both options, select the name you want to work on and Contribute opens it automatically in the main work area.

The Go to Web Address option opens the dialog box shown in Figure 2-7 and enables Contribute to act as a browser capable of displaying any Web site.

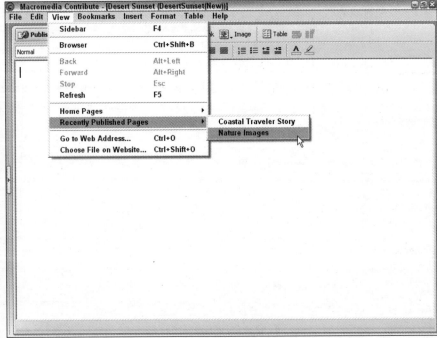

Figure 2-6: The View menu features many options for browsing and loading pages, such as the ability to quickly open recently published pages.

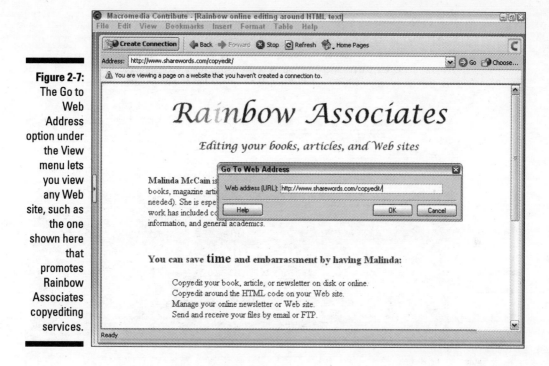

Figure 2-7:
The Go to
Web
Address
option under
the View
menu lets
you view
any Web
site, such as
the one
shown here
that
promotes
Rainbow
Associates
copyediting
services.

The Choose File on Website option opens the dialog box shown in Figure 2-8 and enables you to select a file on the server without using the browse feature to open it. When you double-click a file name, the file opens in Contribute.

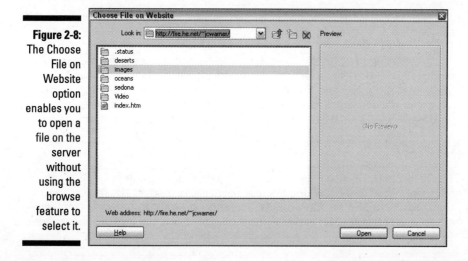

Figure 2-8:
The Choose
File on
Website
option
enables you
to open a
file on the
server
without
using the
browse
feature to
select it.

The Bookmarks menu

The Bookmarks menu, shown in Figure 2-9, works like a limited version of the Bookmarks option in Internet Explorer. You can save pages you want to browse in the future and to return to any page by simply selecting it from the list, but you can't move a bookmark or organize them in subfolders.

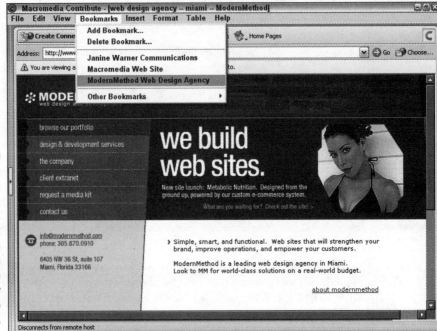

Figure 2-9: The Bookmarks menu enables you to save address you want to easily browse to later.

The Insert menu

As shown in Figure 2-10, the Insert menu offers access to a number of features unique to Web design. From this menu, you can insert images, tables, links, horizontal rules, and line breaks. You can also add special characters, such as the copyright symbol, Yen, or Euro characters. The Insert menu also makes it possible to add a date to your pages and to insert Named Anchors, which are used when creating links within a page (for more on creating links, see Chapter 4).

The Insert menu is also where you can choose to insert content directly from Microsoft Word and Excel documents. To do so, you select the option and then browse to find the file with the contents you want to retrieve. The biggest advantage of this feature is that Contribute automatically formats the content to be as close to the original document as possible. That means you don't have to recreate the formatting in a large file — Contribute does it for you.

The Format menu

You should already be familiar with most of the Format menu options shown in Figure 2-11, such as Bold, Italic, Underline, and Check Spelling (a face-saving option you should never forget to use).

You can also use the options in this menu to format the font face, style, and size and to specify text and highlight colors. You find a Remove Link option here and access to the Properties dialog box for Objects and Templates.

The Keywords and Description option launches a dialog box where you can enter information you want to make available to search engines. For example, you can enter a description that says something like: "Bunny's Guide to Eating Carrots" with the keywords "Bugs, Bunny, Carrots." This information is stored in the Meta data of your page (if you don't know what that means, don't worry too much, it's information stored at the top of the HTML document for search engines and other programs, but it doesn't show up on the page that viewer's see.)

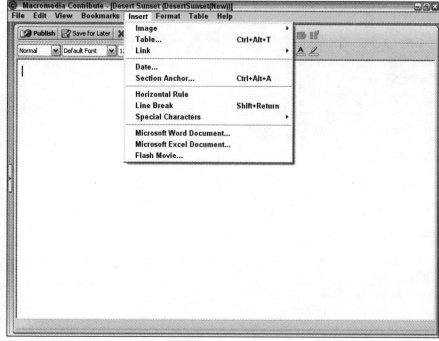

Figure 2-10: The Insert menu includes a number of special Web design features, such as the Insert Microsoft Word and Excel options.

The Page Properties option launches the Page Properties dialog box, shown in Figure 2-12, which enables you to specify the page title, background image, background and link colors, and margin and encoding options.

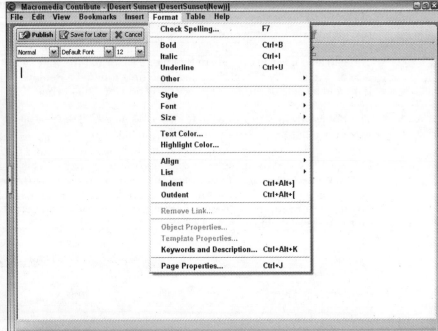

Figure 2-11: The Format menu features many common formatting options, as well as access to Objects, Templates, and Page properties.

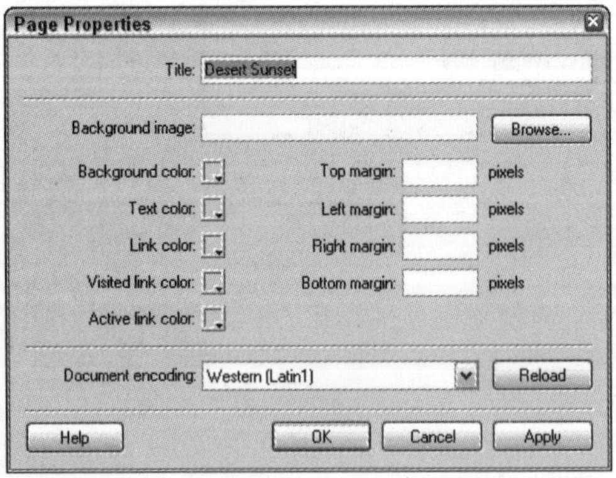

Figure 2-12: Specify background, text, and link colors in the Page Properties dialog box.

The Table menu

On the Web, tables are used for far more than just displaying financial data —
the table formatting options are really important. That's why you find an
entire menu option dedicated to table formatting, from inserting tables to
merging cells, (see Figure 2-13). You find lots more information about creating
and using tables on your Web pages in Chapter 7.

The Help menu

We can all use a little help once in a while. The Help menu provides easy
access to information that can assist you in figuring out how to best use the
many features of Contribute. You also find access to the Contribute Support
Center, shown in Figure 2-14, where you find additional, updated information
on Macromedia's Web site.

Understanding the toolbars

At the top of the Contribute work area, just under the menu, you find a host
of handy toolbars with graphical buttons that provide quick access to the
most common features in Contribute. All of these functions are available
through the Menu options described in the previous section of this chapter,
but you may find them easier to use from the toolbars.

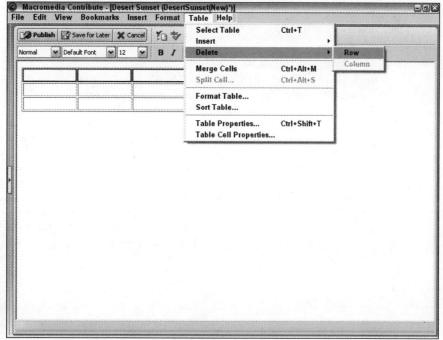

Figure 2-13:
The Table
menu
features
a wide
range of
formatting
options for
working
with Tables.

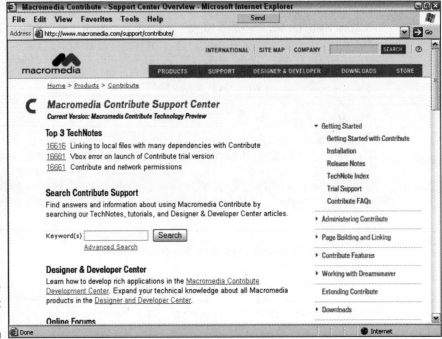

Before I give you descriptions of each of these buttons, let me start by explaining that Contribute has two distinct modes (Browse and Edit) and that each mode has its own toolbar.

Working in Browse mode

In Browse mode, Contribute works much like a Web browser (for example, Internet Explorer) and you can use it to navigate around the Web, enter a URL, move forward and back through sites, and so on.

While you are browsing, notice that at the top left you have one of two button options, depending on whether you have already set up access to work on a site. If you are browsing a Web site that you are not set up to work on, the button in the top left says Create Connection. (You find more about connections in Chapter 3.)

If you are browsing pages on a site that you have already set up to work on in Contribute, then the button in the top left says Edit Page, as you see in Figure 2-15.

Working in Edit mode

When you select Edit Page, Contribute automatically downloads the page you are viewing and saves a copy on your hard drive that you can work on. Simultaneously, Contribute changes the toolbar at the top of the page to reveal the Edit options, shown in Figure 2-16.

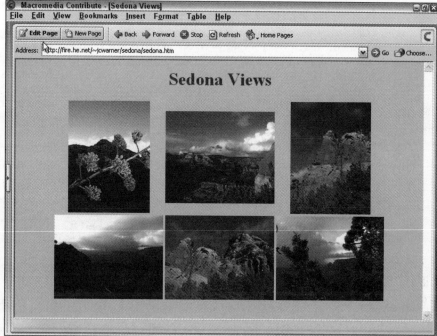

Figure 2-15: You can browse through pages to find the one you want to work on and then select Edit Page to download the page and switch to Edit mode.

The Edit options represent the most common formatting and other features that you are likely to need as you work on your pages. Some should be very familiar, others may be new to you.

I start with the second row of formatting options because they are the easiest and most obvious. Starting from the left, the Heading options include Headings 1 through 6 and Normal. As you might expect, these provide formatting appropriate for headlines and other headings. Heading 1 creates the largest font and Heading 6 the smallest. Normal applies no formatting, meaning the text is displayed in the default font and size of the user's browser.

To the right of the heading options, you find Font options. You can add any fonts you want to this pull-down list, but be aware that if the user who views your pages does not have the font you use, he or she sees the text in the default font of the browser. As a result, you're best to stick with the fonts offered in the predefined list. The numbers to the right of the font enable you to specify the font size from font size 8 to 36.

Following along to the right, you find the bold and italic formatting options, alignment icons for left, center, right, and justified respectively, the numbered and bulleted list options, outdent and indent , and the colored text and highlighted text color options, which open to reveal color palettes and color pickers, such as the one shown in Figure 2-17.

The buttons in the toolbar across the top of the page are unique to Web design so you're less likely to be familiar with them. From left to right, you first find the Publish button, which is how you save your work and load it onto your Web server. The Save For Later button enables you to save a copy of the page on your hard drive with any changes you have made. Then you can return to the page to do more work on it later before you publish it to the live site. The Cancel button closes the page you are working on without saving the changes or loading them on the site. Use this option only if you want to throw away your work.

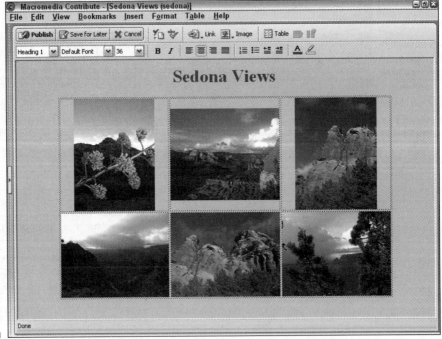

Figure 2-16:
When you choose to edit a page, Contribute automatically downloads the page and switches to display the Edit toolbar options.

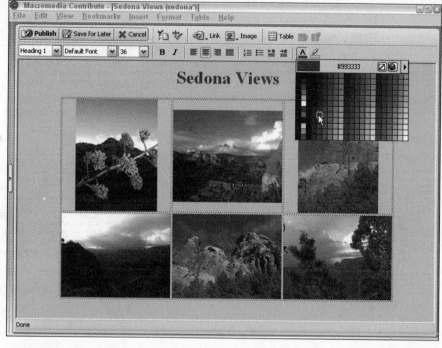

Publish   Save for Later   Cancel   Link   Image   Table

Heading 1   Default Font   36   B   I   #993333

Sedona Views

Figure 2-17:
The Text
Color and
Highlight
options
provide
access to a
color palette
where you
can specify
a color by
selecting it.

Done

You can always cancel a page you're working on and then browse back to it on the server later and download it again. This is a clean way to start over if you have made many changes to a page and want to undo them all.

The next button to the right of the Cancel button is the Page Properties button, which enables you to open the Page Properties dialog box where you specify overall page formatting options, such as link color, text color, and background color or image. The next button launches spell check (and I always recommend you do that before you publish your work). Continuing along, you find an Insert Link button and Insert Image button which make it easy to create links and add images to your pages (more about these two options in Chapter 3). The last buttons in the toolbar are Insert Table, which launches the Insert Table dialog box (see Figure 2-18) and makes it easy to create a table and specify properties, such as number of rows, width and border options. Below that, you find the Insert Row button and to the right, the Insert Column button.

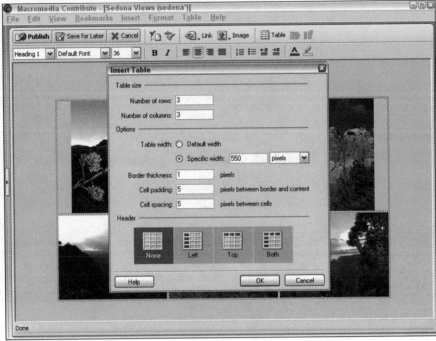

Figure 2-18:
The Insert Table dialog box enables you to specify the size and other attributes of a table when you create it.

Specifying Common Preferences

Before you go too far using any program, you should look for the Preferences option and at least browse through what you can and can't change in terms of settings. Preferences are designed to let you specify certain settings, display options, and other elements that don't have to be a certain way for the program to work so you can have some choice about how you prefer to use it. For example, if you're working on a Web site for Norway, you may prefer to uses the Norwegian spelling dictionary.

General preferences

To open the Preferences dialog box, choose Edit⇨Preferences. The main Preferences dialog box opens with the General options visible, as shown in Figure 2-19. The General preferences include a Faster Table Editing option, which I recommend you keep checked unless you are having trouble formatting tables and want to update your changes more quickly. The Spelling dictionary option features a pull-down list with 14 different spelling dictionaries to choose from, including English [British] and English [Canadian]. If you bought your program in the US, the default option should be English [American].

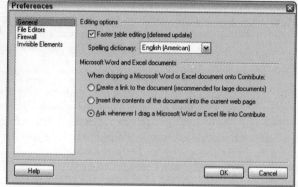

Figure 2-19:
The General
preferences
include the
ability to
choose from
14 different
spelling
dictionaries.

You have three options about how you work with Microsoft Word and Excel files. The safest option, and the one that is automatically selected is "Ask whenever I drag ..." If you choose this option, you see a dialog box just as you start to insert the contents of such a file.

File editors

This complicated-looking dialog box, shown in Figure 2-20, is designed to make it easy to keep track of files and external editors. Set this up in the way you like to work. For example, I like using Macromedia products, but sometimes I want Adobe Photoshop to fix an image. When that happens, I try to relax and be thankful that I have the option.

You can assign image editors to image extensions, such as Macromedia Fireworks with .gif, .jpeg, and other image formats.

Figure 2-20:
The File
Editors
preferences
enable you
to specify
what
extensions
should be
opened by
what
editors.

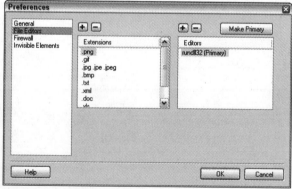

The Firewall preferences have only two fields where you need to enter information unique to your network and any firewall you are using. If you're not sure about this, you may not have a firewall. If you're having trouble connecting to sites, however, check with your system administrator because this may be the problem.

So far, you find only one option in the Invisible Elements preferences (which is quite different from what you find in Dreamweaver where there are many invisible elements.) The Show Section Anchors When Editing a Page option, shown in Figure 2-21, enables you to display a place holder when you use anchors to ensure that you can easily find where you have created them. Anchors are used for jump links, links that go directly to a particular place on a page. You find lots more information about creating links in Chapter 4.

Figure 2-21:
The Invisible
Elements
preferences
enable you
to specify
what
extensions
should be
opened by
what
editors.

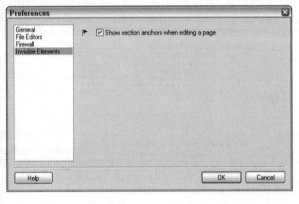

Chapter 3

Working with Contribute

In This Chapter

▶ Connecting to your Web server

▶ Browsing and reviewing pages

▶ Editing existing pages

▶ Creating new pages

*T*his is it — the chapter that delves into all the practical stuff, everything you need to know if you want to jump right in and immediately get to work on your Web site.

Chapter 3 is where you should start if you're on deadline, or if you're just so anxious to get something on the live site you don't care about learning all the cool stuff and you just want to know what you have to know to get up and running with this program.

No, this doesn't mean you shouldn't read the rest of this book or at least refer to the sections you need when you want to get more information on any of the features of this program. I'm sure you'll be pleased to find out how easy Contribute is to use and how much you can do with just this one chapter. Don't worry — when you want to better understand how Contribute works and all you can do with it, the rest of this book will be waiting for you.

This chapter is designed to get you started with the program, so it covers the basics of editing and creating new pages. You find everything you need to know here to edit text on your Web site, add a few pages of information, and upload a new image.

This is where you get started and develop a base of knowledge about what you can do before you explore more of the advanced features, such as image maps and background images (see Chapter 5) or how to create complex designs with tables (see Chapter 7).

If you are building a Web site from scratch, you really need a more robust program, such Macromedia Dreamweaver. But if you just want to help develop an existing site, especially if you are part of a bigger team and you have little or no experience developing Web pages, then Contribute is ideal for you.

Connecting to a Web Site

Contribute is designed to make it easy to work on a Web site that is already on the Internet, but before you can start editing or adding pages to your site, you need to establish a connection. This isn't hard, but it does require some special information, notably a user ID and password that gives you access to the server. Your server is protected by a password because you wouldn't want just anyone to make changes to your site. (If you haven't installed Contribute yet, see Chapter 2 for instructions.)

If you work in one of those places where they send technical staff over to your computer to install and set up software for you, consider yourself lucky because you're probably already be set up and connected to your site. Here's the test: If you can already view the pages on your Web site using Contribute as your browser, and when you view a page the button in the top left of the work area changes to Edit Page, then you're already connected and can skip ahead to the upcoming section, "Browsing and Editing Existing Pages."

Even if you don't have the luxury of a technical staff to set up the software for you, you should be working with someone who knows a lot more about Web design than you do. You may have hired a consultant to build your site and are now using Contribute to maintain it yourself, or you may work for a big company, nonprofit, or educational institution, and someone from the Web design team gave you Contribute to work on your section of the site. Either way, you need one of those people who know more about Web design than you do to help you get connected or at least give you the information you need to set up the connection yourself.

Contribute offers two ways to establish the connection to your server (and you should be pleased to know that this is one of those things you have to set up only once). First, someone else can give you a connection key, a file that contains all the access information for your server and is designed to automatically set you up in Contribute. If you have a connection key, you're golden — it's incredibly easy to import a connection key and get yourself set up (see the next section). If you don't have a connection key, then you need to enter the connection information yourself, but even then it's still easy — Contribute features a special wizard that walks you through the process.

Importing a connection key

If you're working with a good Web site administrator, he or she should send you a Connection key, usually via e-mail, which you can easily import into Contribute to take care of the setup automatically. Here's what to do if someone gives you a connection key:

1. **If you've been e-mailed a connection key, click to download it and save it to your hard disk. If someone gives you a connection key on a disk, copy it to your hard drive.**

2. **Double-click the connection key file.**

   The Import Connection Key dialog box opens, as shown in Figure 3-1.

3. **Enter your name, e-mail address, and password.**

   Get a password from the person who sent you the connection key.

4. **Click OK.**

   The connection to the site is automatically established, and the main page of the site should load in Contribute's main work area.

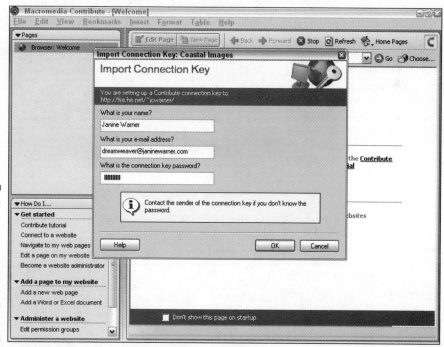

Figure 3-1: You can establish a connection to a Web site by importing a Connection Key.

Using the Connection Wizard

If no one sent you a connection key but you do have the User ID and password for your site, you can establish your own connection using Contribute's Connection Wizard:

1. **Choose Edit⇨My Connections.**

   The My Connections dialog box opens.

2. **Choose New.**

   The Connection Wizard dialog box opens, as shown in Figure 3-2.

3. **Click Next.**

4. **Enter your name and e-mail address, and then click Next.**

5. **Enter the Web address or URL of your Web site and click Next.**

6. **Specify how you connect to your server using the pull-down options, as shown in the dialog box in Figure 3-3.**

   Your options are to connect via a Network or via FTP. (If you're not sure which one you use or you don't have the login information required, ask your Web site's administrator or developer to help you.)

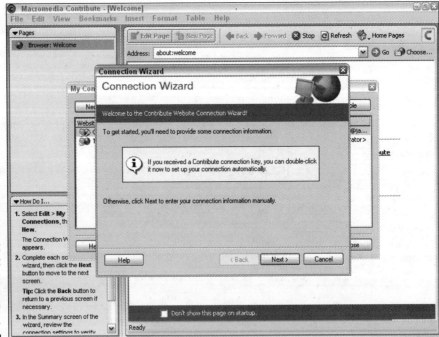

Figure 3-2:
The
Connection
Wizard
makes it
easy to set
up your own
connection
to a Web
site.

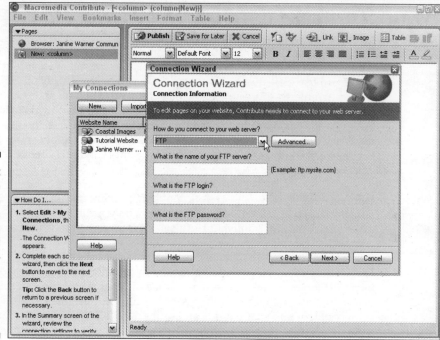

Figure 3-3:
You can use
Contribute
with a
server on
a Local
Network or
via FTP with
a remote
server, such
as an ISP.

Choose FTP if you use a remote server, such as a commercial service provider, and enter the server and login information. If you chose FTP, follow these steps:

    a. Enter the FTP info, including the login and password and click Next.

    b. Enter the folder information and click Next.

    c. Select your group and click Next.

    d. Click Done.

Choose Local/Network if you are working on a site that is hosted on your organization's network. If you chose Network, follow these steps:

    a. Click Next to leave the Connection Information page of the wizard.

    b. Select whether you want to be the administrator or not (entering a password if you do) and click Next.

    c. Click Done.

7. Click Close.

The connection to the site is automatically established and the main page of the site should load in Contribute's main work area.

Browsing and Editing Existing Pages

One of the most intuitive features of Contribute, especially when you compare it to how other Web programs work, is the overall system that makes it so easy to use. Essentially, if you want to work on your Web site, you simply use Contribute to "browse" to any page on your Web site and then click the Edit Page button. When you click Edit Page, Contribute downloads a copy of the page to your hard drive where you can change the text, images, and so on. When you're done, you click the Publish button to apply your changes on the server. It really is that easy if you just want to make a change to a page on an existing site.

Before you start editing pages and publishing them on the site with great abandon, keep in mind that you're working on your live Web site — if you make a mistake and publish it to the site, your errors are visible to anyone who visits your site.

I recommend that you develop a regular system for testing your work and, ideally, that you run it past someone else on your team who can review it for you before you publish your pages (it's almost impossible to catch all of your own mistakes, especially typos and other details.) In Chapter 11, I include some tips and suggestions on how to establish a good testing system, but let me just plant the seed here. Even when you're in a hurry, or on a tight deadline, *always* review your work before you transfer it to the live Web site. If you're really in a hurry, you're much more likely to make a mistake and it will take a lot longer if you have to fix it before you get it right. Just to reassure you a little, Chapter 11 also includes tips about how to use Contribute's Roll Back to Previous Version feature, which at least lets you put things back the way they were if you really screw up.

Making a quick text change

Let's say you want to change a few words on a page on your Web site, and you want to do it as quickly as possible. Perhaps one of your colleagues put up a page of text with a few typos and it's really embarrassing to have it on the site.

First, you need to identify which page you want to download into Contribute. If you're working on only one Web site, Contribute brings you to the main page of your site whenever you launch the program. If you're working on multiple sites, you want to make sure you have the correct site loaded. The easiest way to open a site is to select View⇨Home Pages⇨ and then choose the name of the site you want to open.

In Figure 3-4, you see that I'm selecting my own Web site from a list that includes the Contribute Tutorial site and a Web site called Coastal Images. To demonstrate how to edit text, I'm going to pretend that there is a typo in one of the newspaper columns I feature on my site (of course — ahem — in real life I'd never have typos on my own site).

When you select a home page, Contribute connects to the site and displays the main page. In Figure 3-5, you see the front page of my site displayed. Notice at the top left of the main workspace window the button that says Edit Page. If I wanted to make a change to the front page of my site, I'd click Edit Page, and Contribute would automatically download all the elements so I could work on it. But for this example, I want to edit a page that has one of my columns on it so I need to get to an inside page to make the necessary corrections.

Before you start browsing, I suggest you click that small arrow toward the middle of the page that is between the sidebar and the main workspace to close the sidebar. Clicking that arrow closes the two panels on the left, giving you more room to work on your pages and to browse to find the page you want to work on. (In Figure 3-6, you see a page displayed in Contribute with the sidebar closed.)

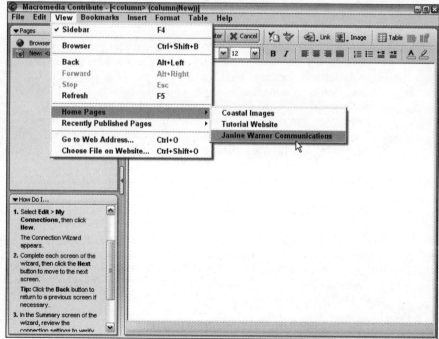

Figure 3-4:
The Home Pages option makes it easy to switch from one Web site to another when you want to work on a different project in Contribute.

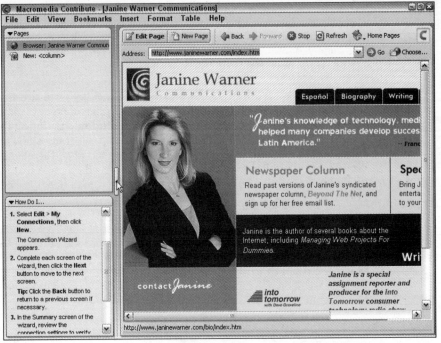

Figure 3-5:
Contribute
displays
pages on a
Web site
just like a
browser
and enables
you to
simply
follow links
to find the
page you
want to
work on.

You browse a Web site with Contribute just like you'd browse with a program like Internet Explorer or Netscape. You can click links, use the forward and back buttons, or enter a URL into the Address space at the top of the work area. Before you start editing, you need to browse to the page you want to work on. In this case, I've browsed to a particular column that I keep in the writing section of my site. Because I'm pretending that I need to fix a typo, I've clicked the Edit Page button on this page, and the HMTL document and related images files are automatically downloading, as you see in Figure 3-6.

After the page is downloaded, the toolbar at the top of the page changes to display the most common editing options. (Chapter 2 includes a comprehensive description of all of the menu and tool items.)

To edit text, simply insert your cursor on the page where you want to make a change. Entering, changing, and deleting text in Contribute works just like it does in a word processing program. You can highlight text sections and use copy and paste to move them, and you delete and replace words with the backspace and delete keys on your keyboard.

The Save For Later button does just that — it saves your changes on your hard drive and switches Contribute back into Browse mode. If you want to keep editing, choose Edit Page and Contribute switches back to Edit mode. If you just want to save your work and keep working, choose File⇨Save or use the key commands Ctrl+S on the PC or ⌘+S on the Mac.

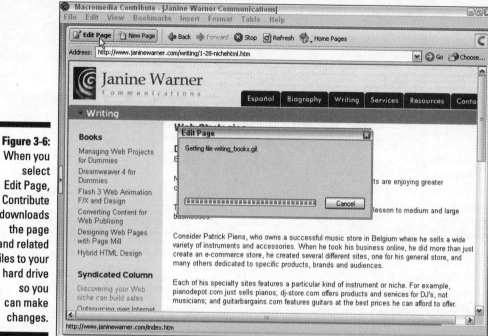

Figure 3-6:
When you select Edit Page, Contribute downloads the page and related files to your hard drive so you can make changes.

When you've made the changes you want, double-check your work and, ide-ally, get someone else to take a quick look and make sure everything is okay. The next step is to publish your changes on the live server, and you want to make sure you're not publishing something you'll regret.

When you are sure you have everything the way you want it on your page, click the Publish button, and Contribute automatically uploads the page to the server. The Congratulations message, shown in Figure 3-7, confirms that the file was sent properly, but it's still a good idea to use a Web browser, such as Internet Explorer, to browse to your site and double-check that the changes were made properly.

Most Web browsers feature a caching system that stores Web pages in short-term memory so that as you surf around a site you don't have to download the same page again when you return to it. However, when you're making changes to a site, this can be problematic because if you use the Publish button in Contribute and then switch over the Internet Explorer to see the changes, they may not show up if the page is cached. The simple solution is to use the Reload or Refresh button on your browser to download the page again so it displays your changes.

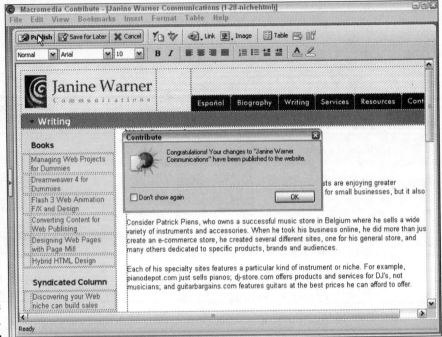

Figure 3-7:
When you use the Publish button to transfer you work to the live server, Contribute provides a confirmation message when it's successful.

Updating existing pages

One of the most common uses of Contribute is to update existing pages by adding or replacing images and inserting text or tables of data. In this section, you find out how to do the basics for each of these activities and find references to more detailed information elsewhere in the book.

Let's start with adding images because that's the fun part. First, you have to download the page you want to work on; then you insert the image on the page, test your work, and publish it to the server — just follow the simple step-by-step instructions that follow.

Before you get started, this exercise assumes you already have an image ready to insert and that the image is the correct size and format. (You find more information about how to edit and create Web graphics in Chapter 5.)

The only image formats that work on the Web are GIF and JPEGs. Before you place an image on your Web page, make sure that it is saved as a GIF or JPEG or it will not display on your page. Although you can also use the PNG format on the Web, it is not supported by all browsers so most designers avoid this option. (See Chapter 5 for more information about images.)

Inserting an image

Follow these steps to add or replace an image on an existing Web page:

1. **Make sure Contribute is connected to your site. (If you need help, see the section "Connecting to a Web site" earlier in this chapter.)**

2. **Browse to the page you want to edit.**

   Use Contribute's browse features to follow links or enter a URL to display the page you want to work on.

3. **Click the Edit Page button.**

   Contribute downloads the page and related files to your hard drive.

4. **Click to insert your cursor where you want to place the image.**

   If you are replacing an existing image, click to select that image, delete it with the delete key on your computer, and then leave your cursor in its place.

5. **Click the Insert Image button in the toolbar above the main work area.**

6. **From the pull-down list shown in Figure 3-8, choose From My Computer if you want to insert an image that is on your hard drive. Choose From Website if you want to insert an image that is on the server.**

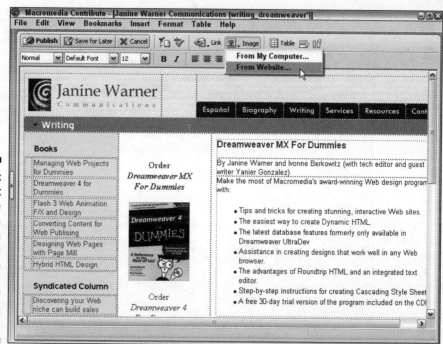

Figure 3-8:
The Insert Image button enables you to select an image from your hard drive or from the Web server.

If you choose From My Computer, the Select Image dialog box opens. If you choose From Website, the Choose Image on Website dialog opens, as shown in Figure 3-9.

7. **Navigate around your hard drive or through the files and folders on the server to find the image you want to insert on your page.**

8. **Double-click the file name of the image to select it.**

Contribute automatically inserts the image on the page.

Changing page properties

The Page Properties dialog box provides access to many of the elements you can change across an entire page. These include background colors, link and text colors, and the page title (the text that appears at the very top of the browser, next to the browser name, and is also the text that is saved in a user's bookmarks list). You find some other options in this dialog box, such as the Background Image feature, covered in Chapter 5. For now, let's keep things simple and just change the page title, background, and text colors.

To change the title, background, and text colors on a page, follow these steps:

1. **Choose Format⇨Page Properties.**

The Page Properties dialog box appears, as shown in Figure 3-10.

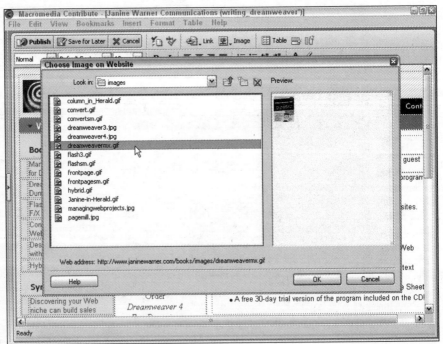

Figure 3-9: The choose Image on Website dialog box enables you to view the files and folders on your server so that you can find the image you want to insert.

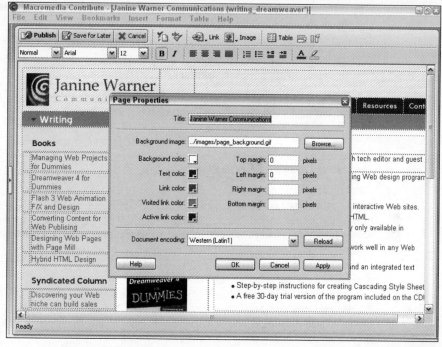

Figure 3-10:
The Page
Properties
dialog box
enables you
to change
text colors,
as well as
specify a
title for the
page.

2. **Click the color swatch box next to Background Color to reveal the color palette. Choose any color you like.**

   Make sure the background color looks good with the text color you select and that your text is still readable. In general, a light background color works best with a dark text color and vice versa.

   The color you selected fills the color swatch box. The color does not fill the background until you click the Apply or OK button.

3. **Click the color swatch box next to Text Color to reveal the color palette. Choose any color you like for the text color.**

   Again, make sure it will be readable against your background color

4. **Click the color swatch box next to Link Color to reveal the color palette. Choose any color you like for the link color.**

   Repeat this step for the Visited Link and Active Link colors. The visited link displays after a user has clicked a link. Because many people are accustomed to links changing color after they visit a page, choosing different colors for Link and Visited Link is a good idea. The Active Link color displays as someone clicks a link (and frankly, most people don't even notice the color difference).

5. **If the page does not already have a title, enter a title at the top of the Page Properties dialog box.**

   The Title doesn't display in the body of the page but is important because it appears at the top of the browser window and is the text that is saved when a user bookmarks a page.

6. **Click Apply to see how the colors look on your page. Click OK to finish and close the Page Properties dialog box.**

Creating New Pages

Although Contribute is not designed to create a new Web site, you can add completely new pages to an existing site. Contribute provides a few options about how to create new pages, from simply creating a blank new page, to creating a page and linking it from another page at the same time, to creating a page based on a template. In the following sections, you find step-by-step exercises to walk you through each of these options.

All the information and exercises in this chapter about inserting images, editing text, and changing page properties work the same whether you are working on an existing page or creating a new one.

Creating a new blank page

The simplest way to create a new page is to create a new, blank document. You can then add text, images, multimedia files, and so on and link the page to and from other pages in the site.

The following steps walk you through the process of creating a new blank page, adding some text, linking it to another page, and publishing it on the site:

1. **Choose File⇨New Page.**

   The New Page dialog box appears, as shown in Figure 3-11.

2. **Select Blank Web Page.**

3. **Enter a title in the Page Title text box at the bottom right of the dialog box.**

   If you do not enter a title, Contribute prompts you to do so. Contribute uses the page title to create the file name, as well as the page title at the top of the browser window.

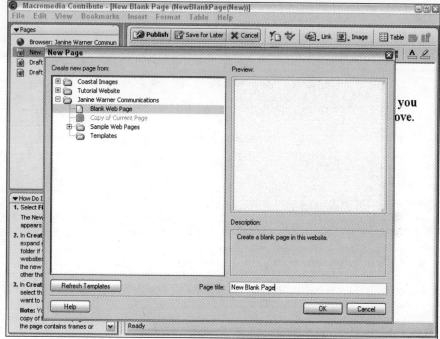

Figure 3-11:
The New
Page dialog
box enables
you to
create a
new blank
page or
to create
pages from
templates.

It's important to avoid spaces and special characters when you name an
HTML page because the name is used in links, and special characters
will cause them to not work properly. You don't have to worry about this
much in Contribute — if you enter a title with special characters or
spaces, Contribute removes them when it creates the file name but
leaves them in the Title area. If you look closely in Figure 3-12, you'll
notice that I named the page New Blank Page, and that is what appears
in the Pages panel on the left of the page, but the file name, listed at the
top of the screen, shows the words NewBlankPage with the spaces
removed.

 4. Click OK.

The new page automatically opens in the main Contribute work area.

 5. Click to place your cursor on the page and enter some text.

You can format text using the buttons in the toolbar along the top of the
page.

 **6. Click and drag to highlight a section of text that you will turn into a
 link.**

You can also click to select an image or other element to make a link.

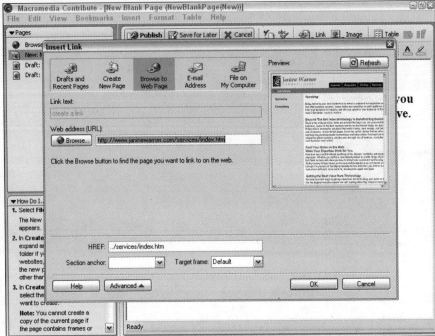

Figure 3-12:
The Insert
Link dialog
box enables
you to link
text or an
image to
another
page.

7. **Click the Link button in the toolbar and select Browse to a Web Page from the pull-down menu.**

   The Insert Link dialog box opens, as shown in Figure 3-12. The Browse to a Web Page option should be highlighted. This enables you to link to another page on the server.

8. **Enter a URL or use the Browse button to launch the Browse to Link dialog box, shown in Figure 3-13, to navigate to the page you want to link to.**

   The Browse to Link dialog box is essentially a mini-browser window that you can use it to surf the Web as you would use a Web browser.

9. **When you find the page you want to link to, click OK in the Browse to Link dialog box, and Contribute automatically inserts the URL in the Insert Link dialog box.**

10. **Click OK.**

    The Insert Link dialog box closes and the link is automatically created.

11. **Choose File⇨Save.**

    The page is saved on your hard drive.

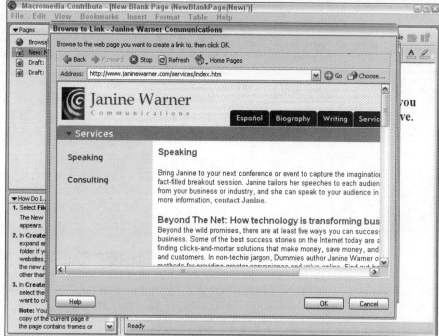

Figure 3-13:
The Browse
to Link
dialog box
serves as
a mini
browser.

12. **Test and review your changes by clicking your links to ensure they are okay.**

    This is a good time to ask someone else to look over your work.

13. **Click the Publish button at the top of the work area.**

    The Publish New Page dialog box opens and prompts you for a filename. Contribute automatically uses the page title as a filename, but before the page is published, offers you this second chance to change it to something else.

14. **Enter a new filename if you want to replace the one that was automatically generated from your page title.**

    You can name the file anything you want, but don't use special characters, such as spaces, exclamation points, and so on.

    Naming files seems simple enough, but when you're working with a team of developers and you're all trying to keep track of a growing number of files on your server, creating a standard naming convention can really help keep you organized. For example, I include the date published in the file name of all my columns. You find more guidelines on filenames and setting links in Chapter 4.

15. **Use the Choose Folder button if you want to save the page to a different folder on the server.**

    This enables you to specify where the new page is stored. In my example, I created a new page for a column I wanted to add to my Web site so I want to store it in the folder where I keep my other columns on the site.

16. **Click Publish.**

    The new page and any related files, such as new images, are automatically uploaded to the server. A confirmation message indicates when the uploading is complete.

After you add a new page to your site, it's always a good idea to use a browser to check your work and make sure that everything displays properly on the server.

Creating a new linked page

The following steps walk you through the process of creating a new linked page, which enables you to create a new page and link it from an existing page on your site at the same time. To use this option, you first browse to the page you want to link the new page from, and then create the new page.

Follow these steps to create a new linked page:

1. **If you are not already in Browse mode, choose View⇨Browser.**

    Contribute has two main modes, Edit and Browse. You need to be in browse to navigate to the page from which you want to create the link to the new page you are about to create.

2. **Browse your site until you find the page you want to link from.**

3. **Click the Edit Page button.**

    Contribute switches to Edit mode, changing the toolbar options across the top of the screen.

4. **Click to place your cursor on the page where you want to create the link.**

    You can select an image or text that you want to become the link, or you can insert the cursor and add text that will become a link at the same time you create the page.

5. **Click the Insert Link button and choose Create New Page from the pull-down list.**

    The Insert Link dialog box opens, as shown in Figure 3-14.

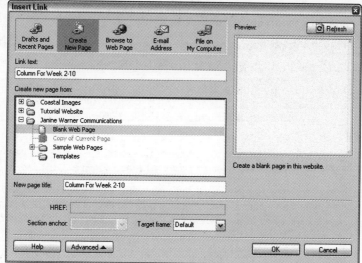

Figure 3-14:
The Insert
Link dialog
box includes
a Link Text
field for
when you
create a
new linked
page.

6. **Enter the text you want to appear on the existing page as the link to the new page.**

   If you selected an image or existing text, this field does not appear because it is not necessary to enter the text you will use.

7. **Enter a title in the Page Title text field.**

   If you do not enter a title, Contribute should prompt you to do so. Contribute uses the page title to create the file name, as well as the page title at the top of the browser window. If you don't enter a Page Title, Contribute automatically inserts the page title "Untitled Document."

8. **Click OK.**

   The new page automatically opens in the main Contribute work area.

9. **Click to place your cursor on the page to enter content.**

   You can now add text, images, multimedia, and any other elements just as you would add them to any document.

10. **You can create new links to or from this page, just as you would any other page.**

    Contribute enables you to create a new linked page so that you can easily add a page and link it in to the site at the same time, but this does not prevent you in any way from creating other links.

11. **Choose File⇨Save.**

    The page is saved on your hard drive.

12. When you have completed your new page, test and review your changes to ensure they are okay.

This is a good time to ask someone else to look over your work.

13. Click the Publish button at the top of the work area.

The Publish New Page dialog box opens, prompting you for a filename. Contribute automatically uses the page title as a filename, but before the page is published, offers you this second chance to change it to something else.

14. Enter a new filename if you want to replace the one that was automatically generated from your page title (see Figure 3-15).

You can name the file anything you want, but don't use special characters, such as spaces, exclamation points, and so on. The best way to break up words in a file name is to use the dash or underscore mark, as shown in Figure 3-15.

15. Use the Choose Folder button if you want to save the page to a different folder on the server.

This enables you to specify where the new page is stored. In my example, I created a new page for a column I wanted to add to my Web site so I want to store it in the folder where I keep my other columns on the site.

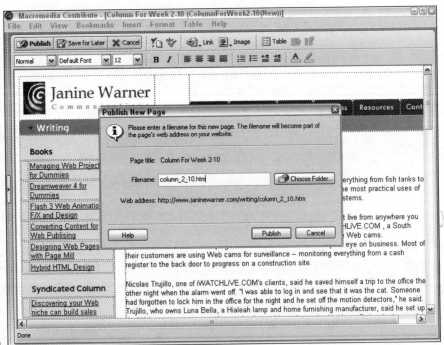

Figure 3-15:
When you publish your new page, Contribute prompts you with a dialog box where you can change the file name and folder the page is stored in on the server.

16. **Click Publish.**

The new page and any related files, such as new images, are automatically uploaded to the server. A confirmation message indicates when the uploading is complete.

Creating a new page with a premade design

Contribute is designed to make your life easier so it should come as no surprise that Macromedia includes a variety of sample page designs that are already formatted, which you can use to create new pages.

In the Sample Web Pages folder, shown in Figure 3-16, you find many great options designed to make it quick and easy to create common page styles, such as calendar pages that come preformatted with boxes for days of the month, and resume pages that make it easy to format the sections common on a professional resume. To use these predesigned pages, simply select the design you want as you are creating a new page and Contribute bases the new page on that design.

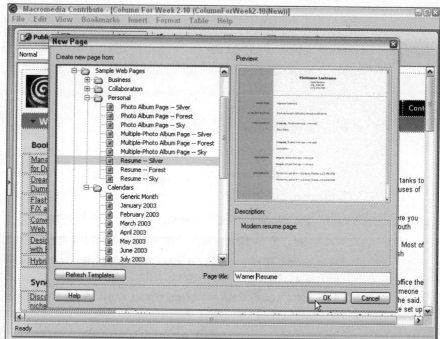

Figure 3-16: Contribute's Sample Web Pages folder contains a variety of page designs you can use when you create new pages for your site.

The following steps walk you through the process of creating a new page based on a sample Contribute page:

1. **Choose File➪New Page.**

   The New Page dialog box appears (refer to Figure 3-16).

2. **Click the plus sign next to the Sample Web Pages folder to open it (refer to Figure 3-16).**

3. **Choose the page design you want to use for your new page.**

   In the example in Figure 3-16, I chose the Silver Resume style.

4. **Enter a title in the Page Title text box at the bottom right of the dialog box.**

   If you do not enter a title, Contribute prompts you to do so.

5. **Click OK.**

   The new page automatically opens in the main Contribute work area with the formatting of the sample page.

6. **Click to place your cursor on the page where you want to add or change text.**

   In the example shown in Figure 3-17, you can see that I am changing the name at the top of the screen.

   You can change the text and other elements on a sample page just as you edit any other content. To change text, for example, highlight the existing text and then delete or replace it with new text that you enter.

7. **Make any other changes you want to make to the file.**

   You can always come back to an existing page and do additional revisions at a later time.

8. **Choose File➪Save.**

   The page is saved on your hard drive.

9. **Test and review your changes to ensure they are okay.**

   Don't ever skip this step, especially if you're in a hurry.

10. **Click the Publish button at the top of the work area.**

    The Publish New Page dialog box opens, prompting you for a filename.

11. **Enter a new filename if you want to replace the one that was automatically generated from your page title.**

12. **Click the Choose Folder button if you want to save the page to a different folder on the server.**

    This enables you to specify where the new page is stored on the server.

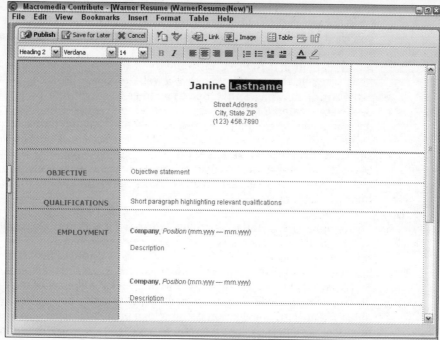

Figure 3-17:
You can edit, delete, or replace the content in a sample page design to customize it with your own information.

13. **Click Publish.**

The new page and any related files, such as new images, are automatically uploaded to the server. A confirmation message indicates when the uploading is complete.

Creating a new page from a template

Of all the different ways that you can create a new page with Contribute, the ability to use templates designed especially for your Web site is the most powerful. Most Web sites are created by a team, and the team members may have very different skills and abilities. Templates enable you to leverage the strength and design skills of some team members and make their work available so that other team members can create new pages more easily.

Here's an example of how this can work. Assume you own a small business and want to create a Web site, but you're not a designer and you don't know much about the Web, so you hire a consulting firm to design and develop the site. But after the site is built and published on the Web, you want to make ongoing changes to pages. For example, you may have a calendar section where you need to update events, or an employee section where you want to note staff changes and promotions. You could hire the same consultants to make all of these little changes for you, but that can get expensive and it's often not very efficient because you have to call the designers, tell them what you want to change, and then wait until they have time to make the change.

A better solution is to use Contribute to make those minor changes and additions yourself. However, if you have a well-designed site, it can get complicated to add new pages that look as good as the ones your professional designers created for you. That's where templates come in. The professional designers can create templates, essentially predesigned pages, for any or all of the sections of your site. For example, in the staff section, you may use a similar design for each staff member that includes a place for a photo, staff bio, contact information, and so on. Those pages may also include all the navigation buttons that appear on all of your pages with links to the main sections of your site.

The template for a staff page such as the one I just described can include all of the main design elements — the logo, navigation bar, and so on — and then include spaces where you can easily add a photo of new staff member and the bio and contact information. Macromedia makes templates even more powerful by including a feature that "locks" any part of the design. So although you may be able to easily change the staff photo, you may not be able to change the navigation bar and logo area at all. This enables your professional designers to create template pages that are easy to update, while protecting important sections of the page that they know should not be changed — especially by accident. When you are working with a team of people with different skill levels and experience in Web design, the ability to lock certain sections of a template can save you lots of grief and frustration by preventing mistakes.

You can't edit or create templates in Contribute. As shown in Figure 3-18, you can use only existing templates to create new pages. Templates must be created in Macromedia Dreamweaver, which is carefully integrated with Contribute. Because templates are such a valuable and important part of getting the most out of Contribute, I've included a chapter on how to create templates in Dreamweaver that can be used in Contribute. You find those instructions, as well as a more detailed explanation of how templates work and when you should use them, in Chapter 10.

The following steps walk you through the process of creating a new page from a template:

1. **Choose File⇨New Page.**

   The New Page dialog box opens.

2. **Click the plus sign next to the Templates folder to open it, as shown in Figure 3-19.**

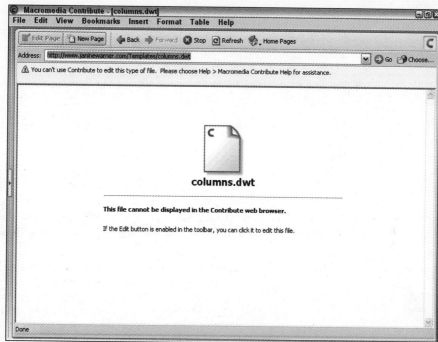

Figure 3-18:
You can't
create or
edit
templates in
Contribute,
but you can
use them to
create new
pages.

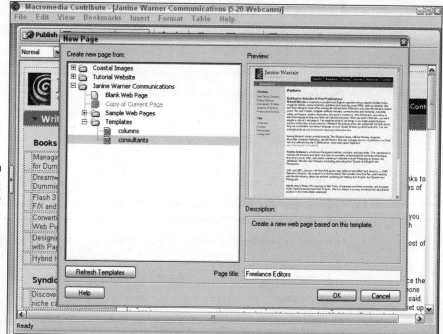

Figure 3-19:
The New
Page dialog
box auto-
matically
includes any
templates
available on
your Web
server.

3. **Choose the Template you want to use for your new page.**

   In the example in Figure 3-19, I chose the Consultants Template, which is designed to make it easy for me to add new resources and people I like to recommend on my Web site.

4. **Enter a title in the Page Title text box at the bottom right of the dialog box.**

   As you can see in Figure 3-19, I entered Freelance Editors in the Title field.

5. **Click OK.**

   The new page automatically opens in the main Contribute work area with the formatting of the template page.

6. **Click to place your cursor in one of the editable regions, indicated by the green tabs and outlining on the page. (See Figure 3-20 for an example.)**

   You can't edit locked regions of a template page. In the example shown in Figure 3-20, the navigation options on the left and top are locked, as is the log area at the top of the page. These are common elements to lock because they should not be changed on individual pages, and locking them ensures you don't change them by accident. The areas of a page that can be edited are designated by an outline and a special tab-shaped header. In the example, shown in Figure 3-20, you see two editable regions, one that is named Partner Heading and one named Partner Description.

7. **Make any changes you want to make to this area of the page, such as changing the heading at the top and inserting a new description.**

8. **Choose File⇨Save.**

   The page is saved on your hard drive.

9. **Test and review your changes to ensure they are okay.**

   Don't ever skip this step, especially if you're in a hurry.

10. **Click the Publish button at the top of the work area.**

    The Publish New Page dialog box opens, prompting you for a filename.

11. **Enter a new filename if you want to replace the one that was automatically generated from your page title.**

12. **Use the Choose Folder button if you want to save the page to a different folder on the server.**

    This enables you to specify where the new page is stored on the server.

13. **Click Publish.**

    The new page and any related files, such as new images, are automatically uploaded to the server. A confirmation message indicates when the uploading is complete.

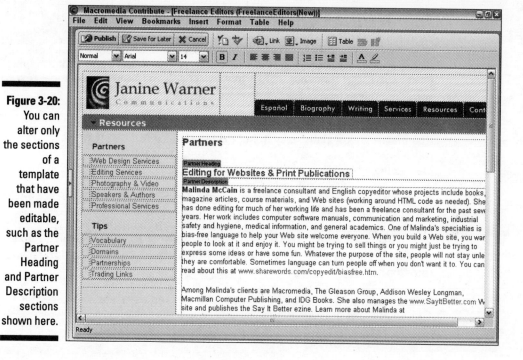

Figure 3-20:
You can alter only the sections of a template that have been made editable, such as the Partner Heading and Partner Description sections shown here.

Importing Existing Content

Typing new text on a page in Contribute is easy enough, but often you want to add content to your Web site that you have already typed into a program like Microsoft Word or Excel. Because these two programs are among the most common word processing and spreadsheet programs, Macromedia includes special features in Contribute to make it especially easy to import content from these programs so you don't have to retype it or even reformat it. Step-by-step instructions for how to do this are in the following section.

Before I get to the good stuff, however, let me warn you that if you have content in a program such as Quark XPress or PageMaker, you can't just easily import this into your Web site. In the case of these programs, often the best option is to just copy and paste the text from one these programs into Contribute. Unfortunately, there is no ideal solution for this kind of content conversion, but keep your eyes on the Adobe and Quark Web sites in case they come out with better solutions in the future. In the meantime, if this is the task you face, make sure you have plenty of time, and if you can get it, plenty of help. This is tedious, time-consuming work.

Importing content from Microsoft Word

I can't even imagine how many billions of pages of text, if not trillions of pages, must exist in Microsoft Word format. And because I know that's true, I can imagine that there is a strong likelihood you will want to add some text to your Web pages from a Microsoft Word document.

Because Word is so commonly used, Macromedia built in a special feature that makes it especially easy to import content for Microsoft Word. To use this feature, simple create a new page or open an existing one, and then choose Insert➪Microsoft Word content.

Although you can save a Word document as an HTML file for the Web, you're better off leaving the conversion to Contribute, because it creates cleaner code and ensures that the file integrates well with the rest of your site. Don't save your Word files as HTML or try to use Word as a Web editor; just create and edit your Word documents as you always would, and then import them into Contribute.

Follow these steps to create a new page from a template and then insert a Microsoft Word document into the file:

1. **Choose File➪New Page.**

   The New Page dialog box opens.

2. **Click the plus sign next to the Templates if you have templates in your site or use the pre-made sample pages provided in the Sample folder.**

   You can also insert Microsoft Word content into an existing page or into a new blank page.

3. **Choose the template you want to use for your new page.**

   In the example shown in Figure 3-21, I'm using the Columns Template from my own site and adding a new column to my writing section.

4. **Enter a title in the Page title text box at the bottom right of the dialog box.**

5. **Click OK.**

   The new page automatically opens in the main Contribute work area with the formatting of the template page.

6. **Click to place your cursor in the editable region, indicated by the green tabs and outlining on the page, where you want to insert the Microsoft Word document content.**

7. **Choose Insert➪Microsoft Word Document (refer to Figure 3-21).**

   The Open dialog box opens.

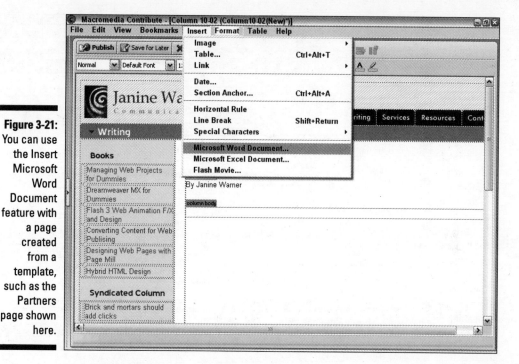

Figure 3-21:
You can use
the Insert
Microsoft
Word
Document
feature with
a page
created
from a
template,
such as the
Partners
page shown
here.

8. **Navigate around your hard drive to find the Microsoft Word document you want to insert on the page.**

9. **Click to select the file name.**

10. **Click Open.**

    The contents of the Microsoft Word file are automatically inserted into your page with all the formatting preserved. (See Figure 3-22 for an example.) You can now edit or format the content as you would any other text in Contribute.

11. **Choose File⇨Save.**

    The page is saved on your hard drive.

12. **Test and review your changes to ensure they are okay.**

13. **Click the Publish button at the top of the work area.**

    The Publish New Page dialog box opens, prompting you for a filename.

14. **Enter a new filename if you want to replace the one that was automatically generated from your page title.**

15. **Use the Choose Folder button if you want to save the page to a different folder on the server.**

    This enables you to specify where the new page is stored on the server.

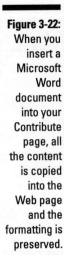

Figure 3-22:
When you insert a Microsoft Word document into your Contribute page, all the content is copied into the Web page and the formatting is preserved.

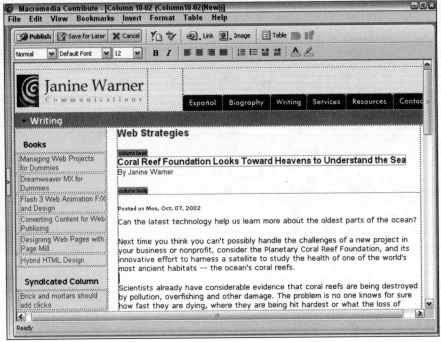

16. **Click Publish.**

    The new page and any related files, such as new images, are automatically uploaded to the server. A confirmation message indicates when the uploading is complete. The original Microsoft Word document is not transferred to the site because the contents were copied directly into the HTML file when you inserted the document.

 If you run into problems because the formatting in the Word document conflicts with style sheets or other formatting you use in your Web site, you may be better off simply copying and pasting content from Microsoft Word to Contribute.

Importing content from Microsoft Excel

If you work with numbers, you're probably very familiar with Microsoft Excel. Much of the content on the Web, from annual reports to sports scores, must be converted from an Excel spreadsheet to an HTML table so that it can be displayed by a Web browser.

In the early days (way back in 1994 when I first started working on the Web), converting financial data from a spreadsheet to a Web page was a tedious task that required a lot of copy and pasting and hitting the tab key more times than you can count. My frustration with this boring task is part of what led me to review Web design programs and ultimately to write books like this one. Even back in the "early days," I knew there had to be a better way, and I was on the lookout when the first Web design programs came on the market.

Unfortunately, it was a few more years before Dreamweaver came along and made the world of Web development so much faster and more efficient, and it was even longer before Contribute came along to make basic page editing even easier. But life is better now and if you're just starting to do Web development work, you should be thankful these tools are here to make it easier.

Just like the Insert Microsoft Word option, you can use this Contribute features to add Excel content to an existing document, to a new page, or to a new page created with a template.

Although you can save an Excel file in HTML format, you're better off leaving the conversion to Contribute, because it creates cleaner code and ensure that the content integrates well with the rest of your site.

Follow these steps to open an existing page in Contribute and insert the contents of a Microsoft Excel document :

1. **Choose View⇨Browser.**

   Contribute changes to Browse mode.

2. **Browse to the page on your Web site where you want to add the Excel content.**

   You can also insert Excel content into a new page.

3. **With the page you want to edit displayed in Contribute, click the Edit button.**

   Contribute automatically downloads the page and changes to Edit mode.

4. **Click to place your cursor on the page where you want to insert the Microsoft Excel content.**

5. **Choose Insert⇨Microsoft Excel Document.**

   The Open dialog box opens, as shown in Figure 3-23.

6. **Navigate around your hard drive to find the Microsoft Excel document you want to insert on the page.**

7. **Click to select the file name.**

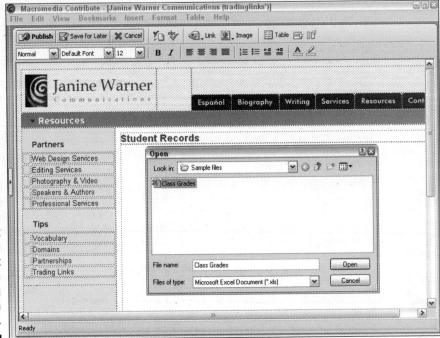

Figure 3-23:
You can use
the Insert
Microsoft
Excel
Document
feature to
add content
to an
existing
page or a
new one.

8. **Click Open.**

   The contents of the Microsoft Excel file are automatically inserted into your page in a table to preserve formatting. (See Figure 3-24 for an example.) You can now edit or format the content as you would any other text in Contribute.

   Although Contribute can recreate the look of the Table you import from Excel, it can not recreate the formulas you may have used to do calculations. If you want to manipulate the data in a table after you've inserted it into your Web page, you may be better of going back to make the calculations in Excel and then importing it again into your Web page.

9. **Choose File⇨Save.**

   The page is saved on your hard drive.

10. **Test and review your changes to ensure they are okay.**

11. **Click the Publish button at the top of the work area.**

   The Publish New Page dialog box opens, prompting you for a filename.

12. **Enter a new filename if you want to replace the one that was automatically generated from your page title.**

13. **Use the Choose Folder button if you want to save the page to a different folder on the server.**

    This enables you to specify where the new page is stored on the server.

14. **Click Publish.**

    The new page and any related files, such as new images, are automatically uploaded to the server. A confirmation message indicates when the uploading is complete. The original Microsoft Excel document is not transferred to the site because the contents were copied directly into the HTML file when you inserted the document.

If you run into problems because the formatting in the Excel document conflicts with style sheets or other formatting you use in your Web site, you may be better off simply copying and pasting content from Microsoft Excel to Contribute.

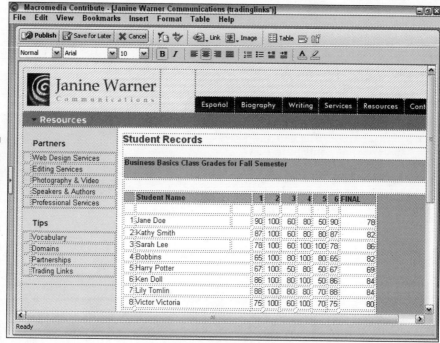

Figure 3-24: Contribute automatically creates a table to store the Excel content when you insert it onto your page.

Editing and Formatting Your Pages

Contribute makes it possible to create a variety of page designs by adding images, formatting text, and using tables to control layout. This chapter is designed to give you an overview of creating and editing pages, but you find lots more details about how to use all of these features later in this book.

- ✔ For more on image editing and placement, check out Chapter 5.
- ✔ To find out how to make the most of tables to create complex page designs, turn to Chapter 7.
- ✔ For more about the different kinds of links you can create, including e-mail links and links to pages on other Web sites, visit Chapter 4.

Part II
"Contributing" to Your Web Site

The 5th Wave   By Rich Tennant

"OK, I think I forgot to mention this, but we now have a Web management function that automatically alerts us when there's a broken link on The Aquarium's Web site."

In this part . . .

No matter how great the content is on your Web site, the first things viewers always notice are the design and the images. This part starts by explaining how links work and how to create them in Contribute. Then you find out about adding images to your pages to bring them to life. You also find a chapter on working with files that are created in other Web design programs to help you avoid some of the potential conflicts and differences among development tools and the pages they create.

Chapter 4

Linking It All Together

● ●

● ●

*L*inks make the Web go 'round. They make it possible to "surf" from one page to another, clicking text or images that are connected to other files on the Web so that you can move from one page to another.

Although links may seem like one of the most magical and complicated elements of the Web, they are really very easy to create, especially with a program like Macromedia Contribute.

You can create links from pages within your Web site as well as from a page on your Web site to a page on a different Web site. You can also create links to e-mail addresses, making it easy for visitors to send messages while they are viewing your site.

Contribute also makes it possible to do something you can't do in many other Web design programs — create a new page and link to it at the same time (you can jump ahead and find out how in the section called "Linking to a new page," later in this chapter). Being able to create a new page as you link to it is useful when you are adding new information to your site and want it to be linked to existing pages.

For example, if you're working on the calendar section and want to add a new event that will be displayed on its own page, you could — while viewing the calendar page — add the text into the calendar, highlight the information you want to link to the new page, and then create the new page and set the link at the same time. Then work on adding the content and formatting it on the new page.

If you're getting a little confused here, don't worry. After you start setting links, it makes more sense. Trust me — this is cool, and it's really easy.

Links are based on the location of a file, an address that includes the name of the file and what folder it resides in. If you rename a file, such as an image or page on your site, you can break the link.

If you create a link to another Web site, you have no control over whether the people who run that Web site change the name of a file or move the page. That's why links to other sites sometimes get broken even if you don't do anything to break the link yourself. Here are two things you can do to try to avoid this problem:

✔ **Check the links on your site regularly.** You can do this by simply browsing your own site and following the links to other sites to make sure they still work. You can do this every week, month, or quarter. Make a note on your calendar to remember to check these links periodically.

✔ **If you link to the main address of a Web site instead of a specific page within a site, it's less likely to change.** For example, I'm not as likely to change my main address, www.JanineWarner.com, as I am to change the address to a specific page on my site, such as a page about a particular book. For example, if the page about my *Dreamweaver MX For Dummies* book is www.JanineWarner.com/books/dreamweavermx, I may change that when the next version comes out, and the link to the specific page could get broken. But if I link to the front page of my site and just instruct readers to look for the latest version of my book, I probably won't ever have to change the link. Now, I know that people link to specific pages so I try not to change them and just add new ones, something you can also keep in mind when you're working on your own site.

Setting Links

Contribute makes it delightfully easy to create all different kinds of links. The most important thing to keep in mind is that a link is essentially an address (URL) that tells a viewer's browser what page to go to when the viewer clicks the text or image with the link.

If the page you want to link to is within your own Web site, you want to create an *internal link* that includes the *path* that describes how to get from the current page to the linked page. The path includes the name of the file and the name or names of the folder or folders that file resides in.

In the example I'm using in this chapter, I'm working on a Web site that features photos I've taken throughout the Southwest. In a site like this, you may have several pages about different kinds of geographic areas, and you may organize those pages in one folder so that you can keep track of them. So you may have folder called "oceans" with a file called "beaches.htm" inside of it. In this case, when you set the link, the text that will appear in the link is "oceans/beaches.htm." Fortunately, you don't have to remember this or know how to write it — you'll use a simple browse button in Contribute to set the link. Find out how in the next section called "Linking pages within your Web site."

If you link to a page on a different Web site, you create an *external link*. An external link must include the full Internet address of the other site. Here's an example of the text that would appear in an external link, also called an absolute link: http://www.coastaltraveler.com.

Although you don't have to type the http:// at the beginning of a Web site address to get to a site in most browsers, you should use the full URL, including the http://, when you create an external link. Otherwise, the browser may think that the www.whatever.com is the name of a folder on your Web server instead of an external site address and will result in a 404, Page Not Found Error. (See Figure 4-4 for an example of how you would set a link to Macromedia's Web site using their full URL.)

Linking pages within your Web site

Linking from one page in your Web site to another page that already exists on your site is easy. Here's how you create a link to another page on your site:

1. **In Contribute, browse to the page on which you want to create a link and click the Edit button to download the page so you can work on it.**

2. **Select the text or image that you want to serve as the link (meaning the text or image that when a user clicks, opens the new page).**

3. **Click the Link icon at the top of the work area.**

   A drop-down window opens, as shown in Figure 4-1.

   Alternatively, if you want to insert new text that will serve as a link, you can enter text into the Link text area on the Insert Link page, and it automatically appears with the link wherever your cursor appears on the page that you are linking from.

4. **Select Browse to Web Page to create a link to another page in your site on the Web server.**

   Alternatively, choose File on My Computer if you know the page is saved on your computer. (*Hint:* If you don't know whether the page is on your computer, stick with my first instruction and Browse to find the page on the server.)

Figure 4-1:
To create
a link in
Contribute,
highlight
the text or
image you
want to
serve as the
link and
then click
the Link
button at the
top of the
page.

The Insert Link dialog box opens, displaying the Browse to Web Page panel, as shown in Figure 4-2.

5. **In the Insert Link dialog box, click the Browse button and navigate to the page you want to link to.**

This works much the way you would navigate around a Web site with a browser. You follow the links until you find the page you want to link to, and the address of the page is automatically inserted into the link box.

Alternatively, you can enter the text manually if you know the name of the file and path.

6. **Click OK.**

The link is automatically set. To test your work, choose File➪Preview in a Browser. When you are finished with the page, you can use the Publish button to save your changes to the server.

If the page is part of a frameset, use the Target field in the Advanced section of the Property Inspector to specify which frame the linked page should open into. (You find out more about setting links in frames in Chapter 8.)

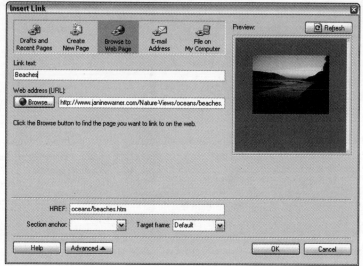

Figure 4-2:
Simply
browse to
find the
page you
want to link
to, and the
link is auto-
matically
set.

Linking to a new page

Often you want to add content to your Web site and find yourself in the position of creating a new link on one page that will go to another page that
doesn't exist yet. Technically, you can't create a link to a page that doesn't
exist, but Contribute was designed to help you overcome the common challenges of Web design, and the folks at Macromedia came up with a special
system that enables you to create a new page at the same time you link to it.
Here's how:

1. **In Contribute, browse to the page on which you want to create a link
   and click the Edit button to download the page so you can work on it.**

2. **Select the text or image that you want to serve as the link (meaning
   the text or image that when a user clicks, opens the new page).**

3. **Click the Link icon at the top of the work area.**

   A drop-down window opens (refer to Figure 4-1).

   Alternatively, if you want to insert new text that will serve as a link, you
   can enter text into the Link text area on the Insert Link page, and it automatically appears with the link wherever your cursor appears on the
   page that you are linking from.

4. **Select Create New Page to create a new page that you will link to.**

   The Insert Link dialog box opens, displaying the Create New Page panel,
   as shown in Figure 4-3.

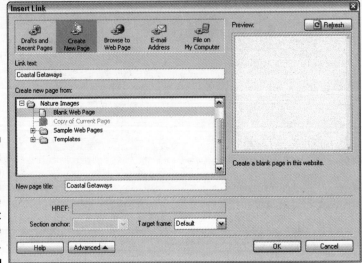

Figure 4-3:
You can
create a
new page
and link to it
at the same
time.

5. **In the Insert Link dialog box, enter a name for the new page in the New Page Title text area.**

6. **Click OK.**

   The link is automatically set, and the new blank page opens in the work area. To test your work, choose File⇨Preview in a Browser. When you are finished with the page, you can use the Publish button to save your changes to the server.

If you want to create a new page by saving a copy of an existing page, do that before you try to set the link. Choose File⇨New Page and then select Copy of Current Page from the New Page dialog box. Note that you can only create a copy of a page if you are viewing it in browse mode, meaning you are not editing the page. Similarly, this is not an option if you are trying to create a new page while linking from an open page or if you create a new page from a template.

Linking to pages outside your Web site

Linking to a page on another Web site — called an *external link* — is even easier than linking to an internal link. All you need is the URL of the page to which you want to link, and you're most of the way there.

To create an external link, follow these steps:

1. **In Contribute, browse to the page on which you want to create a link and click the Edit button to download the page so you can work on it.**

2. **Select the text or image that you want to serve as the link (meaning the text or image that when a user clicks, opens the new page).**

3. **Click the Link icon at the top of the work area.**

   A drop-down window opens (refer to Figure 4-1).

   Alternatively, if you want to insert new text that will serve as a link, you can enter text into the Link text area on the Insert Link page, and it automatically appears with the link wherever your cursor appears on the page that you are linking from.

4. **Select Browse to Web Page to create a link to a page on another Web site.**

   The Insert Link dialog box opens, displaying the Browse to Web Page panel, as shown in Figure 4-4.

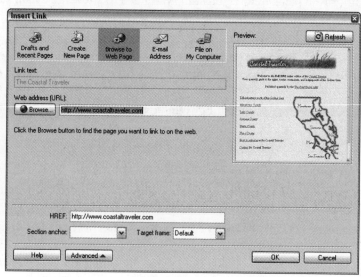

Figure 4-4:
To link to another Web site, use the Browse button or simply enter the URL in the Insert Link dialog box.

5. **In the Insert Link dialog box, enter the URL of the site you want to link to in the Web address text area.**

   Make sure you type in the entire URL, including the `http://` part, at the beginning. Alternatively, you can click the Browse button and navigate to the page you want to link to. You can use this feature to browse the Web as you would if you were using a regular browser. You can go to a search engine and look for a page you want to link to, or you can follow links on a site to get to an internal page. Just keep surfing until the page you want to link to is displayed in the Browse to Link dialog box.

6. Click OK.

The link is automatically set. To test your work, choose File⇨Preview in a Browser. When you are finished with the page, you can use the Publish button to save your changes to the server.

Setting a link to an e-mail address

Another common link option goes to an e-mail address. E-mail links make it easy for visitors to send you messages. I always recommend that you invite visitors to contact you because they can point out mistakes in your site and give you valuable feedback on how you can further develop your site.

Setting a link to an e-mail address is almost as easy as setting a link to another Web page. Before you start, you need to know the e-mail address to which you want to link.

To create an e-mail link in Contribute, follow these steps:

1. **In Contribute, open the page on which you want to create a link and click the Edit button to download the page so you can work on it.**

2. **Select an image or highlight the text that you want to act as the e-mail link.**

3. **Click the Link icon at the top of the work area.**

   A drop-down window opens (refer to Figure 4-1).

4. **Select E-mail Address to create a link that automatically launches an e-mail message with the e-mail address you specify.**

   The Insert Link dialog box opens, displaying the E-mail Address panel, as shown in Figure 4-5.

5. **In the Insert Link dialog box, enter the e-mail address you want messages to automatically be addressed to.**

6. **Click OK.**

   The e-mail link is automatically created. When a visitor to your Web site clicks an e-mail link, the browser automatically launches an e-mail program and opens a new e-mail message with the specified address so the visitor can simply type a subject and message and then send it. To test your work, choose File⇨Preview in a Browser. When you are finished with the page, you can use the Publish button to save your changes to the server.

   Even if the page is part of a frameset, you don't need to specify a target for an e-mail link. (To find out more about framesets and targets, see Chapter 8.)

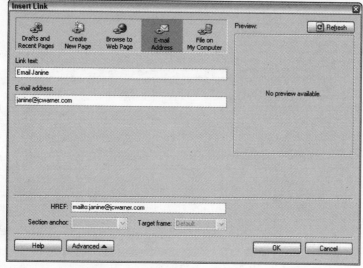

Figure 4-5:
To create an
e-mail link,
enter the
e-mail
address in
the Insert
Link dialog
box.

Changing Page Properties

Contribute provides access to many of the elements you can change across
an entire page, such as text and link colors, in the Page Properties dialog box.
You can also change the background color, background image, margins, and
page title (the text that appears at the very top of the browser, next to the
browser name; this is also the text that is saved in a user's bookmarks list.)
Page Properties are covered in Chapter 3 and Background Images are covered in Chapter 5. For now, let's keep things simple and just change the link
colors.

To change the Link Colors on a page, follow these steps:

1. **In Contribute, create a new page or open an existing page on which
   you want to change the page properties; then click Edit to download
   the page so you can work on it.**

2. **Choose Format➪Page Properties.**

   The Page Properties dialog box appears, as shown in Figure 4-6.

3. **Click the color swatch box next to Link color to reveal the color
   palette (you see the color palette open for the Active link color in
   Figure 4-6).**

   The Link color option controls what color links are displayed in on
   your page.

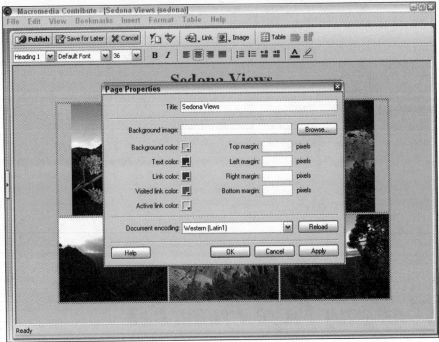

Figure 4-6:
The Page
Properties
dialog box
enables you
to change
link colors,
as well as
specify a
title for the
page.

4. **Choose any color you like. (Just make sure it will look good with the text color you select and that your text will still be readable against the background color or image on the page.)**

   The color you selected fills the color swatch box. The link color is not changed until you click the Apply or OK buttons.

5. **Click the color swatch box next to Visited link color to reveal the color palette for that option.**

   The Visited link color option controls what color links are displayed on your page after they have already been selected by a user.

6. **Choose any color you like, (But again, make sure it will be readable against your background color. In general, a light background color works best with a dark text color and vice versa.)**

7. **Click the color swatch box next to Active link color to reveal the color palette for that option.**

   The Active link color option controls what color links are displayed in on your page when they are being clicked by a visitor.

8. **Choose any color you like, (Again, make sure the color will be readable.)**

9. **Click Apply to see how the link and text colors look on your page.**

   Note that the Text and Link colors will be visible only in Contribute. The Visited Link and Active Link colors are visible only in a browser because the Visited Link color displays only after the link has been visited in a browser. The Active Link color displays only when the link is actively being selected.

10. **Click OK to finish and close the Page Properties dialog box.**

    To test your work, choose File➪Preview in a Browser. When you are finished with the page, you can use the Publish button to save your changes to the server.

Testing Links

You should always test your work, but especially when you create links. It's just so easy to get them wrong or to have them work on your computer but then not work properly on the server.

To test your links, you must first publish the pages you've created or revised on the server and then use the Browse feature to navigate around your site, clicking all of your links to make sure they work. Check out Chapter 11 for more information on how to publish your pages.

Chapter 5

Bringing Pages to Life with Images

*T*he beauty of the Web is that you can combine images and text — creating complex messages and using a wide range of graphics to illustrate key concepts — and make your pages look more aesthetically pleasing.

Adding graphics to a Web page, such as the one shown in Figure 5-1, is a lot easier than most people think, and Contribute makes it click-of-a-button easy. The first step is to collect the images you want to use and ensure that they are in the correct *format*. When we're talking about images, *format* refers to whether the image is a GIF, JPG, or some other format, such as a TIF or PSD file, more commonly used for print. This chapter starts with some general information about image formats and how images are displayed on a Web page to help you get the general concepts before you start putting images on your pages.

If you have the image you want to use and it's the right size and format already, you can skip ahead to the section "Inserting Images on Your Pages" for step-by-step instructions designed to get your images online quickly and easily.

Figure 5-1:
Even on Web sites that aren't designed to showcase images, the photographs and other graphics are what bring a site to life.

Understanding Web Graphics

Images come in many formats, sizes, and shapes (see Table 5-1), but on the Web you have limited options — you can use only GIF and JPEG images on Web pages, and you want the images to be as small as possible because that's what makes them load faster for your viewers.

Table 5-1	Image Formats and What They're Good For		
Image Format	*Full Name*	*Pronounced*	*Best Used For*
GIF	Graphic Interchange Format	*giff* (*g* as in golf) or *jiff* (*j* as in jump) Both pronunciations are used commonly.	Graphic format designed for the Web. Best choice for line art, such as one- or two-color logos, simple drawings, and basically any image that has no gradients or blends.

Image Format	Full Name	Pronounced	Best Used For
JPG (also JPEG)	Joint Photographic Experts Group (The extension comes from the name of the development group that created this compressed color image storage format)	*j-peg*	Graphic format designed for the Web. Best choice for colorful, complex images, such as photographs and any images containing gradients or color blends.
PNG	Portable Network Graphics	*ping*	A relatively new format designed for the Web. Unfortunately, it's not widely used because it is not supported by all browsers.
TIF	Tagged Image File	*tiff*	Does not work on the Web. This image format is well suited for designs that will be printed and need high resolution.
PICT	Picture	*pict*	A Macintosh graphic file format well suited for print but not supported on the Web.
BMP	Bitmap Graphic	*B-M-P*	An image format developed by Microsoft that is not supported on the Web.
PSD	(Adobe) Photoshop Data file	*P-S-D*	The default format for images created in Photoshop. Does not work on the Web, but is ideal for original image versions because it maintains all Photoshop layers and other formatting that can be lost when converted for use on the Web.

In print, images often come in TIF, PICT, or BMP formats, but on the Web images saved in those formats won't work — they have to be converted to GIFs or JPEGs before you load them on a Web site.

If you have the right software, the conversion isn't too hard to do, but Contribute is not an image program, so it won't help you. Fortunately, Macromedia makes a wonderful image program for the Web called Fireworks, which is ideally suited to the task of creating or converting images for the Web and includes an easy-to-use wizard that walks you through the conversion process effortlessly, even if you're new to using image programs. Adobe also makes a program, called ImageReady, specifically for designing and converting images for the Web.

You'll also hear people talk about *optimizing* images for the Web. In this context, *optimizing* means making the image load as quickly as possible by making it as small as possible. *Small* on the Web has two meanings: physical size and file size, which are determined by factors such as the number of colors used and the level of compression.

The most important thing to keep in mind when placing images on a Web page is that you want to keep your file sizes as small as possible. You may ask, "How small is *small?*" The best answer is usually as small as you can stand it (again, we're talking about file size, not just physical size, and much of that is about the quality of the image and how good it looks).

Before you demand that all of your images look picture-perfect online, remember that the larger your graphics files are, the longer people have to wait for them to download before they can see them. You can have the most beautiful picture of Mount Everest on the front page of your Web site, but if it takes forever to download, most people aren't going to be patient enough to wait to see it.

More about GIFs

GIFs, aside from the barely-supported PNG format, is the only file format widely accepted that can have an invisible color to create a transparency effect. GIFs can also have multiple frames, so you can create small animated loops with this format. Ads on the Web, generally referred to as *banners,* are often made in GIF or animated GIF formats.

Designers who want to create buttons or banners with text for a Web page most often create these elements as GIFs. The GIF format is ideal for stylized text because you can often create text images with only a few colors, and because GIF offers the option of transparency, you can make it appear that the text floats on the page by making the background invisible.

Also remember that when you build pages with multiple graphics, you have to consider the cumulative download time of all the graphics on the page. So if you want more than one picture on one page, smaller is definitely better. Most Web pros consider anything from about 60K to 80K a good maximum *cumulative* size for all the graphics and other elements on a given page. With the increasing popularity of DSL and cable modems, however, many Web sites are starting to become a bit more graphics-heavy. However, anything over 150K is definitely a no-no if you expect people with dial-up modems (56K and under) to stick around long enough to view your pages.

Achieving small file sizes requires using compression techniques and color reduction, tasks that can be achieved using any of the graphics programs mentioned in the preceding section. Whatever program you use, you should understand that image sizes can be reduced to varying degrees and that the challenge is to find the best balance between small file size and good image quality. If you really want to find out the best ways to create graphics for the Web, read *Web Design For Dummies* by Lisa Lopuck (published by Wiley Publishing, Inc.). It has a fantastic section on designing Web graphics.

Inserting Images on Your Pages

Contribute makes placing images on your Web pages easy. Whether you are creating a new page or adding an image to an existing page, the basic steps are the same.

To place an image in a *new* file, follow these steps:

1. **Choose File➪New.**

   The New Page dialog box opens.

2. **Select Bank Web Page to create a new page.**

   You can also create a new page using a template if your site has been set up for with Templates. Templates are accessible from the Templates folder in the New Page dialog box.

3. **Enter a name in the Page Title text field.**

   The name you enter will be displayed in the title area of the page in the top of the browser when it is displayed. Contribute also uses this name as the file name for the HTML document.

   Because most servers don't support file names with spaces or special characters, Contribute automatically removes them from the file name but leaves the title exactly as you wrote it.

4. **Click the Insert Image icon at the top of the Contribute work area (the icon with the small tree on it).**

5. **If the image you want to use is on your computer, but not on the Web server, choose From My Computer and follow the next step. If the image you want to insert is already on the server, choose From Website and skip to Step 7.**

6. **In the Select Image dialog box (see Figure 5-2), browse your local drive until you locate the image you want to place on the page and then skip to Step 8.**

   Alternatively, you can insert images simply by choosing Insert⇨Image⇨ From My Computer, which brings up the same dialog box.

   You can only use images in GIF, JPEG, or PNG formats on the Web. If you use another format, such as a TIF or PICT file, Contribute will not display it in the Select Image dialog box.

7. **In the Choose Image on Website dialog box, browse the server until you locate the image you want to place on the page.**

   Alternatively, you can insert images simply by choosing Insert⇨Image⇨ From Website, which brings up the same dialog box (see Figure 5-3).

8. **Double-click to insert the image you want or click once and then click the Select (or Open) button.**

   The image automatically appears on your page.

Figure 5-2:
Use the
Select
Image
dialog box,
available
when you
choose
Insert⇨
Image⇨
From My
Computer, to
insert an
image from
your hard
drive.

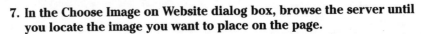

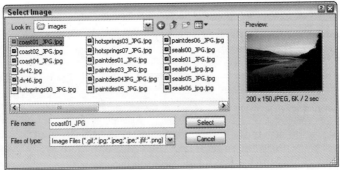

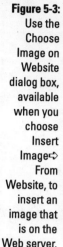

Figure 5-3:
Use the
Choose
Image on
Website
dialog box,
available
when you
choose
Insert
Image⇨
From
Website, to
insert an
image that
is on the
Web server.

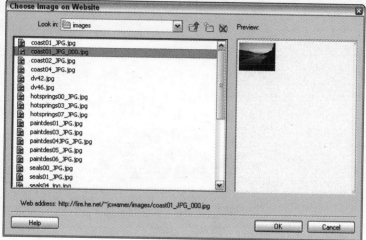

Aligning Images on a Page

After you place an image on your Web page, you may want to center it, place it next another image, or align it so that text can wrap around it. In the following two sections — "Centering an image" and "Aligning an image with text wrapping" — you discover how to alter the alignment of an image.

Centering an image

To center an image on a page, follow these steps:

1. **Click to select the image that you want to center.**

2. **From the icons for alignment options at the top of the Contribute workspace, shown in Figure 5-4, click the Center Alignment icon.**

   The image automatically moves to the center of the page. Beware that alignment options adjust the alignment of everything on that same line.

Figure 5-4:
Use the alignment icons at the top of the Contribute workspace to center, left, or right-align an image.

Aligning an image with text wrapping

To align an image to the left or right of a page and wrap text around it, follow these steps:

1. **Insert the image immediately to the left of the first line of the text.**

   The easiest way to do this is to place the cursor before the first letter of text; then select Insert➪Image.

   Don't put line breaks between the image and the text.

2. **Click to select the image.**

3. **Choose Format➪Image Properties.**

4. **In the Image Properties dialog, choose the alignment option you want from the Align drop-down list, as shown in Figure 5-5.**

5. **Click to Apply to view changes; click OK to apply the changes and close the dialog.**

   The image aligns to the left or right as specified, and the text automatically wraps around it, as shown in Figure 5-6.

To prevent text from bumping right up against the image, add horizontal or vertical padding. As you can see in Figure 5-5, I've added five pixels of padding in the Image Properties dialog box to achieve the result you see in Figure 5-6.

Figure 5-5:
Use the alignment options in the Image Properties dialog box to align an image in a way that enables text wrapping.

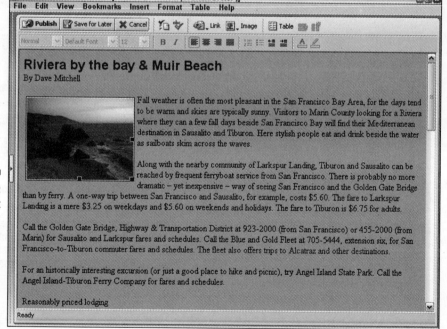

Figure 5-6:
To wrap text around an image, use the Image Properties dialog box to alter alignment.

Adding a Background

Background images can bring life to a Web page by adding color and fullness. When you insert an image into the background of a page, the image repeats across and down the entire screen area. Used cleverly, a background image can help create the illusion that the entire page is one large image while still downloading quickly and efficiently. The trick is to use a relatively small background image that creates a dramatic effect when it *tiles* (repeats) across and down the page (see Figures 5-7 and 5-8).

Beware that certain backgrounds can make it hard to read text that's placed on top of them. Choose your background images carefully and make sure there is plenty of contrast between your background and your text — it's hard enough to read text on a computer screen as it is.

When you set an image as the background for your Web page, the browser repeats it across and down the page, as you see in Figure 5-7. This is why background images are often called *tiles,* because they repeat like tiles across a kitchen floor. However, if you use a long, narrow image as a background or a large image that's small in file size, you can create many effects beyond a repeating tile. The image shown in Figure 5-7 was intentionally created to be wider than most computer screens so that the colored area would repeat on the left but the white area would fill the right. This is a great way to divide up sections of page.

If you don't want a background image to tile, your only option is to use an image that is taller and wider than most monitors. For this effect, you need to create a background image that is as large as 1200 x 1600 pixels in size. The key here is that you must be careful to keep your image file size very small. Background images of these dimensions work well only if you are using GIFs with very limited numbers of colors in them or highly compressed JPEG images. Because GIFs can use only a couple of colors, their files sizes stay small even though their physical dimensions are huge, so they generally work best for this.

Whether you create a small square or rectangle image that you want to tile across your page, or one large image that you want to fill the entire screen by itself, you follow the same steps in Contribute to apply it to your page.

To set a background on a Web page, follow these steps:

1. **Choose Format⇨Page Properties.**

   The Page Properties dialog box appears, as shown in Figure 5-9.

2. **Click the Browse button to the right of the text box next to Background Image.**

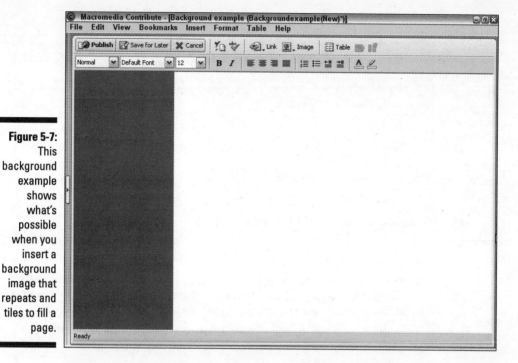

Figure 5-7:
This background example shows what's possible when you insert a background image that repeats and tiles to fill a page.

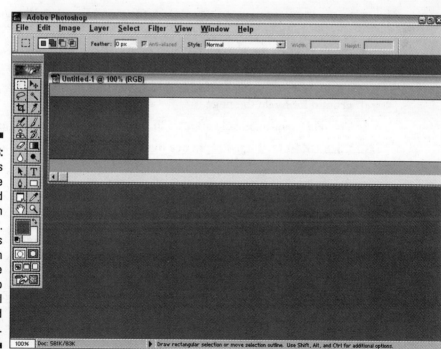

Figure 5-8:
This tile is used as the background image in Figure 5-7. Here it is shown in Adobe Photoshop in its actual size and shape.

3. **If the image you want to use is on your computer, choose From My Computer and follow the next step. If the image you want to insert is already on the server, choose From Website and skip to Step 5.**

4. **In the Select Image dialog box, browse your local drive until you locate the image you want to use for your background on the page and skip to Step 6.**

5. **In the Choose Image on Website dialog box, browse the server until you locate the image you want to use for your background.**

6. **Click to select the image you want to insert and then double-click it to insert or click once and then click the Select (or Open) button.**

7. **Click Apply in the Page Properties dialog box to see how the background looks on the page.**

   The image automatically appears in the background of your page.

8. **Click OK in the Page Properties dialog box to finish.**

Creating Your Own Images

The best way to get original images is to create your own. If you're not graphically talented or inclined, consider hiring someone who can create images for you. If you want to create your own images for use in Contribute, Fireworks is a good program to start with because of its tight integration with Contribute and overall "dummy-proof" features — no pun intended!

Fireworks is a perfect tool for making Web graphics and is easy to learn because it shares a common interface with Contribute. However, you can use any other image-editing programs on the market either separately or in unison with Fireworks. The following list of image-editing programs shows you a little of what's out there. Most of these programs also allow you to scan photographs and logos using a scanner.

The last few years have seen a tremendous advancement in the features and capabilities of specialized Web graphics programs as well as increased competition between application vendors, especially the heavyweights like Adobe and Macromedia. Consequently, the current "best of the crop" graphics program is a toss-up between Macromedia's Fireworks and Adobe's Photoshop. One of these two programs will come out on top of almost any comparison of features and ability to produce the smallest Web graphics. If you're serious about Web graphics, I highly recommend getting one of these two programs — they're the cream of the crop and can easily pay for themselves by giving you the most professional and efficient results on your Web projects.

However, if you don't have the budget or the time to learn more complex programs, you may be better off with a more limited photo-editing program such as Adobe PhotoDeluxe, which is a capable yet far less expensive option, costing only around $49. For creating buttons, banners, and other Web graphics on a budget, consider Jasc Paint Shop Pro, MicroFrontier Color It!, or Microsoft Image Composer.

Unless otherwise indicated, all of these programs are available for both Mac and Windows and all offer free trial or demo versions on their respective Web sites:

- **Macromedia Fireworks** (www.macromedia.com): Fireworks was one of the very first image-editing programs designed specifically to create and edit Web graphics. Fireworks gives you everything you need to create, edit, and output the best-looking Web graphics, all in one well-designed product. Besides sharing a common interface with Contribute, Fireworks also integrates extremely well with Contribute to speed up and simplify the process of building a Web site. In Chapter 11, I cover some of the special features of Fireworks and Contribute that help you to work together with these two programs.

- **Adobe Photoshop** (www.adobe.com): Adobe calls Photoshop the "camera of the mind." This is unquestionably the most popular image-editing program on the market and a widely-used standard among graphics professionals. With Photoshop, you can create original artwork, correct color in photographs, retouch photographs and scanned images, and do much more. Photoshop has a wealth of powerful painting and selection tools in addition to special effects and filters to create images that go beyond what you can capture on film or create with classic illustration programs. The latest versions of Photoshop also add a wealth of features for creating and editing Web graphics, putting it on par with Fireworks in this department.

✔ **Adobe Photoshop LE and PhotoDeluxe** (www.adobe.com): For novices or users who don't need all the bells and whistles offered in the full-blown version of Photoshop, Adobe offers two products that provide just the basic features — Photoshop LE and PhotoDeluxe. One or the other often comes bundled with a scanner or printer. While you can still accomplish a lot with Photoshop LE, it's not great for preparing Web images. However, PhotoDeluxe *is* geared for Web graphics output and is very easy to learn and use.

✔ **Adobe Illustrator** (www.adobe.com): Illustrator is one of the industry standards for creating illustrations. You can drag and drop illustrations that you create in Illustrator right into other Adobe programs, such as Photoshop or PageMaker. Illustrator also comes with an export feature that enables you to export your illustrations in GIF or JPEG format with a browser-friendly palette of colors so that your illustrations look great on the Web.

✔ **Corel Photo-Paint** (www.corel.com): Widely used, though definitely not an industry standard, Corel Photo-Paint offers almost all the same features and capabilities as Adobe Photoshop for a fraction of the price. Photo-Paint comes with a generous clip art and royalty-free photography collection. One of the best things about Photo-Paint is that for about $50 less than Photoshop, you can get the complete Corel Draw Graphics Suite, which includes Photo-Paint, Draw and RAVE 3D. Undoubtedly, this is a great set for home users who want professional-grade graphics and page layout capabilities at a more affordable price.

✔ **Equilibrium DeBabelizer** (www.equilibrium.com): DeBabelizer, by Equilibrium Technologies, is a graphics-processing program capable of handling almost every image format ever used on a computer. This one probably isn't the best program to use for creating images from scratch, but it does excel at some of the highly specialized tasks of preparing and optimizing images for the Web. One of the best features of DeBabelizer is its capability to convert images from just about any format to just about any other. If you have a bunch of images to convert, you can use DeBabelizer's *batch convert* feature, which enables you to automatically convert hundreds of photographs into JPEGs or convert many graphics into GIFs all at once without having to open each file separately. Be aware, though, that DeBabelizer has a pretty steep learning curve and isn't recommended for someone just starting out in creating Web graphics.

✔ **Jasc Paint Shop Pro** (www.jasc.com): Paint Shop Pro, by Jasc Software, is a fully featured painting and image-manipulation program available only for Windows. Paint Shop Pro is very similar to Photoshop, but on a more limited scale because it doesn't offer the same range of effects, tools, and filters. However, it costs less than Photoshop and may be a good starter program for novice image-makers. You can also download an evaluation version for free from the Jasc Web site.

✔ **Macromedia Freehand** (www.macromedia.com): Macromedia Freehand is an illustration program used widely both on the Web and in print. Freehand has many excellent Web features, including support for Web file formats such as GIF89a, PNG, and JPEG, as well as vector formats such as Flash (.SWF) and Shockwave FreeHand (.FHC).

✔ **MicroFrontier Color It!** (www.microfrontier.com): This low-cost, easy-to-use graphics program is available only for the Macintosh and is a great tool for beginners, as well as those on a tight budget. Although it's much more limited than many of the other programs in this list, it provides enough features to create basic banners and buttons for a small business Web site.

Getting Great Graphics: Royalty-Free Clip Art and Graphics

You want your Web graphics to look good, but where do you get them? If you have any design talent at all, you can create your own images with Fireworks or any of the other image programs that I describe in "Creating Your Own Images," earlier in this chapter. If you're not an artist, you may be better off gathering images from *clip art collections* (libraries of ready-to-use image files) and using royalty-free or stock photography, as I describe in this section. If you have a scanner, you can also scan in existing photographs or logos to use.

Unfortunately, Contribute doesn't have any image creation or editing capabilities of its own, so you have to use a different program if you want to create or edit images.

If you don't want the hassle of creating your own images (or, like me, you lack the artistic talent), you may be happy to find many sources of clip art available. Royalty-free images, which include clip art and photographs, are generally sold for a one-time fee that grants you all or most of the rights to use the image. (Read the agreement that comes with any art you purchase to make sure that you don't miss any exclusions or exceptions.) You can find a wide range of CD-ROMs and Web sites full of clip art, photographs, and even animations that you can use on your Web site. Speaking of animations, nowadays you can even find Web sites that sell Flash files, animations, buttons, and other artistic elements that you can edit and integrate into your Web site. (For more on creating a multimedia Web site, see Chapter 12.) Many professional designers buy clip art images and then alter them in an image program — such as Macromedia Fireworks, Adobe Illustrator, or Adobe Photoshop — to tailor them for a specific project or to make an image more distinct. Here are some clip art suppliers:

- **Artville** (www.artville.com): Artville is an excellent source of quality illustrations and a great place to find collections of artistic drawings and computer-generated images that can provide a theme for your entire Web site.

- **Eyewire** (www.eyewire.com): One of the world's largest sources of clip art, Eyewire includes illustrations as well as photographs.

- **PhotoDisc, Inc.** (www.photodisc.com): PhotoDisc is one of the leading suppliers of royalty-free digital imagery, specializing in photographs of a wide variety of subjects.

- **Stockbyte** (www.stockbyte.com): Stockbyte is a great source for international royalty-free photos.

- **Web Promotion** (www.webpromotion.com): A great source for animated GIFs and other Web graphics. Artwork on this site is free provided you create a link back to Web Promotion on your Web site, or you can buy the artwork for a small fee.

Chapter 6

Working with Other Web Editors

*I*n theory, all Web design programs should be compatible because HTML files are, at their heart, just ASCII (or plain-text) files. You can open an HTML file in any text editor, including Macintosh SimpleText and Windows Notepad. However, HTML has evolved dramatically over the years and different Web programs follow different standards, which can cause serious conflicts when a page created in one program is opened in another.

One of the reasons Dreamweaver is so popular is because it creates very clean code and is considered more accurate and more respectful of HTML standards than other programs. Dreamweaver is also better at creating pages that work in different browsers and on different platforms.

Contribute was designed much like Dreamweaver, with the same attention to creating clean and universal code. And although you can use Contribute to edit any HTML files, working on pages created in another Web program can be challenging.

If you do use Contribute to edit Web sites that are created in any program other than Dreamweaver, you won't be able to take advantage of all the Dreamweaver integrated features, such as templates, which can be designed to lock certain sections of a page so you can't alter them by accident. If you are working on a site created in Adobe GoLive, for example, there may be no safeguards to keep you from altering any of the page design. If you are working on a page designed in FrontPage, you may find that there are some features you can't edit with Contribute, including FrontPage's interactive features, such as the discussion area and search engine elements.

The following sections describe the most popular HTML editors and are designed to help you appreciate some of the differences between them and Dreamweaver so that you can better use Contribute to edit sites created in these programs.

Microsoft FrontPage

Microsoft FrontPage is one of the most popular HTML editors on the market, in large part because Microsoft office is so popular. FrontPage also offers some powerful features as well as an attractive bundle of programs for Web developers, including Image Composer, a bundled graphics program designed for creating images for the Web. FrontPage also includes *extensions* that you can use to add interactive features, such as a simple search engine or a discussion area, to your Web site. FrontPage Extensions work only if their corresponding programs reside on the Web server that you use, but many commercial service providers now offer FrontPage Web components.

If you've used the Dynamic HTML features in FrontPage, you won't be able to edit those at all in Contribute and need to pay special attention to those features if you decide to convert your site to Dreamweaver (which you may want to consider because Microsoft FrontPage isn't as good as Dreamweaver at creating DHTML features that work in both Netscape Navigator and Microsoft Internet Explorer). Overall, you'll probably improve your DHTML code if you work with Dreamweaver instead of FrontPage. Because DHTML is much more complex than HTML, you probably don't want to edit this code manually — converting from other editors to Dreamweaver can get pretty tricky. You may find that the simplest solution is to delete the DHTML features that you created in FrontPage and re-create them in Dreamweaver.

For more information about Microsoft FrontPage, visit Microsoft's site at `www.microsoft.com/frontpage`, shown in Figure 6-1.

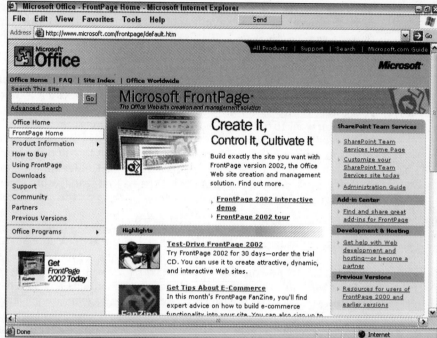

Figure 6-1:
Microsoft's
Web site
features an
extensive
section
about
FrontPage.

Microsoft Word

Although Microsoft Word is a word processor and is not considered an HTML editor per se, it does have HTML output capabilities. As a result, you're likely to encounter pages that have been output from Microsoft Word at some point. The problems you find in HTML code generated from Word are similar to the problems generated from FrontPage: They both tend to output verbose and redundant code that deviates from HTML standards. Because Word-generated HTML is so common, Dreamweaver includes a special Clean Up Word HTML command and Contribute also has some special features for working with Word, as well as content created in Excel. More about this in Chapter 3.

Adobe GoLive

Previously called GoLive CyberStudio, GoLive is Adobe's flagship HTML editor, replacing the earlier PageMill program. GoLive offers some great features for easy page design and a lot of similarities with Dreamweaver, but it also brings a few special challenges of its own. GoLive uses a grid to provide down-to-the-pixel layout control, but as a result, GoLive often outputs very complex code that is difficult to edit in other programs.

The grid feature in GoLive is optional, and if the site you are working on was created without this feature, editing your pages in Contribute should be a much easier task. If the site was created using the grid, you may find that re-creating your pages from scratch in Dreamweaver is your best option and that if you want to use Contribute, you should convert the entire site to Macromedia Dreamweaver. The code used to create the complex HTML tables that GoLive uses in its grids are extremely difficult to edit outside of GoLive. If you're working with people who insist on using GoLive (it is a good program, overall), try to get them to avoid using the Layout Grid feature when designing their pages and you'll have an easier time working on the site with Contribute.

If you've added any JavaScript actions to your pages in GoLive, you won't be able to edit them in Contribute, either, but the actions should still work. Likewise, Dynamic HTML features and animations created in GoLive can't be edited in Contribute or even Dreamweaver, for that matter. You'd really have to work with the coding manually. If your page contains any actions or DTHML features, you may find it easiest to re-create the page in Dreamweaver.

For more information about Adobe GoLive, visit Adobe's Web site at `www.adobe.com/products/golive`, shown in Figure 6-2.

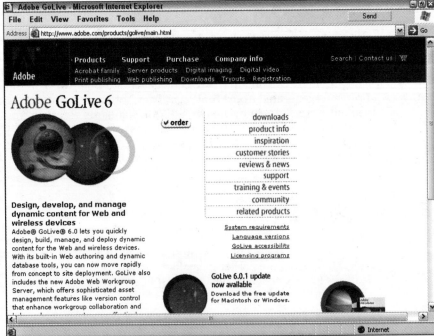

Figure 6-2:
Adobe's Web site features an extensive section about GoLive in the Adobe Products section.

NetObjects Fusion

If you're working on a site created in NetObjects Fusion, you face a more difficult compatibility challenge than you'd have with almost any other HTML editor on the market. That's because Fusion takes a unique approach to Web design and HTML code output.

The biggest challenge with Fusion sites is that Fusion uses complex HTML tables and a transparent graphic to control spacing. The down-to-the-pixel design control enticed many graphic designers because they could create complex layouts with less effort, but the page designs they created are not well supported by all browsers — meaning that the designs didn't work well for broad audience sites.

The problem if you are working on a Web site created with Fusion is that it has very complex code that doesn't lend itself easily to further editing in any other program. Unfortunately, if you want the cleanest HTML code possible, which speeds up download time and makes editing pages easier in the future, your best bet is to recreate your designs from scratch in Dreamweaver and then use Contribute for quick updates or to enable more people to work on the site.

I'm sorry to break this to you, but if you want to use Contribute, you should give up on Fusion. And, if you're importing a site created in Fusion, you should probably start over with Dreamweaver; the transition process is just too daunting to be worth it. Move all of your images into new image directories, set up a new site in Dreamweaver, and start over with your design work.

For more information about NetObjects Fusion, visit their Web site at www.netobjects.com, shown in Figure 6-3.

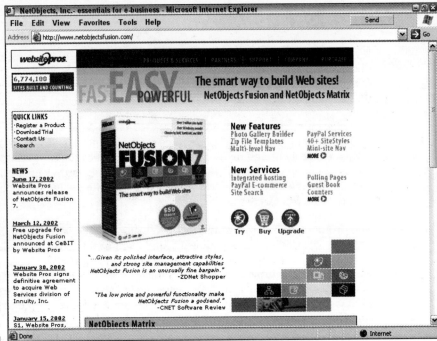

Figure 6-3:
The
NetObjects
Fusion
Web site
provides
extensive
information
about this
Web
development
program.

Other HTML Editors

A few years ago there were lots of different visual HTML editors being used. Today there are only a few major ones left. The few that I discuss here seem to have captured most of the market. Still, you may find yourself inheriting sites built in older visual editors such as Adobe PageMill, or Claris HomePage, to name a few. Each of these should present fewer problems than either FrontPage or GoLive, which tend to be the hardest to work with. In any case, as you consider how best to convert your work into Dreamweaver and Contribute, pay special attention to unusual code output, non-standard rules about HTML tags and syntax, and sophisticated features such as Dynamic HTML and CGI scripts. These are the elements of an HTML page that are most likely to cause problems when you import them into Dreamweaver.

For the most part, you can open any HTML page with Contribute and continue developing it with little concern. If you run into problems, remember that you always have the option of recreating the page from scratch in Contribute or Dreamweaver — a sure way to get rid of any unwanted code. You may also want to use Dreamweaver's Clean Up HTML feature to identify potentially problematic code from another editor. To use this feature in Dreamweaver, choose Commands⇨Clean Up HTML and then select the elements you want to alter in the Clean Up HTML dialog box.

Also be careful if you are use Adobe ImageReady to automatically output HTML with images — for example, if you use the slicing feature to break up a large image into smaller images arranged in an HTML table. ImageReady also relies heavily on the transparent image trick for alignment and makes heavy use of the COLSPAN attribute in Tables. Both of these tricks can be problematic if you change the table width values. If you are having trouble getting your images to align the way you intend, you may again be better off deleting the original page and re-creating the table without these elements.

Working with Dynamic Web Sites

What Contribute loses in its inability to edit complex and dynamic sections of a site, it makes up for by protecting those elements so that if you are editing other content on a page with these features, you can't alter (read: *screw up*) the code those programmers worked so hard to create.

Contribute can edit only HTML content, but you can use it to edit content around dynamic document code so that non-programmers can make some contributions, even to a dynamic Web site.

Dynamic Web sites can be created using a variety of different technologies these days, but most are developed around a database where all of your content is stored and then use sophisticated programming code to generate some or all of the pages of the Web site *dynamically*, meaning the pages are created automatically by pulling the content from a database and inserting it into a template that controls the design and placement.

You should also appreciate the browser that is built into Contribute is capable of displaying dynamic pages, entering data into forms, and even submitting those forms.

Contribute can also be used to create new pages from templates that include dynamic elements, such as ColdFusion tags, includes, and dynamic data elements. Contribute users can also copy existing dynamic pages.

Using templates, you can even enable users to edit content within a dynamic page while protecting the code for the dynamic portions of the page.

Contribute also includes some automatic protections; for example, users cannot edit source code, nor can they edit anything outside of the <body> and <title> tags of a page, so don't even try to work on those elements from within Contribute.

If you're working on a large, database-driven site, such as those created with a program like Vignette (see Figure 6-4), you should probably stick with the content management interface that came with that program. Contribute is not designed to work with a third-party system that is this complex.

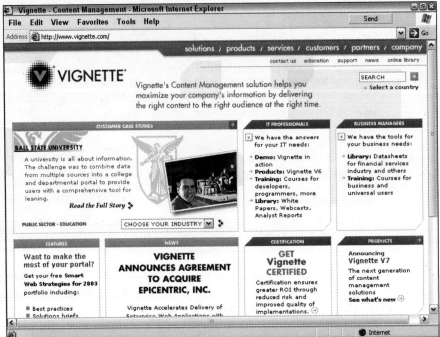

Figure 6-4:
Contribute
is not
designed to
work on
sites
developed
with content
management
systems,
such as the
one created
by Vignette.

Part III

Looking Good (Even if You're Not a Designer)

The 5th Wave By Rich Tennant

@RICHTENNANT

"I can't really explain it, but every time I animate someone swinging a golf club, a little divot of code comes up missing on the home page."

In this part . . .

*I*f you want to create compelling designs within the con-
fines of the rules of HTML, you need to use HTML
tables, frames, and Cascading Style Sheets (CSS). This
part walks you through the maze of nested tables and
merged cells, split pages framed with links, and the power
and design control that you can achieve only with CSS.
You also get a bonus chapter about templates, which
require Dreamweaver to create but are especially powerful when combined with Contribute. Finally, you also get a
chapter about how to publish your work when you're
ready to go public with your new Web design talents.

Chapter 7

Designing Pages with Tables

• •

• •

*E*ven experienced Web designers get frustrated with the limitations of Web design. You just can't do some of the things that are easy to do in print when you're working on a Web page.

For example, you can't just place an image wherever you want on a page by dragging it into place, and you don't have line spacing control in text the way you're used to. Many of the other design features common in a program like Microsoft Word or Quark XPress that are designed for print are lacking in Web design.

As HTML evolves, creating designs precisely the way you want them using Dynamic HMTL features — such as layers — that enable the placement of elements anywhere on a page is becoming possible. The problem is, DHTML is not universally supported by browsers, so what you gain in easy design control, you lose with the risk that someone using an old browser won't be able to view your work as you intended it. That's part of why Macromedia didn't include some of these advanced Web design features in Contribute. Just because it's possible to use some of these new design features doesn't mean it's a good idea. Macromedia is trying to keep Contribute really simple to use, so it's best that there aren't a lot of extra features you shouldn't use, anyway.

So for now, you're going to find that the only way you have to provide much design control in your pages is to use HTML tables — a trick good designers have been using on the Web for years, and one that is still the most popular approach today.

If you've ever used a desktop publishing program such as QuarkXPress or Adobe PageMaker, you've probably used text and image boxes to lay out pages. DHTML layers work much like this, but tables can be used to achieve a similar effect. You use the table cells (the "boxes" created by the intersection of each row and column in a table) to control the placement of text and images. Because you can make merge and split cells, you can use a table to create almost any kind of design. And because you can make the borders of a table invisible, your viewers don't see the underlying structure of your table when they look at your Web page in a browser.

For example, you can use a table to align elements side by side on a page and create columns of text. You still won't get the design control you're used to in a desktop publishing program, but with a little ingenuity, you can create the same effects.

This chapter is designed to show you how to use HTML tables for everything from columnar data to complex page designs. You explore a wide range of uses for HTML tables and find step-by-step instructions for how to create and edit a variety of designs for your Web pages.

Working with tables is one of the most complex things you'll have to do with Contribute, but it's also one of the most valuable tools for creating good design.

Understanding Table Options

You insert elements such as text, images, and multimedia files into cells just as you would insert them on a page without tables. Click to place your cursor in the cell and type to enter text, use the Insert Image icon to add images, and use the multimedia icons in the Insert Media panel to add multimedia.

Whether you are creating a new table or editing one that is already on a page, you should know what's possible before you get started. You can change all the HTML table attributes, including the number of rows and columns, as well as height, width, border size, and cell padding and spacing.

In Contribute, you access these options by clicking the border of a table to select it and then choosing Table➪Table Properties, as shown in Figure 7-1. (Even if the borders are not visible in a table when it's displayed in a browser, Contribute displays tables with a thin, dotted line so you can see what you're doing when you work on them.)

To access the options for an individual cell, place your cursor in the table cell, and select Table➪Table Cell Properties, as shown in Figure 7-2.

Figure 7-1:
To access table options, click the table and open Table Properties.

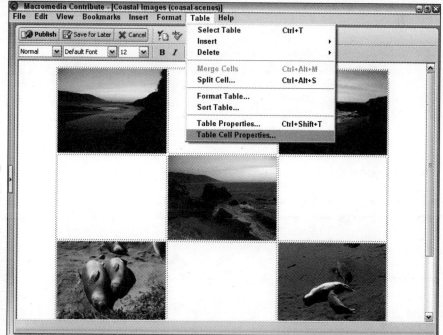

Figure 7-2:
To access individual table cell options, click on the table and open Table Cell Properties.

Sometimes selecting a table with the mouse can be a bit tricky. Here are a couple of tips for selecting a table more easily:

✔ Make sure you are clicking directly on top of the border of the table, which works best for simple tables.

✔ For nested tables, where one table is inside of another table and there can be many confusing borders touching each other, try clicking inside any cell that belongs to the table you want to select and then from the menu, choosing Table⇨Select Table.

Creating a table

Contribute makes it click-of-a-button easy to add a new table to a Web page. Follow these instructions to create a simple new table:

1. **Place your cursor on the page where you want the table**

2. **Click the Table icon at the top of the work area.**

   The Insert Table dialog box opens, as shown in Figure 7-3.

3. **Enter 3 for the Number of rows and 3 for the Number of columns.**

4. **Choose Specific width, enter 300, and choose Pixels from the drop-down menu.**

5. **Enter 0 for Border thickness (this makes the borders invisible).**

Figure 7-3:
The Insert
Table dialog
box makes
it easy to
create a
new table.

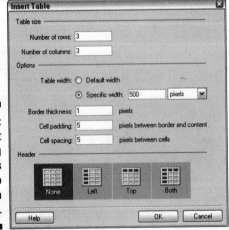

6. **Enter 5 for Cell Padding and 5 for Cell Spacing.**

7. **Click the Top option under Header.**

8. **Click OK**

   A new table appears on the page.

That's it — that's all there is to creating a simple table, but there are many ways you can alter that simple table. The following section is designed to introduce you to the many formatting options you can apply to tables. Review this list to get an idea of what's possible, but don't feel like you need to memorize it — you can always refer back to it, and after you've worked with tables for a while, you start to recognize these options without even thinking about them.

Table formatting choices

The table formatting options listed below are available in the Insert Table dialog box, shown in Figure 7-3, the Table Properties dialog box, shown in Figure 7-4, and the Table Row and Column Properties dialog box, shown in Figure 7-5. Some of the options below are available in more than one dialog box. These options can be used to alter the attributes of tables and their cells when creating or editing a table. The descriptions below explain what each of these options does and how they apply to both creating and editing tables.

- **Rows:** Determines the number of rows in the table. You can alter the number of rows in a table by changing the number. Be careful, though: If you enter a smaller number than already exist, Contribute deletes the bottom rows — contents and all.

- **Columns:** Determines the number of columns in the table. You can alter the number of cells by changing the number. Be careful, though: If you enter a smaller number than already exist in a table, Contribute deletes the columns on the right side of the table — contents and all.

- **Table Width:** Determines the width of the table. You can alter the width by changing the number. The width can be specified as a percentage or a value in pixels. Values expressed as a percentage increase or decrease the table's size relative to the size of the user's browser window, meaning they will expand or shrink to fill the specified percentage of the space available. Values expressed in pixels remain constant no matter how large the viewer's browser window. Pixel sizes are preferable if you want to ensure that the table is always be the same size, but a user may have to scroll to see the entire table.

✔ **Row Height:** Determines the height of the table row. You can alter the height by selecting the radio button next to the pixels text box and entering a or changing the number. Values expressed in pixels remain constant no matter how large the viewer's browser window. Pixel sizes are preferable if you want to ensure the table row will always be the same size, but a user may have to scroll to see the entire table. If you specify Fit to Contents, Contribute will automatically adjust the row height to fit the text, images, or other elements in the row.

Table dimensions expressed as a percentage enable you to create a table that changes in size as the browser window is resized. If you want a table to always take up 75 percent of the browser window no matter how big the user's monitor or display area, percentages are a good way to specify table size. If you want a table to always take up a specific number of pixels — that is, to remain the same size regardless of the browser window size — choose pixels instead of percentages for your table dimensions.

✔ **Cell Padding:** Specifies the space between the contents of a cell and its border.

✔ **Cell Spacing:** Specifies the space between table cells.

✔ **Table Alignment:** Controls the alignment of the table. Options are left, right, center, or default, which aligns the table left in most browsers.

✔ **Border Thickness or Width:** Controls the size of the border around the table. The larger the number, the thicker the border. If you want the border to be invisible, set the border to 0.

✔ **Background Color:** Controls the background color. Click the color square next to this label and select a color from the box that appears. When you click the color square, the cursor changes to an eyedropper, enabling you to pick up a color from anywhere on the page by clicking the color. You can apply this option to a single cell or to the entire table.

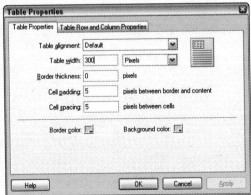

Figure 7-4:
The Table
Properties
dialog box.

✔ **Border Color:** Controls the border color. Click the color square next to this label and select a color from the box that appears. When you click the color square, the cursor changes to an eyedropper, enabling you to pick up a color from anywhere on the page by clicking the color. You can apply this option to a single cell or to the entire table.

Figure 7-5:
The Table
Row and
Column
Properties
dialog box.

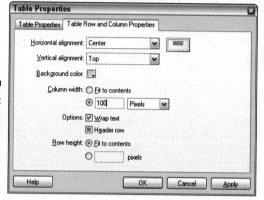

Controlling Cell Options

If you want to alter individual cells, use the Table Cell Properties dialog box, where the following options are available:

✔ **Merge Cells:** To merge cells, you must first select two or more cells by clicking and dragging or by holding down the Shift or Command keys while clicking to select multiple cells. Only contiguous cells can be merged. With the cells selected, choose Table⇨Merge Cells to merge them together.

✔ **Split Cell:** Click inside a cell to select it and then choose Table⇨Split Cells. When you use this option, a dialog box lets you specify if you want to split the row (meaning split the cell horizontally) or the column (meaning split the cell vertically). You can then specify the number of columns or rows, which controls how many times the cell is divided. *Note:* The Split Cell option can be applied to only one cell at a time.

✔ **Horizontal Alignment:** Controls the horizontal alignment of the cell contents. Options are left, right, and center.

✔ **Vertical Alignment:** Controls the vertical alignment of the cell contents. Options are Top, Middle, and Bottom. This is useful if you are trying to ensure that the contents of multiple cells align evenly even if they are different sizes.

- ✔ **W:** Controls the width of the cell.
- ✔ **H:** Controls the height of the cell.
- ✔ **Wrap Text:** Select Wrap Text to enable word wrapping within the cell.
- ✔ **Header:** Use to format a cell's contents using a Header style, which makes the text bold and centered. Only available when an entire row or column is selected.

Using the Format Table Feature

One of the best reasons for using tables is to present lots of data in a clear and structured way. Tables accomplish this because the use of rows and columns allows the reader to follow along easily when there is a lot of data to represent. One of the ways to make your data even more presentable and attractive is to colorize the rows and columns in the table. In the previous section, I show you how to change the attributes of individual cells. In this section, I show you a really great Contribute feature that allows you to select predefined table formats with great color schemes to enhance your presentation. Figure 7-6 shows the advanced table formatting options.

To use the Format Table dialog box:

1. **Select an existing table in a document.**

2. **Choose Table⇨Format Table.**

   The Format Table dialog box appears.

3. **Select one of the color schemes by scrolling the list or modify any of the parameters to create your own scheme.**

4. **Click the Advanced tab to reveal additional formatting options as shown in Figure 7-6.**

5. **Click OK.**

   The color scheme and other formatting options are applied to the table.

These color schemes were created by professional designers so you can be sure they'll look good on your Web page. You can also modify any of the attributes in the Format Table dialog box and create your own color schemes.

Using low-contrast color schemes in tables is considered the most effective way to present content in a table. (Just look at Intuit's Quicken software, E-Trade, Amazon, and so on for real-life examples.) High contrast colors in tables are usually reserved for site menus and submenus or other elements you want to call more attention to.

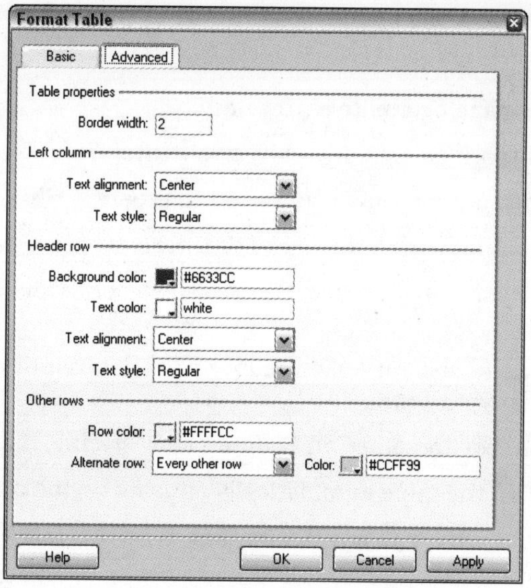

Figure 7-6:
The
Advanced
tab in the
Format
Table dialog
box.

Formatting and Sorting Columns

When you're working with lots of cells in a table, you may want to format multiple cells in the same way. Contribute makes it easy to do that, whether you want to align numbers, make the headings bold, or change the color scheme. But before you start planning how to line up all of your numbers perfectly, be aware that you don't have as much control in HTML as you have in a program such as Excel, where you can align numbers to the decimal point. You can align the content of columns left, right, or center. However, even if you use the same number of digits after the decimal point in all of your numbers, you can't get them to line up precisely unless you use a monospace font (monospace fonts are not very pretty and they're not available from the font list provided in Contribute). Still, if one price is $12.99 and another is $14, express it as $14.00, and when you align right, the numbers will line up relatively well.

In the following steps, I show you how to create a table of financial data in Standard View and align all the data cells on the right so that the numbers align. You can also use these steps to align the contents of table cells to the left, center, or top, or to apply other formatting options, such as bold or italic. In these steps, I insert the data into the table after I create it in Contribute.

To create a table of financial data and align and sort the data, follow these steps:

1. **Open an existing page or create a new one.**

   If you are working with an existing table, skip to Step 7.

2. **Click to place your cursor where you want to create a table.**

3. **Click the Insert Table icon at the top of the work area.**

   Alternatively, you can choose Insert➪Table. The Insert Table dialog box appears.

4. **In the appropriate boxes, type the number of columns and rows you want to include in your table.**

5. **Specify the width, border, and Cell Padding and Spacing; then click OK.**

   When you click OK, the table automatically appears on the page.

6. **Click to place your cursor in a cell, and then type the data that you want in each cell.**

7. **Select the column or row for which you want to change the alignment.**

   Place your cursor in the first cell in the column or row that you want to align; then click and drag your mouse to highlight the other columns or rows that need to be changed.

8. **Choose the desired alignment option from the alignment icons at the top of the screen.**

   If you are sorting financial data, Align Right is usually your best option.

9. **Choose Table➪Sort Table.**

   The Sort Table dialog box opens, as shown in Figure 7-7.

10. **Specify sorting options by using the pull-down menus.**

    These options enable you to sort data alphabetically or numerically, in ascending or descending order. You can sort by row or column.

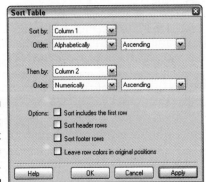

Figure 7-7:
The Sort
Table
dialog box.

Using Tables for Spacing and Alignment

As you get more adept at creating Web pages, you may find that HTML tables are a crucial part of creating almost any design that requires more than basic alignment of elements on a page. Using tables, you can get around many of the limitations of basic HTML and accomplish some of the following design feats:

✔ Evenly-spaced graphic bullets (little GIFs that can take the place of bullets) next to text

✔ Text boxes and fields properly aligned in a form

✔ Images placed wherever you want them on a page

✔ Columns of text that don't span the entire page

✔ Myriad intricate layouts that are impossible to accomplish with HTML alone

In the rest of this chapter, I show you how to use tables to create a variety of page designs, including a few of the ones I just listed.

When you use a table for design control, turn off the border so that it's not visible in the design. You do that by typing 0 in the Border Thickness text box of the Table Property Inspector dialog box while the table is selected.

Why use tables instead of frames?

Some people don't like frames because they can be difficult to create and confusing for users to navigate, and some older browsers can't display frames. So tables provide a more universally accessible design element.

Frames can save a little time because the entire page doesn't have to reload every time a user clicks a link; only the new frame has to load. With a navigation bar, for example, the images and text of the navigation bar stay in their own frame while new material appears in another frame. If you design your page carefully with tables, you can achieve a similar effect, and the download time can be minimal. If you use text

links instead of images, they load so quickly that it doesn't matter. And if you use the same graphics on every page (as most people do in a navigation bar), the linked images reload quickly because they're *cached* (stored in temporary memory on the visitor's computer) the first time the user visits the page.

You can create very similar designs using tables or frames, so you make your choice based on your goals and your audience. If you want to make sure that the largest possible audience can see your page, use tables; if you want to change only part of a page and keep some of your page elements visible at all times, use frames.

Aligning a navigation bar

A common element on Web pages is a *navigation bar* — a row of images or text with links to the main sections of a Web site. Navigation bars are usually placed at the top, bottom, or side of a page where users can easily access them but where they're out of the way of the main part of the page design.

Designers often use HTML frames (see Chapter 8) to insert a navigation bar, but you can effectively place a navigation bar on a page by using tables. The sidebar "Why use tables instead of frames?" can help you make the right choice for your Web site.

Merging and splitting table cells

Sometimes the easiest way to modify the number of cells in a table is to *merge* cells (combine two or more cells into one) or *split* cells (split one cell into two or more rows or columns). This technique makes it possible to vary the space in table sections and customize their structure. For example, you may want a long cell space across the top of your table for a banner and then multiple cells underneath it so that you can control the spacing between columns of text or images. The following two sets of steps show you how to merge and split cells in a table:

To merge cells, create a new HTML page and follow these steps:

1. **Choose Insert⇨Table and create a table with four rows and four columns, width 75 percent, and border 1. Click OK, and the table appears on the page.**

2. **Highlight two or more adjacent cells by clicking and dragging the mouse from the first cell to the last**

   You can only merge cells that are adjacent to one another.

3. **Choose Table⇨Merge Cells.**

   The cells are merged into a single cell using the colspan or rowspan attribute, which makes a single cell merge with adjacent cells by spanning extra rows or columns in the table.

To split a cell, follow these steps:

1. **Click to place your cursor inside the cell you want to split.**

2. **Choose Table⇨Split Cell.**

   The Split Cell dialog box appears.

3. **Select Rows or Columns in the dialog box, depending on how you want the cell to be divided.**

   A cell can be split into however many new rows or columns you want.

4. **Type the number of rows or columns you want to create.**

   The selected cell is split into the number of rows or columns you entered.

Using nested tables: Tables within tables

Placing tables within tables, called *nested tables,* can help you create the most complex designs. You create nested tables by inserting a table within a cell of another table. In the days when you had to write your own code, this was a daunting task. Today, Contribute makes nesting tables easy, enabling you to create complex designs without ever looking at the HTML code.

Nested tables can get pretty messy. As with all design tricks, don't get carried away and overuse nested tables just because Contribute makes them easy to create. The best Web designs are those that communicate the information to your audience in the most elegant and understandable way. Try to avoid nesting your tables too many levels deep. A table within a table within a table is nested three levels deep. Anything more than that gets a bit hairy. Pages that use too many nested tables take longer to download because browsers have to interpret each table individually before rendering the page.

One situation that makes a nested table worth the added download time is when you want to place a table of financial or other data in the midst of a complex page design.

To place a table inside another table, follow these steps:

1. **Click to place your cursor where you want to create the first table, which will be come the outer table.**

2. **Choose Insert⇨Table.**

   The Insert Table dialog box appears.

3. **Type the number of columns and rows that you need for your design.**

4. **Set the Width to whatever is appropriate for your design, and click OK.**

   The table is automatically sized to the width you set.

5. **Click to place your cursor in the cell in which you want to place the second table.**

6. **Repeat Steps 2 through 4, specifying the number of columns and rows that you want and the width of the table.**

   The new table appears inside the cell of the first table.

7. **Type the information that you want in the nested table cells as you would enter content into any other table.**

Tables are designed to automatically adjust to fit their contents. Thus, if you create a table and make it 300 pixels wide and then insert a graphic or another table that is more than 300 pixels wide, the first table adjusts itself to accommodate the contents you have inserted. If you specify fixed sizes and then insert larger contents, Contribute may have trouble managing the conflicting specifications. This can get a bit confusing so it's important to keep track of the contents of a table and to try to design tables to accommodate the contents of all of its cells.

Chapter 8

Working within Frames

*F*rames provide another way to develop site navigation because they enable you to display multiple HTML pages in one browser window and control the contents of each framed area individually. Designers commonly use frames to create a page with two or more sections and then place links in one section that, when selected, displays information in another section of the same browser window. Figure 8-1 shows an example of how frames look with navigation options down the left side of the page that open content in the main area of the page to the right of them.

Web pages that use frames are split into separate sections — or individual *frames*. All the frames together make up a *frameset*. Behind the scenes, each frame of the frameset is a separate HTML file, which makes a page with frames a little complicated to edit, even with Contribute.

At least with the visual editor in Contribute you can view all the HTML files that make up the frameset at the same time and select which one you are going to edit while they are displayed in the way in which they appear in a browser. (If you're starting to get confused, hang in there, frames make a lot more sense when you see them in action.)

Should your site use frames at all?

No one wants to be "framed," whether that means being falsely accused of a crime or trapped in the HTML frameset of a Web site with no escape. That's why it's important to appreciate not only the best way to edit frames, but when to use them to enhance site navigation and how to take best advantage of them if you do use them. You can't create frames in Contribute, so some of the following points won't apply to your work, but it's still good for you to know about the potential problems with frames and you can us this list as a guide to talk with whoever is using Contribute to design your site.

Here's a list of guidelines to follow when using frames:

✔ **Don't use frames just for the sake of using frames.** If you have a compelling reason to use frames, then create an elegant and easy-to-follow frameset. But don't do it just because Contribute makes it easy.

✔ **Limit the use of frames and keep files small.** Remember that each frame you create represents another HTML file. Thus, a frameset with three frames requires a browser to display four Web pages, the three frames pages, plus the frameset page, which can dramatically increase download time.

✔ **Turn off frame borders.** Newer browsers support the capability to turn off the border that divides frames in a frameset. If the section has to be scrollable, the border is visible no matter what. But if you can turn the borders off, your pages look cleaner. Frame borders are thick and an ugly gray in color, and they can break up a nice design. Use them only when you feel that they're really necessary.

✔ **Don't use frames when tables are better.** Tables are easier to create than frames and can provide a more elegant solution to your design needs because they're less intrusive to the design. I include lots of information on creating tables in Chapter 7.

✔ **Don't place frames within frames.** The windows get too darned small to be useful for much of anything, and the screen looks horribly complicated. You can also run into problems when your framed site links to another site that's displayed in your frameset. The sidebar "Resist using frames when you link to other people's Web sites" later in this chapter provides many more reasons to limit using frames inside of frames.

As a navigational feature, frames enable you to keep some information constant, while changing other information on the same page. For example, you can keep a list of links visible in one frame and display the information each link brings up in another frame, as the site shown in Figure 8-1 does.

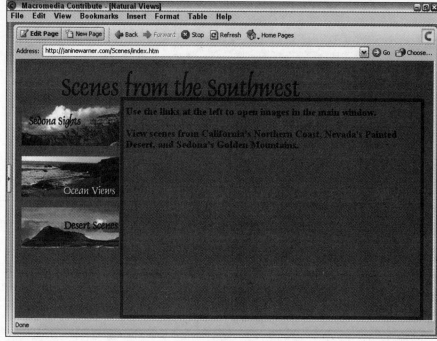

Figure 8-1:
The Nature
site shown
in this image
uses
navigation
buttons in
the left
frame area
that open in
the right
area.

Understanding How Frames Work

Frames are a bit complicated, but Contribute helps to make the whole process somewhat easier. When you edit a Web page with frames in Contribute, you need to remember that each frame area is a separate HTML file, and you need to work on each frame separately. You also want to keep track of which file is displayed in which section of the frame so that you can set links.

Figure 8-2 shows a simple frameset example with three frames, each containing a different HTML page and different text *(Page 1, Page 2, and Page 3)* so that I can clearly refer to them in the numbered steps that follow.

In addition to the files that display in each frame, a separate HTML file needs to be created to generate the frameset. This page isn't visible in the browser, but it describes the frames and instructs the browser how and where to display them. This gets a little complicated, but don't worry. Contribute creates these pages for you. I just want to give you a general understanding of all the files that you're creating so that the steps that follow make more sense.

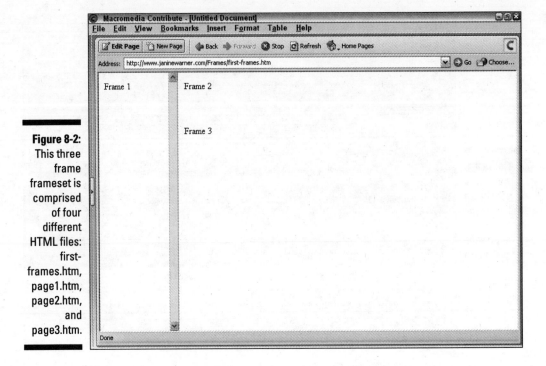

Figure 8-2:
This three
frame
frameset is
comprised
of four
different
HTML files:
first-
frames.htm,
page1.htm,
page2.htm,
and
page3.htm.

To help you understand how this works, take a look at the example in Figure 8-2. In this document, you see three frames, each displaying a different HTML page. The fourth HTML file that makes up the frame page *contains* the other frames but doesn't show up in the browser, even though you see it in the title bar (it's called first-frame.html). This file is the frameset file, and it describes how the frames should be displayed, whether they should be on the left side of the page or the right, the top or bottom, and how large they should be. The name of each frame is used to set links so that you can specify which frame a new HTML file should *target,* or open into. I cover more about linking frames in the "Setting Targets and Links in Frames" section later in this chapter.

Editing a Frame Page

You edit a frame page (that is, a page within a frameset) just as you would any other page. The only thing to keep in mind is that when you use Contribute's browse feature to navigate to the page you want to edit, you see the entire frameset, but you can edit each frame only within the set individually, so you need to specify which frame you want to work on when you select it. Follow these steps to edit a page within a frameset.

1. **Browse to the frameset you want to work with on the server.**

   The frameset displays in Contribute just as it would in a Web browser.

2. **Click the Edit Page button.**

   The Select a Frame to Edit dialog box opens, as shown in Figure 8-3.

3. **Click to select the page you want to work on.**

   Notice that when you select the name of a page, it is highlighted in the display area so you can identify which file name corresponds to which page in the frameset.

4. **Click Edit.**

   The page you selected from the frameset opens in the Contribute work area. You can now edit it like any other page. When you save the changes and publish this page, it is incorporated back into the frameset on the site.

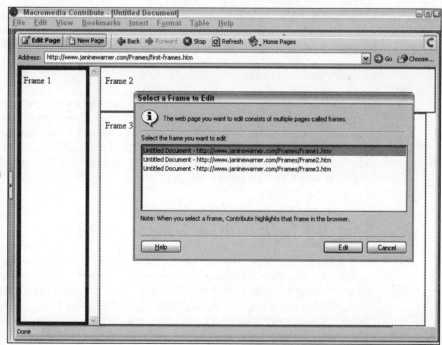

Figure 8-3:
The Select a Frame to Edit dialog box opens when you are viewing a frameset and choose Edit Page.

Setting Targets and Links in Frames

One of the best features of frames is that you can change the contents of each frame separately within the Web browser. This feature opens a wide range of design possibilities that can improve navigation for your site. One very common way to use a frameset is to create a frame that displays a list of links to various pages of your site and then open those links into another frame on the same page. This technique makes it possible to keep a list of links constantly visible and can make navigation a lot simpler and more intuitive.

Setting links from a file in one frame so that the pages they link to open in another frame is like linking from one page to another, and that's essentially what you're doing. What makes linking a frameset distinctive is that, in addition to indicating which page you want to open with the link, you have to specify which frame section it should *target* (open into).

The other thing you have to do before you can set links is to name each frame so that you can specify where the linked file should load. If you don't, the page just replaces the frameset altogether when someone clicks the link — which defeats the purpose of using frames in the first place. Naming the *frame* is different from naming the *file* that the frame represents; the *frame name* is like a nickname that allows you to distinguish your frames from one another on a page and refer to them individually. The *filename* is the actual name of the HTML file for the frame. This makes more sense after you see how it works, as I show in the next section.

Because you won't be creating new frames pages in Contribute, what you need to be concerned with is identifying the names already assigned the pages you are working on so that you can set new links. You find these names automatically displayed in the Target frame pull-down section of the Insert Link dialog box. Follow the steps in the "Setting links with frame targets" section to see how this works.

Setting links with frame targets

Setting links in a frameset is like setting any other links between pages, except that you need to specify the target frame, meaning the frame where the link will be displayed. For example, if you want a link in the right frame to display in the main frame, you need to specify the main frame as the target in the link. If you don't specify a target, the link opens in the same frame the link is in. Because the most common reason to use frames is to keep navigation links in one frame and open them in another, knowing how to target a frame when you set a link is good information to have.

For the purposes of this exercise, I'm going to walk you through creating three text links in the left frame that open in the main frame of a frameset as shown in Figure 8-4. If you're working on your own frameset, use this as a guide to follow along and set the links as they correspond to your frameset.

If this seems confusing, don't fret. It's easier to understand after you try the following steps:

1. **Click the Edit Page button and select the frame that you want to link from.**

   In the example in Figure 8-4, I selected the left frame that has the three Cool links in it.

   The frame page opens in the Contribute work area just like any other page.

2. **Highlight the text you want to link.**

   For this exercise, I highlighted the words *Cool Link 1*. Note that this works the same way if you want to link an image.

3. **Click the Link icon and select Browse to Web Page to link to another page on your site or to another Web site.**

   The Insert Link dialog box opens.

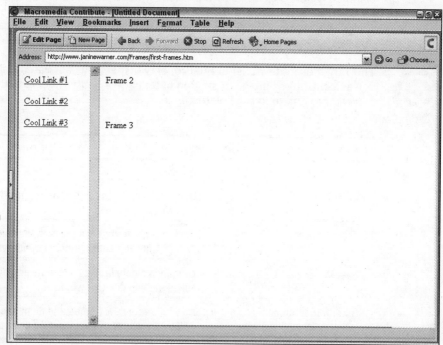

Figure 8-4:
You can create links in one frame that open in another frame.

4. **Use the Browse button to navigate to a page you want to link to or enter the URL of a Web page in the text area.**

   The ULR you want to link to appears in the Web address field. As you see in Figure 8-5, I'm creating a link to www.macromedia.com.

5. **Select the frame name from the Target frame pull-down as shown in Figure 8-5. (Make sure you have selected the Advanced button at the bottom of the dialog to reveal the Target options.)**

   Note that the names should automatically appear in the Target pull-down. Frame names are created when the frames are developed and vary depending on what the person who created the frames chose to call them. If you're not sure what the frame targets are, you can use trial and error to deduce the right one or ask your site administrator for assistance.

Comparing target options

You have many options when you target links in a frameset. As shown in the preceding section, "Setting links to a target frame," you can specify that a linked page open in another frame within your frameset. In addition, you can set linked pages to open in the same frame as the page with the link, to open a completely new page in its own browser window, and even to open a second browser window on top of the browser window that is displaying the frameset. Table 8-1 provides a list of target options and what they mean. You can find all of these options in the Target drop-down list of the Property Inspector.

The Target drop-down list in the Property Inspector is activated only when you select a linked image or section of text and specify the link in the page you want to link to in the link text box.

Table 8-1	Understanding Frame Target Options
Target Name	**Action**
Default	Opens the linked document in the same frame as the link.
Entire Window	Replaces the frameset page with the linked page so that it fills the entire browser window.
New Window	Launches a new browser window and opens the linked page in the new window.
Other target options	As you create new frames and name them, the names are added to the target list so that you can specify them by selecting them from the pull-down list.

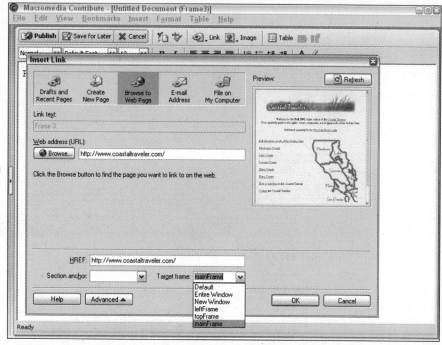

Figure 8-5:
Use the
Target
frame
options in
the bottom
of the Insert
Link dialog
box to set
frame links.

Resist using frames when you link to other people's Web sites

I understand that most people don't want to lose viewers to another site when they set a link, but that's the nature of the Web. If your site is designed well, you shouldn't have to worry about losing people. Instead, you should guide them around your informative site and then politely help them to other resources that they may find of interest — and let them go. Frames keep users captive and usually leave them annoyed with you for taking up part of their browser area with your site. By displaying content from other sites within one or more of the frames in your site, you do yourself more harm than good in trying to keep them.

If you insist on using frames when you link to another site, do so discretely by placing a small,

narrow frame across the bottom of the screen or the left side — not a wide band across the top, and certainly not more than one frame that still contains information from your site. Not only is this rude and ugly, but it's gotten a few Web sites sued because the people they linked to felt that the designers were making it look like their content belonged to the site using the frames.

An additional reason not to use frames when you link to another site is that many other sites use frames, too. You can quickly create a mass of frames within frames that makes it difficult for users to find their way through information.

Chapter 9

Formatting Text in HTML and CSS

· ·

In This Chapter

▶ Appreciating Cascading Style Sheets

▶ Applying CSS with Contribute

▶ Creating HTML styles with Dreamweaver

▶ Using Dreamweaver to create CSS styles

· ·

*T*ext is at the heart of nearly every Web page. In fact, HTML was originally developed as a way to exchange text-only files between scientists and researchers, not to design pretty pages. Graphics didn't come along until later. Before graphical HTML editors like Macromedia's Contribute or Dreamweaver, even formatting text for things like bold and italic required a pretty thorough knowledge of HTML tags, and there were lots of tags to memorize.

After you figure out how to work with text in Contribute, you'll probably conclude that HTML doesn't give you a whole lot of typographic control over your page designs. Welcome to the world of HTML design. Fortunately, things in the HTML world have progressed a lot since the early days of Web design, and thanks to some new technologies, today's Web designers have a lot more control over type than they did even a few years ago.

The evolution of HTML text formatting means that today you can use specific font faces, control size and style more precisely, and even create style sheets. Cascading Style Sheets *(CSS)* are a kind of extended HTML that enable greater style control and the ability to specify formatting features for types of text, such as headlines, even across multiple pages. Because CSS are such a valuable feature for teams working with Contribute, you find out how to use Macromedia's Dreamweaver to create Cascading Style Sheets that can be used by Contribute in the second part of this chapter. But don't worry — you find all you need to know to apply style sheets in Contribute in the first part of this chapter, and if that's all you need to do, you don't need to read any further.

If you don't already have Dreamweaver, you can download a free, 30-day trial version from www.macromedia.com and use it to follow along with the second part of this chapter. But again, don't worry, you don't need Dreamweaver to use style sheets in Contribute. The material in the second part of this chapter is a bonus in this book, designed to give you the instructions you need to create and edit styles using Dreamweaver because they are so valuable in Contribute. In addition to CSS, you find out how to create HTML styles, a unique feature of Dreamweaver that provides an alternative to CSS and enables you to save and apply repetitive text attributes to documents — things like type size, color, bold, italic, and so on.

Appreciating Cascading Style Sheets

CSS provide a whole new level of control over page design. By using CSS, Web page designers can gain control over such things as font type, sizing, spacing, and even exact positioning of page elements in a way that is much more consistent across computer platforms. If you're sure your Web audience can view CSS and you want to learn how to do some really cool stuff with type, read on.

A Cascading Style Sheet is basically a list of rules defined in HTML. HTML already contains a bunch of rules of behavior, but you can neither see them (unless you read a very technical HTML manual) nor alter them — they're kind of like the grammar rules in a language. CSS, however, lets you create your own rules and override the rules of HTML, which are very limited in terms of page design. These new rules determine how the browser renders certain page elements. Imagine if you could invent a bunch of new words and grammar rules for the English language. Now imagine that everyone else can do that, too. What keeps the communication from breaking down is that every time you invent these new rules, you include a dictionary and a grammar guide to go along with each document. That's what CSS is all about.

The term *cascading* refers to the way in which the general CSS rules within a style are overridden by local rules. With CSS, you can create general rules or local rules. Because local rules override the general rules, they are referred to as cascading. This definition becomes clearer as you read on and become more familiar with how CSS operates.

Have you ever used a style sheet in a word processor or desktop publishing application? If so, you can appreciate how style sheets make life easier. CSS is a powerful tool because with it, you can define a set of formatting attributes and then apply them to as many elements on a page or throughout a Web site as you want.

The most powerful aspect of CSS is the ability to make global style changes across a site. Suppose, for example, that one fine day you decide that all of your headlines should be purple rather than blue. You can change the style definition for Headline, and all the text on your page or site that you formatted with the Headline style changes from blue to purple. One simple change to the style can save you hours, even days, if you ever find yourself in a redesign (and believe me, every good site goes through periodic redesigns).

Contribute does a wonderful job of hiding the complexities of using CSS from you. Formatting text is as simple as selecting the text and choosing the desired style from a menu. Contribute lets you choose from a list of default styles and from any additional styles that have been associated with a Web page through Dreamweaver or some other means.

Using Styles in Contribute

Contribute lists seven predefined styles that can be applied to text. These styles are named: Normal, Heading 1, Heading 2, Heading 3, Heading 4, Heading 5, and Heading 6 (see Figure 9-1). Contribute also lists any CSS styles that have been associated with a Web page by some other means (such as through Dreamweaver).

Contribute lets you apply styles to text. You cannot, however, create new styles or attach an external style sheet to a Web page in Contribute. The second part of this chapter explains how to do this using Dreamweaver instead.

Contribute will not display HTML styles if your administrator has disabled them. Find out more about how to disable HTML styles in Chapter 13.

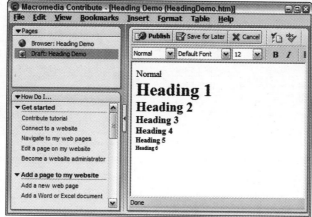

Figure 9-1: Contribute has seven default styles that can be applied to text.

Applying Styles to Text in Contribute

In order to apply styles to text in Contribute:

1. **Open a draft of the Web page you want to edit.**

2. **Select and highlight the text you want to change.**

3. Choose a style for the text by doing one of the following:

- Choose a style from the Style pop-up menu in the toolbar, as in Figure 9-2.

- Select Format⇨Style from the main menu and choose one of the listed styles (see Figure 9-3).

If you choose one of the built-in heading styles, the entire paragraph is changed — not just the text you selected.

Figure 9-2:
The Style
pop-up
menu is on
Contribute's
toolbar.

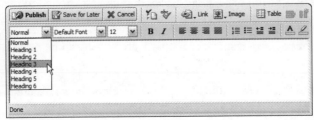

Figure 9-3:
Styles can
be chosen
from
Format⇨
Style.

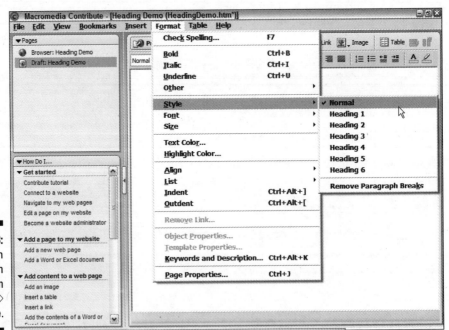

Cascading Style Sheets and Dreamweaver

Contribute makes applying existing styles extremely easy. In order to keep things simple, Contribute was not designed to define or edit styles. A separate Web page editor like Macromedia's Dreamweaver is needed to do this.

If you don't have Dreamweaver on your computer, Macromedia lets you download a trial version on their Web site. Go to www.macromedia.com and follow the links to the download section.

You can get more information about Dreamweaver by checking out *Dreamweaver MX For Dummies* (Wiley Publishing, Inc.) by Janine Warner and Ivonne Berkowitz.

The next few sections of this chapter show you:

- ✔ How to work with Dreamweaver to create and apply style and formatting attributes
- ✔ The challenges involved when formatting documents to work with various Web browsers like Internet Explorer and Netscape Navigator
- ✔ The difference between internal and external styles sheets
- ✔ How to create and link external style sheets

Formatting text in Dreamweaver

Before you find out about HTML styles and CSS, this section makes sure you understand how to use the text formatting features using the Property Inspector. This section shows you about the Property Inspector, how to apply text formatting with Dreamweaver and ensures you have the basics down before you get into the more complex aspects of style sheets.

The Property Inspector

The Property Inspector is docked at the bottom of the page in Dreamweaver. The Property Inspector displays the properties of a selected element on the page. A *property* is a characteristic of HTML — such as the alignment of an image or the size of a cell in a table — that you can assign to an element on your Web page. If you know HTML, you'll recognize these as HTML *attributes*.

When you select any element on a page (such as an image), the Inspector changes to display the properties (attributes) for that element, such as the height and width of an image or table. You can alter those properties by changing the fields in the Property Inspector. You can also set links and create image maps using the Property Inspector.

In Figure 9-4, the image in the upper-left corner has been selected, so the Property Inspector reveals the characteristics for that image: its height and width, its alignment, and the *URL* (Uniform Resource Locator or, more simply, Web address) to which it links.

TIP

At the bottom-right corner of the Property Inspector, you can see a small arrow. Click this arrow to reveal additional attributes that let you control more advanced features.

Figure 9-5 shows the Property Inspector when a table is selected. Notice that the fields in the Inspector have changed to reflect the attributes of an HTML table, such as the number of columns and rows.

Figure 9-4:
The Property Inspector displays the attributes of a selected element, such as the image shown here.

Figure 9-5:
The Property Inspector displays the attributes of the selected HTML table.

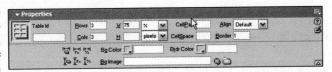

Understanding the <FONT> tag

HTML is really all about tags. Whenever you make changes to a type selection in Dreamweaver, you alter the contents of the HTML <FONT> tag or add additional tags that control things like bold and italic. Changing the contents of the <FONT> tag allows you to specify size, font, color, and tells the browser how to display the type. All of these options are attributes of the <FONT> tag, so you specify them in the Property Inspector in Dreamweaver. But before you start applying these options, you need to understand a little about how they work.

Regarding font sizes, HTML may be different from what you're used to if you've been formatting text in a word processor or graphics program. HTML only uses a limited list of sizes, which range from 1 to 7, with 7 being the largest. HTML can also specify font sizes relative to a given browser's default font size. The actual size of the default font varies from browser to browser and from platform to platform. In most browsers, the standard default size is HTML Font Size 3, but users can change the default to any font and size in the browser's preferences. If you're used to regular font sizes, 3 sounds like it's a really tiny font size. But, actually, it's about the same size as Times 12 point on the Mac and Times Roman 14 point on the PC. That's why the default size option in the Property Inspector in Dreamweaver is the equivalent of font size 3.

In addition to setting absolute font sizes, you can also set relative font sizes. *Absolute* font sizes keep their size no matter what; *relative* sizes adjust according to users settings, always keeping their relative size in relation to other sizes on the page. HTML gives you the option of setting the font size using +1 through +7 or –1 through –7. Using these options enables you to specify a font size relative to the default of the browser, even if it's something other than font size 3. For example, if you set the font size to +2, it is displayed at +2 larger than whatever the default font size is, even if the viewer made the default size in her browser the equivalent of Times 24 point. This enables you to create relative sizes in HTML so that you can ensure that one section of text is larger than another, even though you can't control the exact font size.

When you specify a font face in Dreamweaver, you override the default font of the browser (the default font and size can be changed in the browser's preferences). But for the font to be displayed, it must be available on the viewer's computer. If you specify that you want to use Helvetica but your viewer's computer doesn't have Helvetica, the browser reverts to the browser's default font.

To help get around the problem of specifying specific fonts, HTML lets you specify multiple font faces and then prioritize their use. For example, if you specify Helvetica, you may also specify a similar font, such as Arial, as your second choice. Then, if Helvetica isn't available, the browser looks for Arial. If Arial is on the viewer's hard drive, the browser uses it to display the text instead. You can even take this a step further and choose a family of fonts, such as serif or sans serif, as one of your options. Then the browser at least tries to use a font in the same family if none of the fonts you've chosen is available. (*Serif* fonts have the little curly edges, like Times Roman; *sans serif* fonts, such as Helvetica and Arial, don't have the curly edges.)

To help you specify multiple font choices, Dreamweaver provides a list of common fonts and families in the font drop-down list in the Property Inspector. These are organized into groups of three or four fonts that you can apply to text, and they include some of the most popular and useful combinations of font choices. You can also edit this list to add fonts and combinations of fonts of your own choosing. Figure 9-6 shows the drop-down list for font choices in the Property Inspector. In this example, I've chosen the Arial, Helvetica, sans-serif option. The browser that displays this text first tries to display it in Arial. If Arial isn't available on the computer, the text is displayed in Helvetica, and if that's not available, it uses the third option and displays the text in any sans-serif font available on the user's computer.

Figure 9-6:
Click the
arrow in the
font drop-
down list of
the Property
Inspector to
choose a
font or font
family.

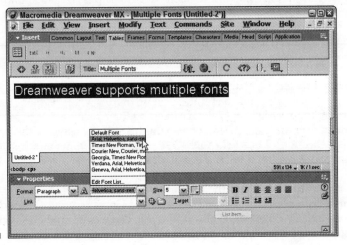

HTML font sizes display differently when viewed on Macintosh and PC computer systems. A given font size viewed on the Mac usually appears about two point sizes smaller than the same font size viewed on a PC because of a difference in the display standards of the two systems. Unfortunately, this is not something you can control (unless you literally create two different pages, one for each system your visitors may use). Most designers choose to create their page for the Windows system, because that is the most commonly used system, but good designers also test their work on Mac systems to ensure the page looks good on both, even if it's not exactly the same.

The most important thing is to be sure to take this difference into consideration, especially if you're designing a site on a Mac. Ideally, you should view the results on both platforms during development of your site in order to find a size that works best, knowing that the size you choose will look smaller on a Mac or bigger on a PC.

Applying font attributes

With Dreamweaver, applying a font or combination of fonts and setting font sizes and colors is easy.

To apply font attributes to text, follow these steps:

1. **Highlight the text that you want to change.**

2. **In the Property Inspector, choose a set of fonts from the font drop-down list (click the button to the right of where it says Default Font).**

   The font is automatically applied to the text. If you don't see the fonts you want to apply, you can create your own set by choosing Edit Font List from this drop-down list and adding fonts in the order you want them to display.

3. **With the text still highlighted, choose the size you want from the Size drop-down list in the Property Inspector (button to the right of the Size field in the Property Inspector).**

   You can choose a size from 1 to 7 or specify sizes relative to the default font size by choosing + or –1 through 7. You can also choose None to use the default size.

4. **With the text still highlighted, click the color square in the middle of the Property Inspector, just to the right of the Size text box.**

   When you click the color square, a pop-up color palette appears so you can select a font color.

5. **Choose any color from the color palette (see Figure 9-7) by clicking the eyedropper over the appropriate color.**

   The color palette is limited to Web-safe colors (those that best display on both the Macintosh and Windows operating systems). The arrow in the top right of the color palette provides access to other color palette options, including those best suited to Mac, those best suited to PC, and grayscale. As a general rule, the Web-safe palette is your best option because it displays most consistently across different monitors and platforms.

   If you want to create a custom color, click the icon that looks like a rainbow-colored globe in the top-right corner of the color palette, just be aware that your custom color may not appear exactly as you created it because Dreamweaver converts RGB colors into hexadecimal codes. If you click the first icon, the square with a diagonal red line, the color reverts to the default text color for the page (the color specified as text color in Page Properties). You can also pick up a color from anywhere on the screen simply by dragging the eyedropper icon over any part of the screen and clicking over a desired color.

6. **You can also click Bold (B) or Italic (I) in the Property Inspector to change the font style accordingly.**

Figure 9-7:
Click the
color square
in the
Property
Inspector to
open up the
color
palette.

Creating your own HTML styles

Now that you know how to control font attributes, you'll probably find that making font changes throughout a site can become rather boring and repetitive, especially if you need to make the same changes over and over. If you want to save some time, you can easily save commonly used attributes as particular styles and then use them over and over again. This is what HTML styles are about. Don't confuse HTML styles with Cascading Style Sheets; HTML styles are simply a collection of <FONT> tag and other style attributes that you can save in Dreamweaver and then easily reuse.

HTML styles are convenient, and they are better suited to consistent display across different browsers, but they are more limited than Cascading Style Sheets. First of all, they let you apply only those font attributes that are available as part of regular HTML. This means that you can't specify font sizes based on pixels, picas, or any other measurement other than the normal, very limited, HTML sizes. HTML styles also can't be shared among sites unless the other sites are also being edited in Dreamweaver. No other HTML program can use or modify Dreamweaver HTML styles.

Perhaps the greatest limitation of HTML styles compared with Cascading Style Sheets, however, is that if you format text to a certain style and later change the style definition, the text you formatted earlier doesn't update automatically to reflect the changes to the style. Still, in many cases, HTML styles can save time and increase productivity if your needs aren't that demanding and automatic updating isn't critical to your needs.

Here's an example of how you might use HTML styles. Say you want all the headlines on your site to be font face Arial, size 5, and bold. You can create a style called Headline and apply all of those formatting options at once when you use the Headline style. If you want different size headlines, you can create a style sheet that defines Headline 1 as one size and Headline 2 as a smaller size for subheads.

To create a new HTML style, follow these steps:

1. **Choose Text➪HTML Styles➪New Style.**

   A submenu appears offering you a list of predefined styles, along with the New Style option.

2. **Choose New Style.**

   The Define HTML Style dialog box opens, as shown in Figure 9-8.

3. **Enter a name in the text box.**

   You can name the style anything you want. In this case, I've chosen to name a style Headline. The name you enter appears in the style menu after you create the style.

4. **Specify if the style should be applied only to selected text elements or to all elements separated by the paragraph tag.**

5. **Specify the behavior of the style when it is applied.**

   If you want the style you create to be applied in addition to existing formatting, choose Add to Existing Style (+). If you want to clear any existing formatting before applying the new style, choose Clear Existing Style.

6. **Select all formatting attributes, including font, size, color, style, and alignment, that you want to include in this style.**

   The Paragraph attributes are available only if you have selected Paragraph in the Apply To section at the top of the dialog box.

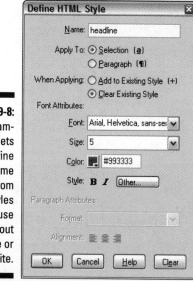

Figure 9-8:
Dreamweaver lets you define and name custom HTML styles to use throughout your page or Web site.

7. **Click OK to save the style.**

   Your new style now appears in the submenu when you choose Text⇨HTML Styles. Any time you want to apply this style to a selected area of text, you can simply choose the style from the submenu and your text changes to reflect that style. When you quit Dreamweaver and start it up again, or even restart your computer, the HTML Style you created remains as an option in the HTML Styles menu until you remove it.

To apply an existing HTML style, follow these steps:

1. **Highlight the text you want to modify and choose Text⇨HTML Styles.**

   A submenu appears offering you a list of predefined styles that ship with Dreamweaver or any custom styles that you have created.

2. **Click to select one of the styles from this list, and the style is applied to your selected text.**

HTML styles are stored on your hard drive in a file called `styles.xml`. This folder is located either in the site folder (in the Library subfolder) or in the Dreamweaver configuration folder if the site root folder has not been defined. Because of this, styles you define for one site are not necessarily available when working with other sites.

Working with Cascading Style Sheets

The addition of Cascading Style Sheets *(CSS)* to HTML has many people with graphic design backgrounds excited. Finally, you can have real design control on the Web and apply global style settings across multiple pages — or even an entire site.

If you're not familiar with the concept of style sheets, you're sure to appreciate the benefits. Cascading Style Sheets, more commonly referred to by the acronym *CSS,* enable you to define styles with multiple text formatting options in HTML. CSS goes a long way toward giving you real typographic control and a consistent look and feel throughout a Web site, as well as saving time in designing your Web page.

Before you get too excited, however, I have to warn you that CSS is not supported by many of the browsers still in use on the Web. Because CSS is a relatively new addition to HTML, older versions of Web browsers like Netscape and Internet Explorer won't display formatting that is designed as a CSS. Even newer browsers won't always display CSS the same way. (You find more on browsers in the following section, "Understanding the Differences among Web Browsers.")

As a result, many sites on the Web still use regular HTML formatting options, which you find explained earlier in this chapter.

The main reason to create CSS today is that the future benefits are so appealing. In another year or so, it will probably be safe to rely on CSS for most of your users. If you know that most of the people who are visiting your site have recent browsers, it may already be reasonable for you to just use CSS, but most general-audience sites are better off using regular HTML formatting or the HTML styles feature of Dreamweaver described in the previous section.

You should also know that Cascading Style Sheets are much more complex to create than basic HTML formatting. Dreamweaver makes it much easier than writing the codes by hand, but you'll still want to take some time to discover the best way to create CSS with the fonts, colors, styles, and other formatting you want in your styles.

Understanding the differences among Web browsers

The differences in the way that Netscape Navigator and Internet Explorer support Cascading Style Sheets can be extremely frustrating, to say nothing of the differences between different versions of the same browsers. The good news is that style sheets are great for design consistency and for making fast changes throughout a page and even an entire site. The bad news is that style sheets are one of the newer additions to HTML, and some older browsers don't support them. The worse news is that style sheets aren't *backward compatible,* meaning that if you use this cool new design feature and visitors view your site using an older browser, such as Netscape Navigator 3.0, they won't be able to see any of the formatting that you created with a style sheet. They will be able to see the text — and it'll just look like plain old HTML text.

Now for even worse news: Even if your viewers use the latest browser, they won't necessarily see the same formatting because Netscape and Microsoft haven't agreed on how to implement and support style sheets. Ironically, even Microsoft hasn't been able to get CSS to work consistently in Internet Explorer on both Mac and PC computers.

For example, in Internet Explorer 4 and 5, you can use JavaScript to change attributes, such as font color and size, after a page has loaded. This feature can add powerful effects to your site, such as changing the color of a link when a user moves the cursor over it. But this feature doesn't work the same way in Navigator because Navigator 4.0 doesn't support changes to attributes, though Navigator 6, the latest version from Netscape, does offer support. On the other hand, version 3.0 and above of both Internet Explorer and Netscape Navigator enable you to swap images, so you can create a similar effect by using two images of different colors. Fortunately, you don't have to know what browser supports what features. Dreamweaver takes care of that for you by enabling you to target browsers and limit design options to features supported by target browsers.

Dreamweaver works hard to try to solve these problems with browser differences. When you work with Dynamic HTML (DHTML), Dreamweaver creates complex code in the background that is designed to take best advantage of the features supported by each browser. If you look at the code, it may look a bit more complex than necessary sometimes, but that's because Dreamweaver creates these tags in ways that both browsers can interpret them.

Creating CSS in Dreamweaver

When you get into creating and using Cascading Style Sheets, you use one of the most complex and advanced features of Dreamweaver. Consequently, creating style sheets takes a little more time to grasp than applying basic HTML tags or using HTML styles. Still, Dreamweaver makes it much easier to define style sheets than to write them by hand — a task that is a lot closer to writing programming code than to creating HTML tags.

To help you get the hang of using Dreamweaver to create style sheets, I first walk you through the screens that define styles and give you an overview of your options as you create styles. After the following sections on each aspect of style sheet creation, you find specific numbered steps that walk you through the process of creating and applying your own CSS styles.

Understanding CSS style types

You can create two types of style sheets with CSS and Dreamweaver: internal style sheets and external style sheets. An *internal style sheet* stores its data within the HTML code of a page and applies styles to only that page. An *external style sheet* is a text file that you create and store outside of your HTML page. You then reference it as a link, much like you do any other HTML page on the Web. In this way, you can apply style sheets to an entire Web site or to any page that links to the external style sheet, which also means that you can have many different pages referencing the same style sheet. You create these two kinds of style sheets in much the same way, as you see in the following step-by-step exercises.

You can define two different kinds of CSS styles to use in either an internal or external style sheet: custom styles and redefined HTML tag styles. The difference is that a *custom style* is a completely new set of formatting attributes that you can apply to any text selection. Custom styles in CSS are referred to as *classes.* Don't worry about this too much because I get into it in more detail later in the chapter. For now, just know that when you define a custom style, you give it a class name and then you use that name to apply the style to any text block on the page. So you can call a custom style anything you want, you can create a new custom style any time you want, and the new style doesn't necessarily affect anything else on the page. Creating a custom style is a little bit like making up your own HTML tag, with formatting rules that you can define yourself.

In contrast, you create redefined HTML tag styles by *redefining* how *existing* HTML tags are rendered by the browser; you are changing existing rules instead of creating new ones. This means that you change how common HTML tags format text throughout your page — or throughout your Web site if you want to define it that way. The result is that if you redefine a tag, such as the <BLOCKQUOTE> tag, all the text already formatted with the <BLOCKQUOTE> tag automatically changes to reflect your new style definition.

Suppose that you define the <BLOCKQUOTE> tag to render text in blue at 12-point italic. Normally, *blockquoted text* simply creates an indent on the right and left margins — great for setting off quoted text on a page. Because you've redefined the <BLOCKQOUTE> tag, it's going to also add the new attributes of blue and 12-point italic. But there's more. Because style sheets are cascading, any styles applied to tags *within* the <BLOCKQUOTE> tag override the <BLOCKQUOTE> tags that enclose it. So, if you placed a set of <B> tags (that normally indicate bold text) inside the <BLOCKQUOTE> tag and defined the <B> tag as red text, any text falling inside the <B> tags would be red instead of blue, in addition to bold. The <B> tag would override the enclosing <BLOCKQUOTE> tags. This is illustrated in Figure 9-9. This is true for any tag that you modify using CSS.

The style information would be contained in a separate style sheet document or in the head section of the page if it were assigned only to that document. In the main body of your HTML page, this would look like the following:

```
<BLOCKQUOTE>Content formatted by the blockquote style
        <B>content formatted by the bold style</ B> more
        content formatted by the blockquote style
        </BLOCKQUOTE>
```

Creating a new CSS style

To create a new CSS, open any HTML document or create a new file in Dreamweaver and choose Window⇨CSS Styles to open the CSS Styles panel at the right of the display area. In the lower-right corner of this panel you can see four small icons (really small). From left to right, these icons represent Attach Style Sheet, New Style, Edit Style Sheet, and Delete Style (resembles a trash can). Choose Text⇨CSS Styles⇨New CSS Style.

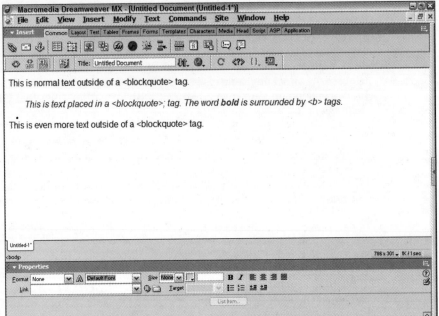

Figure 9-9:
<B> within
<BLOCK
QUOTE>.

The New CSS Style dialog box, shown in Figure 9-10, opens, giving you the following options:

- **Name:** Although the first field in this box is titled Name, when you first bring it up, its title actually changes depending on which of the CSS types you select using the three radio buttons beneath it. Read the description for each of the CSS types in the following three bullets to see how to fill out this field.

- **Make Custom Style (class):** Enables you to define a new style that you can apply to any section of text on a page by using the class attribute. When you select this option, the first field asks for a name. All custom style names must begin with a period, which Dreamweaver automatically inserts as you name the style. This kind of style is also referred to as a *class*. If you choose this option, after clicking OK another dialog box appears, allowing you to define the different options for the style, which I explain in the section "Creating a custom style" later in this chapter.

- **Redefine HTML Tag:** Enables you to create a style that changes the formatting associated with an existing HTML tag. When you select this option, the first field asks for a tag name. Clicking the pop-up menu next to the tag field allows you to select from a huge list of HTML tags (the default one is the <BODY> tag). For more information on this option, see "Redefining HTML tags" later in this chapter.

✔ **Use CSS Selector:** Enables you to define a kind of pseudoclass that combines a custom style with a redefined HTML tag. CSS Selector styles apply only to the <A> tag and enable you to do things such as change the color of a link when the mouse hovers over it. When you select this option, the first field asks for the Selector name. Choices in the pop-up list are a:active, a:hover, a:link, and a:visited.

- • a:active affects an active link, which is triggered while someone is actually clicking on the link.

- • a:hover is triggered while the mouse is directly over the link.

- • a:link is applied to any text link.

- • a:visited affects links that have already been visited by the user.

Please note that CSS Selector styles work only in Internet Explorer 4 and above browsers.

✔ **Define In:** This option lets you choose whether your style sheet exists within the current page or in a separate file. When you select a new style sheet file, you're creating an external style sheet. If you select "This document only," you're creating an internal style sheet, meaning defined styles will be available only for the page you are working on.

Defining styles

When you choose to make a new style and select one of the three style options in the New CSS Style dialog box, the CSS Style Definition dialog box opens. This is where you decide how you want your style to look by selecting the attribute options. This dialog box includes eight categories, each with multiple options that you can use to define various style elements. In this section, I discuss each of these eight categories.

You don't have to make selections for all the options in each category. Any options that you leave blank remain at the browser's default. For example, if you don't specify a text color, the text is displayed as black or whatever the page's default color is.

Don't be frustrated by options in these categories that Dreamweaver doesn't display. If they don't display in Dreamweaver, they almost certainly won't work in any of the current browsers. The good news is that Macromedia is looking ahead and building these options into Dreamweaver so that they'll be ready when these features are supported. Keep an eye on the Macromedia Web site at www.macromedia.com and Macromedia's DHTML information site at www.dhtmlzone.com for changes and updates to Dreamweaver, as well as for news about changing standards and support for these CSS features. Right now, Microsoft Internet Explorer 5 and above provide the most complete CSS support.

The Type category

After you name your style and specify the fields described in the earlier section, click OK and the CSS Style Definition dialog box appears (Figure 9-11). When you choose Type from the Category panel on the left, the Type options are visible, as shown in Figure 9-11, and you have the following formatting options:

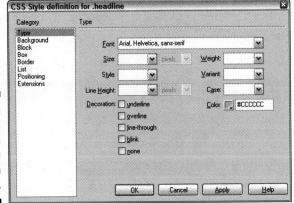

Figure 9-11:
The Type page of the CSS Style Definition dialog box.

  ✔ **Font:** Specifies a font, font family, or series of families. You can add fonts to the list by selecting Edit Font List from the drop-down list.

  ✔ **Size:** Defines the size of the text. You can choose a specific point size or use a relative size, expressed as small, extra small, and so on.

  ✔ **Style:** Enables you to choose whether the text appears as Normal, Italic, or Oblique.

  ✔ **Line Height:** Enables you to specify the height of a line that the text is placed on (graphic designers usually call this *leading*). The 4.0 browsers don't support this feature, and it can cause problems in older browsers. So, for now, you should probably avoid this one.

✔ **Decoration:** Enables you to specify whether text is underlined, overlined (the line appears over the text instead of under it), or displayed with a strikethrough. You can also choose blink, which makes the text flash on and off.

Use the Decoration options sparingly, if at all. Links are automatically underlined, so if you underline text that isn't a link, you risk confusing viewers. Overlined and strikethrough text can be hard to read. So use these options only if they enhance your design. And, by all means, resist the blink option; it's distracting and can make the screen difficult to read. (Overline and blink do not yet display in Dreamweaver.)

✔ **Weight:** Enables you to control how bold the text is displayed by using a specific or relative boldness option.

✔ **Variant:** Enables you to select a variation of the font, such as small caps. Unfortunately, this attribute is not yet supported.

✔ **Case:** Enables you to globally change the case of selected words, making them all uppercase or lowercase or with initial caps. Unfortunately, this attribute is not yet supported.

✔ **Color:** Defines the color of the text. You can use the color well (the square icon) to open a Web-safe color palette in which you can select predefined colors or create custom colors.

The Background category

The Background category of the CSS Style Definition dialog box (see Figure 9-12) enables you to specify a background color or image for a style. You can choose from the following options:

✔ **Background Color:** Specifies the background color of an element, such as a table.

✔ **Background Image:** Enables you to select a background image as part of the style definition.

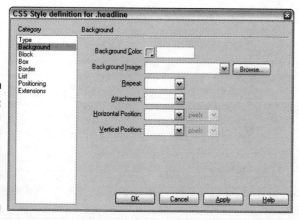

Figure 9-12:
The Background page of the CSS Style Definition dialog box.

✔ **Repeat:** Determines how and whether the background image tiles across and down the page. In all cases, the image is cropped if it doesn't fit behind the element.

The Repeat options are as follows:

- **No repeat:** The background is displayed once at the beginning of the element.

- **Repeat:** The background tiles repeat vertically and horizontally behind the element.

- **Repeat-x:** The background repeats horizontally, but not vertically, behind the element.

- **Repeat-y:** The background repeats vertically, but not horizontally, behind the element.

✔ **Attachment, Horizontal Position,** and **Vertical Position** options control alignment and positioning of the background image.

The Block category

The Block category (see Figure 9-13 defines spacing and alignment settings for tags and attributes. You can choose from the following options:

✔ **Word Spacing:** Can be specified in points, millimeters (mm), centimeters (cm), picas, inches, pixels, ems, exs.

✔ **Letter Spacing:** Can be specified in points, millimeters (mm), centimeters (cm), picas, inches, pixels, ems, exs.

✔ **Vertical Alignment:** Works only with the `<IMAGE>` tag in Dreamweaver. It specifies the vertical alignment of an image, usually in relation to its parent.

✔ **Text Align:** Specifies how text aligns within an element.

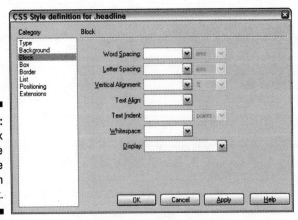

Figure 9-13:
The Block page of the CSS Style Definition dialog box.

✔ **Text Indent:** Specifies how far the first line of text indents.

✔ **Whitespace:** Options are normal, pre (for previous), and nowrap.

✔ **Display:** Indicates how an element should be rendered. An element can be hidden by choosing "none."

The Box category

The Box category (see Figure 9-14) defines settings for tags and attributes that control the placement of elements on the page. You can choose from the following options:

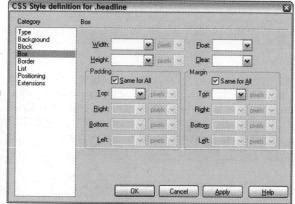

Figure 9-14:
The Box page of the CSS Style Definition dialog box.

✔ **Width, Height:** Enable you to specify a width and height that you can use in styles that you apply to images, layers, or any other element that can have its dimensions specified.

✔ **Float:** Enables you to align an image to the left or right so that other elements, such as text, wrap around it.

✔ **Clear:** Sets the side (left or right) on which layers are not allowed to be displayed next to the element. The element drops behind the layer if the layer intersects the selected side. (Doesn't currently display in Dreamweaver.)

✔ **Padding:** Sets the amount of space between the element and its border or margin.

✔ **Margin:** Enables you to define the amount of space between the border of the element and other elements on the page.

The Border category

The Border category defines settings, such as width, color, and style, for the borders of elements on a page. Options are Style, Width, and Color. (See Figure 9-15.)

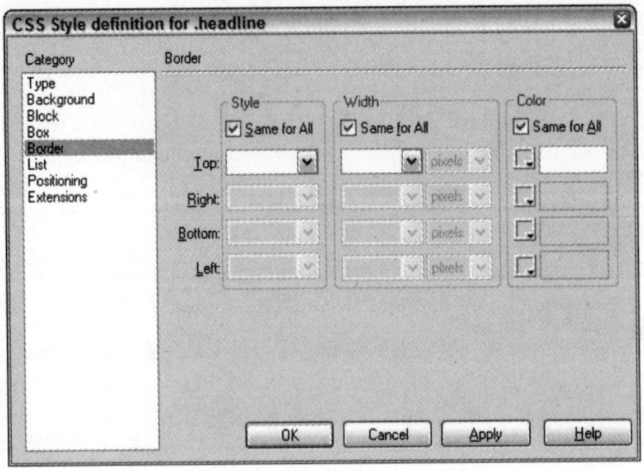

Figure 9-15:
The Border
category
of the
CSS Style
Definition
dialog box.

The List category

The List category defines settings, such as bullet size and type, for list tags. You can specify if bullets are disc, circle, square, decimal, lower-roman, upper-roman, upper alpha, lower alpha, or none. If you want to use a bullet, you can use the Browse button to locate an image to be used as the bullet. You can also specify the Position inside or outside to control positioning. (See Figure 9-16.)

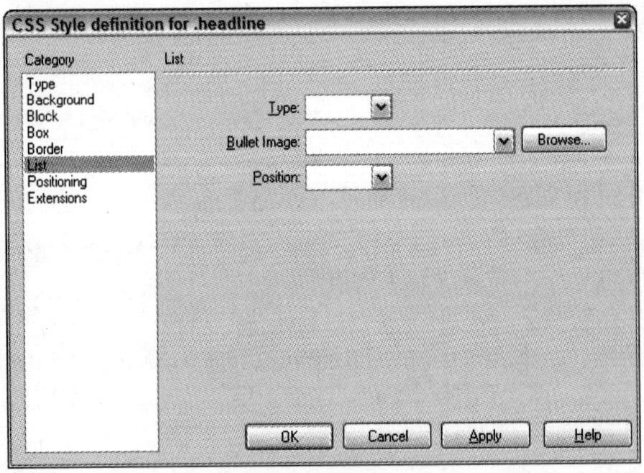

Figure 9-16:
The List
category
of the
CSS Style
Definition
dialog box.

The Positioning category

The Positioning category (see Figure 9-17) enables you to change a tag or block of text into a new layer and specify its attributes. When applied, this style uses the tag specified for defining layers in the Layer preferences. The default in

Dreamweaver for layers is the `<DIV>` tag. You can change this by editing the Layer preferences, but the `<DIV>` tag is the most universally supported, so you're best to stick with it. You can choose from the following options:

- **Type:** Enables you to specify the position of a layer as absolute, relative, or static.

  - **Absolute:** This positioning uses the top and left coordinates entered in the Placement text boxes on this screen to control the position of the layer relative to the top-left corner of the Web page.

  - **Relative:** This positioning uses a position relative to the current position of the layer instead of the top-left corner of the page.

  - **Static:** This positioning keeps the layer in the place where you insert it on the page.

- **Visibility:** Enables you to control whether the browser displays the layer. You can use this feature, combined with a scripting language such as JavaScript, to dynamically change the display of layers. The default on most browsers is to inherit the original layer's visibility value.

  - **Inherit:** The layer has the visibility of its parent.

  - **Visible:** The layer is displayed.

  - **Hidden:** The layer isn't displayed.

- **Z-Index:** Controls the position of the layer on the Z coordinate, meaning how it stacks in relation to other elements on the page. Higher-numbered layers appear above lower-numbered layers.

- **Overflow:** Tells the browser how to display the contents of a layer if it exceeds its size. (Doesn't currently display in Dreamweaver.)

  - **Visible:** Forces the layer to increase in size to display all of its contents. The layer expands down and right.

  - **Hidden:** Cuts off the contents of the layer that don't fit and doesn't provide any scroll bars.

  - **Scroll:** Adds scroll bars to the layer regardless of whether the contents exceed the layer's size.

  - **Auto:** Makes scroll bars appear only when the layer's contents exceed its boundaries. (Doesn't currently display in Dreamweaver.)

- **Placement:** Defines the size and location of a layer, in keeping with the setting for Type. The default values are measured in pixels, but you can also use pc (picas), pt (points), in (inches), mm (millimeters), cm (centimeters), or % (percentage of the parent's value).

- **Clip:** Enables you to specify which part of the layer is visible by controlling what part of the layer is cropped if it doesn't fit in the display area.

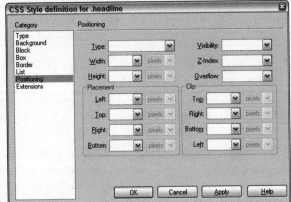

Figure 9-17:
The
Positioning
page of the
CSS Style
Definition
dialog box.

The Extensions category

Extensions (shown in Figure 9-18) include filters and cursor options, most of which aren't supported in any browser or are supported only in Internet Explorer 4.0 and above:

✔ **Pagebreak:** Inserts a point in a page where a printer sees a page break.

✔ **Cursor:** Defines the type of cursor that appears when a user moves the cursor over an element.

✔ **Filter:** Enables you to apply to elements special effects such as drop shadows and motion blurs.

Creating a custom style

The following steps tell you how to use Dreamweaver to create a custom style. In this example you define a style for headlines using CSS. If you want to create a style for another element, follow these same steps but change the specific attributes.

You can leave attributes unspecified if you don't want to use them. If you don't specify them, the browser uses its own default. For example, I don't recommend using any of the Decoration options because they can distract and confuse viewers.

To define a style for a headline, follow these steps:

1. Choose Text➪CSS Styles➪New CSS Style.

The New CSS Style Sheet dialog box appears. The new style is automatically called .unnamed1.

2. **In the Name text box, type a new name for the style.**

   Dreamweaver gives you a default name that begins with a period (.) because class names must begin with a period. You can name the style anything you want as long as you don't use spaces or punctuation. Dreamweaver adds the initial period to the class name if you omit it.

3. **Next to Type, select Make Custom Style (class).**

4. **Next to Define In, select This Document Only to create an internal style sheet.**

5. **Click OK.**

   The CSS Style Definition dialog box opens.

6. **From the Font drop-down list, choose a font or font set.**

   If you want to use fonts that aren't on the list, choose the Edit Font List option from the drop-down list to create new font options.

7. **From the Size drop-down list, choose the size you want for your headline.**

   Large headlines are generally 24 or 36 point. You may prefer to choose a relative size, such as large or larger.

8. **From the Style drop-down list, choose a style.**

   Italic and Oblique are both good for making text stand out on a page.

9. **From the Weight drop-down list, choose Bold to make your headline thicker and darker.**

10. **Ignore Variant and Case because these attributes aren't well supported by current browsers.**

Figure 9-18:
The
Extensions
page of the
CSS Style
Definition
dialog box.

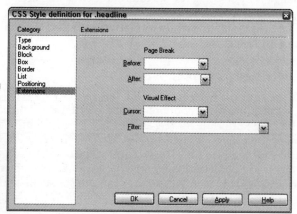

11. Click the Color well and choose a color from the color well.

Sticking to the default color swatches in the color well is best because it ensures that you use a Web-safe color. You can also create a custom color by clicking the icon that looks like a rainbow-colored globe in the upper-right corner of the color well.

12. Click OK when you're finished.

Your style is automatically added to the Styles list.

You can apply styles in the Styles list to any Web page or selected text block. After you create your style, it appears in the submenu under Text⇨CSS Styles. Any text that you apply it to takes on the formatting attributes you just specified. For more on how to use styles, read "Applying Styles" later in this chapter.

Redefining HTML tags

When you create a custom style, as I explain in the preceding section, you start a completely new style with its own unique name. When you redefine an HTML tag, however, you begin with an existing HTML tag, such as <B> (bold), <HR> (horizontal rule), or <TABLE> (table), and change the attributes associated with that specific tag. Any new attributes that you apply through CSS to an existing tag override the existing attributes.

To redefine a tag, start a New CSS Style and select the Redefine HTML Tag option in the New CSS Style dialog box. When you choose this option, a list of tags appears at the top of the dialog box. Choose the tag that you want to change from the Tag drop-down list shown in Figure 9-19. Then define how you want to change it by altering the various categories and attributes in the CSS Style Definition dialog box. Be aware that when you redefine an existing HTML tag, any text that you've already formatted with that tag changes to reflect the new definition.

Eliminating underlines from links

Now that you know how to redefine an HTML tag, here's your chance to put it into practice. One of the most commonly used HTML tag modifications involves disabling the underline for the anchor tag, <A>, so that hypertext links are no longer underlined in the browser. Many Web designers like to remove the underline because they think it detracts from the design and also because the cursor changes to a hand over any link, they consider the underline unnecessary. This technique works in both Netscape and Internet Explorer 4.0 (and above) browsers.

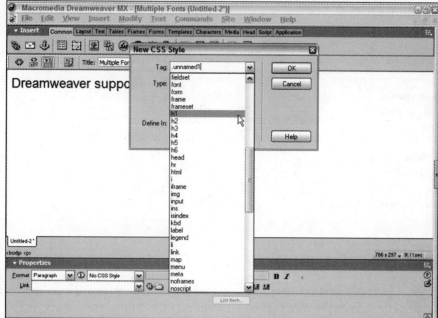

Figure 9-19:
The
Redefine
HTML Tag
option gives
you a list of
the HTML
tags that
you can
redefine
using CSS.

To disable underlining for hypertext links, follow these steps:

1. **Choose Text➪CSS Styles➪New CSS Style.**

2. **Select the Redefine HTML Tag option and choose the anchor tag <A> from the drop-down list.**

3. **Next to Define, select This Document Only.**

4. **Click OK.**

   The CSS Style Definition dialog box opens.

5. **Make sure that the Type category is selected; then check the none option under the Decoration section, as shown in Figure 9-20.**

6. **Click OK to apply the changes.**

After you click OK, active links are no longer underlined on the page, even when displayed in a browser (as long as it's 4.0 or higher). In older browsers, the links appear with underlines, but otherwise are unaffected. You can make more modifications to the <A> tag in this manner, or you can apply the same principles to any of the other HTML tags available in the New CSS Style dialog box. Remember, any time you redefine an HTML tag using CSS, the changes are visible in your page only if those tags are actually used.

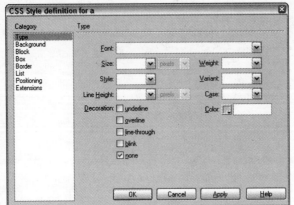

Figure 9-20:
Using CSS
to disable
underlining
of hypertext
links.

Conflicting styles

Be careful when you apply more than one style to the same text (something that is easier to do than you may realize). The styles may conflict, and because browsers aren't all consistent in the way in which they display styles, the results can be inconsistent and unexpected.

For the most part, Netscape Navigator 4.0 and above and Internet Explorer 4.0 and above display all the attributes applied to an element, even if they're from different styles, as long as the styles don't conflict. If they do conflict, browsers prioritize styles depending on how they're defined.

Here's an example to help you get the idea. You define a custom style called .headline as red and centered, and you apply it to a selection of text. Then you decide that you want that text to be bold, so you apply the bold tag independently by selecting it from the Property Inspector. You have now used two different types of styles. Because they don't conflict, all of them take effect and your text becomes bold, centered, and red. If, however, you decide that you want this text aligned left, instead of centered, and you apply left alignment directly from the Property Inspector, you have a conflict.

If a direct conflict exists, custom styles overrule regular HTML tag styles. The browser also gives priority to the attribute of the style that's inserted closest to the text. This can get really hard to juggle if you're applying defined styles, trying to keep track of standard HTML tags, and then trying to sort out how the browser prioritizes them. It gets worse with time, too, because these styles and priorities are sure to change and evolve. Your best bet is not to apply conflicting styles. Go back and redefine an existing style, apply regular HTML tags individually, or create a new style. Remember that you can use the Duplicate option from the Edit Style Sheet dialog box to create a new duplicate style, and then make minor alterations. (For more on the Edit Style Sheet dialog box, see the upcoming section, "Editing an Existing Style.")

Applying Styles in Dreamweaver

Defining styles in Dreamweaver is the complicated part. Applying them after you've defined them is easy. You simply select the text that you want to affect and choose the predefined style that you want to apply.

To apply a style in Dreamweaver, follow these steps:

1. **Highlight the text to which you want to apply a style.**

2. **Select the style that you want to apply from the list that appears in the white area of the CSS Styles panel.**

   The style is automatically applied to the selection. If the Style panel is not visible, choose Window⇨CSS Styles to open it.

You can also apply a custom style by selecting the text that you want to change, choosing Text⇨CSS Styles, and choosing a style from the submenu.

Editing an Existing Style

You can change the attributes of any style by editing that style. This is a major advantage of Cascading Style Sheets: You can make global changes to a page or even to an entire Web site by changing a style that you applied to multiple elements with an external style sheet. Be aware, however, that everything you defined with that style changes.

Remember that you can also create new styles by duplicating an existing style and then altering it. Then you can apply that new style without affecting elements that are already formatted on your pages with the original version of the style.

The Edit Style Sheet dialog box, shown in Figure 9-21, includes the following options:

✔ **Link:** Enables you to link to or import an external style sheet (a separate text file that defines a style) so that you can apply it to the page or even to the entire site that you're working on. You can find more information on external styles in the section "Using External Style Sheets" later in this chapter.

✔ **New:** Enables you to define one of three types of style sheets (Custom CSS Styles, HTML Tag Styles, and CSS Selector Styles). You can find these explained in detail in the section "Defining styles" earlier in the chapter.

✔ **Edit:** Enables you to change an existing style. For more information, see the steps following this bulleted list.

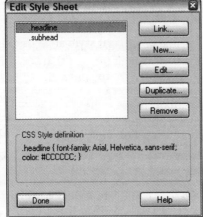

Figure 9-21:
The Edit
Style Sheet
dialog box.

✔ **Duplicate:** Creates a copy of a selected style that you can then redefine as any one of the three style options.

✔ **Remove:** Enables you to delete a defined style.

The Undo feature doesn't work with the Remove option from the Edit Style Sheet dialog box. If you delete a style by mistake, close the dialog box by pressing Done and then choose Edit➪ Undo Remove CSS Style from the main menu before doing anything else.

Duplicating a style with a new name and deleting the old one is a quick way to disable an unwanted style without losing the code. This way you don't have to recreate it should you ever want it back.

To edit an existing style, follow these steps:

1. **Choose Text➪CSS Styles➪Edit Style Sheet.**

   Alternatively, you can click the Open Style Sheet icon (the second from the right) near the bottom-right corner of the CSS Styles panel.

2. **Select the style that you want to change in the Edit Style Sheet dialog box and click the Edit button.**

   The Style Definition dialog box for that style appears.

3. **Choose a category that you want to change, such as Type or Background, from the Category panel; then specify the style changes you want to make.**

   You can find descriptions of all the style options in the section "Defining styles" earlier in this chapter.

4. **When you've made all the changes you want, click OK.**

    The style automatically redefines to reflect your changes. At the same time, all elements that you defined with that style automatically change.

Using External Style Sheets

Up to now, you've been using CSS only in the context of internal style sheets. Internal style sheet information is stored in the HTML code of the document you are working on and applies only to that document. If you want to create styles that you can share among documents, you need to use external style sheets. External style sheets enable you to create styles that you can apply to pages throughout a Web site by storing the style sheet information on a separate text page that can be linked to from any HTML document.

External style sheets are where you can realize the greatest time savings. You can define styles for common formatting options used throughout an entire site, such as headlines, captions, and even images, which makes applying multiple formatting options to elements faster and easier. Big news- and magazine-type Web sites often use external style sheets because they need to follow a consistent look and feel throughout the site, even when many people are working on the same site. Using external style sheets also makes global changes easier because when you change the external style sheet, you globally change every element to which you applied the style throughout the site.

Creating and Editing an External Style Sheet

You create external style sheets almost exactly the same way you create internal style sheets, except external style sheets need to be saved in separate text files. When you use Dreamweaver to create an external style sheet, Dreamweaver automatically links the style sheet to the page that you're working on. You can then link it to any other Web page in which you want to apply the style definitions.

To create an external style sheet, follow the same steps for creating an internal style sheet, except that in the New Style dialog box, select New Style Sheet File instead of This Document Only. When you click OK, you're prompted to save the style sheet somewhere on your drive as an external file.

To link an existing external style sheet to the current page, follow these steps:

1. **Select Window⇨CSS Styles.**

   The CSS Styles panel appears.

2. **Click the Attach Style Sheet icon in the CSS Styles panel (the first button on the bottom right).**

   The Select Style Sheet dialog box appears, prompting you to identify the location of the external style sheet.

3. **After you select the external file name, click the Select button (Open button on a Mac).**

   The dialog box disappears and the external CSS file is automatically linked to your page. Any styles that you've defined in the external style sheet now appear in the CSS Styles panel and any redefined HTML styles are automatically applied to the page. Because you've established a link on this page to the external style sheet, the styles in the external style sheet always appear in the CSS Styles panel whenever you open this file.

4. **To apply a style on your page, select the text you want to apply the style to and click the appropriate style in the CSS Styles panel.**

Chapter 10

Creating and Using Templates

· ·

In This Chapter

▶ Using template features to control development

▶ Creating special template designs

▶ Locking template areas

· ·

*T*emplates are especially well suited to a collaborative work environment where you have a team of people with varying skill levels. For example, at a university, the technical staff may build the main framework of a Web site, but then they may want to enable each department to create their own subsection, and even within the departments, there may be many different people who should contribute to the site. Administrative staff may be best suited to keeping up the calendar section and special announcements while interns may handle student sections. This is where templates are ideal because the technical staff or experienced designers can create templates that can be used by others, such as administrative staff and interns, to make updates simple enough for non-Web designers.

Many Web design programs boast about their HTML templates, which are a common feature. But what they really mean is that they include some ready-made page designs with the program or at least the ability to create simple skeleton pages.

Macromedia takes this concept a few leaps farther by providing template design features that enable you to create the design of a page in a reusable format and even limit which sections of that page other developers can and can't alter. By "locking" certain sections of templates, you can make your pages "idiot proof" and help ensure that key elements or complex programming sections aren't altered accidentally by less experienced developers.

Templates become even more powerful now that Macromedia has created Contribute. Because Contribute is so easy to use, you can give it to almost anyone on your team to work on your Web site right away, and because it's integrated with Dreamweaver, you can use it to work on sites that use Dreamweaver templates.

Contribute is so easy to use in part because it has such limited features. As a result, you can't create templates in Contribute, even though you can edit pages designed with templates and create new pages from templates in Contribute. In Chapter 3, you find instructions for using templates in Contribute. This chapter is focused on how to create templates in Dreamweaver that can be used in Contribute.

You have to create templates in Dreamweaver, and because this feature is so key to getting the most out of Contribute, I've included this chapter as a sort of bonus in this book. You'll have to have a copy of Dreamweaver to follow the steps in this chapter (you can download a fully-functional 30-day trial version from www.macromedia.com/software/dreamweaver).

Understanding How Templates Work

When you create a template, you essentially create the outline of what the page should look like. Usually a template represents a design with placeholders but no actual content. You can use templates to create documents for your site that have a common structure and appearance. And here's a great bonus: When you're ready to redesign your site, simply go back and edit the template itself, and then you can automatically apply the changes to every page on the site that uses that template (for example, if you change the logo for your company or add a new navigation element that you want to appear on every page in a section).

Templates are best used when you are creating a number of pages that share certain characteristics, such as background color or image placement. Rather than setting the correct properties for every new page or making the same changes on page after page, you can use a template to make changes to several pages at once. For example, if you have a section with all the bios of your staff, you can create a template and just replace the image and text on each page.

Dreamweaver MX includes a wealth of ready-to-use Web Components. You'll find these in the new document dialog box when you choose File↪New. These components can help you get your site designed quickly, using sample layouts, Dream Templates, framesets, and many other goodies.

Controlling templates

One of the greatest advantages of using the Dreamweaver template feature is that you can specify which areas of the template can be changed. This is especially useful if you're working with people who have various skill levels in Web development, and you want a more advanced designer to create a page that a less experienced person can't mess up later. With that goal in mind, a template has editable regions and locked (noneditable) regions. Use *editable regions* for content that changes, such as a product description or events in a calendar. Use locked regions for static, unchanging content, such as a logo or site navigation elements.

For example, if you're publishing an online magazine, the navigation options may not change from page to page, but the titles and stories do. To indicate the style and location of an article or headline, you can define *placeholder text* (an editable region, with all the size and font attributes already specified). When you're ready to add a new feature, you simply select the placeholder text and either paste in a story or type over the selected area. You do the same thing to create a placeholder for an image. By default, templates are locked. You can add content to the template, but when you save the template, all content is automatically marked noneditable. If you create a document from such a template, Dreamweaver warns you that the document will not contain any editable regions. To make a template useful, you must create editable regions or mark existing content areas as editable. (The step-by-step instructions in the following section, "Creating templates," walk you through the process.)

You can modify a template even after you've used it to create documents. Then when you update documents that use the template, the noneditable sections of those documents are updated to match the changes you made in the template.

While you're editing the template itself, you can make changes to any part of the file, be it the editable or locked regions. While editing a document made from a template, however, you can make changes only to the editable regions of the document. If you go back and change a template after it is created, Dreamweaver gives you the option of having those changes reflected in all the pages you've created with that template or only the page you are currently editing.

Creating templates

Creating a template is as easy as creating any other file in Dreamweaver, as you can see in the following steps. You can start with an existing HTML document and modify it to suit your needs, or you can create a completely new document. When you save a file as a template, the file is stored automatically in the Templates folder of the main folder for the Web site. Templates must be saved in this common folder for the automated features in Dreamweaver to work properly. If you don't already have a Templates folder in your Web site, Dreamweaver automatically creates one when you store your first template.

The Template features work only if you have defined your Web site in Dreamweaver. If you aren't sure how to do this, refer to the program's help files or pick up a copy of *Dreamweaver MX For Dummies* (Wiley Publishing, Inc.).

All elements in a template are locked by default, except the document title section, which is indicated by the `<TITLE></TITLE>` tags. For the template to be of any use for building new pages, you must make other areas of the page editable as well. Remember that you can always return to the template and make more areas editable or remove the capability to edit certain areas later.

To create a new template with editable regions, follow these steps:

1. **From the Files panel, choose the Assets tab and then select the Templates icon (see Figure 10-1).**

   The Templates category in the Files Assets panel opens in the right side of your screen.

2. **In the Templates panel, click the icon that is an arrow with dots in the top-right corner and choose New Template from the drop-down menu that opens.**

   A new, untitled template is added to the list of templates in the panel.

3. **With the template still selected, type a name for the template just as you would name any file in the Finder on a Mac or the Explorer on a PC.**

   The new template is added to the Templates for Site list, as shown in Figure 10-2.

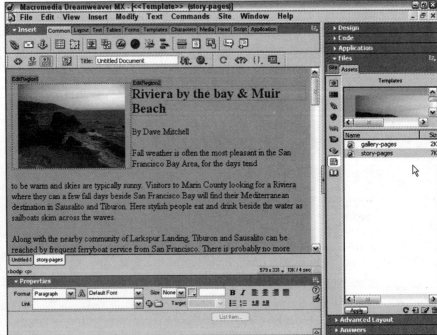

Figure 10-1: The Templates category in the Files Assets panel makes it easy to create and organize templates.

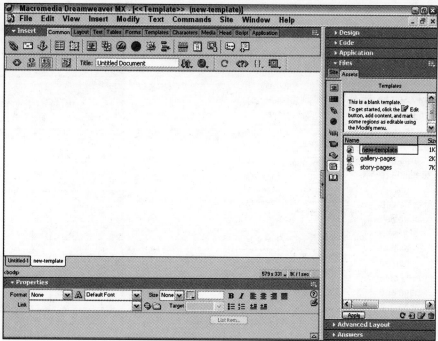

Figure 10-2:
Adding a
new
template.

4. **After you name the new template, double-click the name to open it.**

   The template page opens in Dreamweaver as any other HTML page would, except that the filename ends with the extension .dwt.

   You can now edit this page as you would any other HTML page, inserting images, text, tables, and so on.

5. **Choose Modify⇨Page Properties to specify the page title, background, text, and link colors.**

   Again, this works just like it would in any other Dreamweaver document.

6. **To make an area of the template editable, click to place your cursor in the area you want editable and choose Insert⇨Template Objects⇨ Editable Region (shown in Figure 10-3).**

   The New Editable Region dialog box opens, prompting you for a name for the editable region. Editable region names are used as identifiers so you can name them anything you want, but don't use spaces or special characters. Dreamweaver automatically names these regions "EditRegion1," "EditRegion2," and so on if you do not enter your own name.

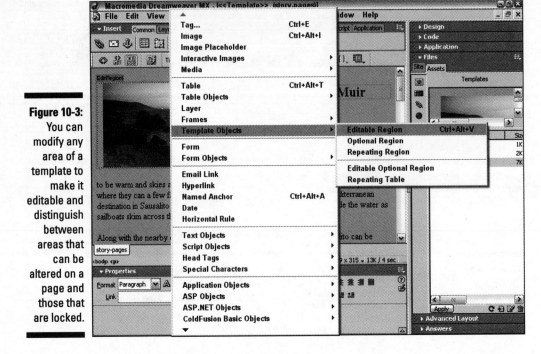

You can
modify any
area of a
template to
make it
editable and
distinguish
between
areas that
can be
altered on a
page and
those that
are locked.

7. **To make an image or text area editable, select the image or text and choose Insert⇨Template Objects⇨Editable Region.**

As in Step 6, the New Editable Region dialog box opens and prompts you for a name for the editable region.

8. **Repeat Step 6 or Step 7 to continue to make regions of the page editable.**

9. **When you are finished creating the template, choose File⇨Save to save your changes and then choose File⇨Exit to close the file, just as you would with any other Dreamweaver document.**

You can make an entire table or an individual table cell editable, but you can't make multiple cells editable all at once, unless you have merged them first. You have to select each cell one at a time if you want to make some of the cells in a table editable, but not others. Layers and layer content are also treated as separate elements, but they can also be modified to be editable. Making a layer editable enables you to change the position of that layer. Making layer content editable means that you can change the content of the layer, such as the text or image in the layer.

Creating a template from an existing page

Sometimes you get partway through creating a page before it occurs to you that it would be better to make the page a template. Other times, you may have a page that someone else created, and you decide that you want to make it into a template. Either way, it's as easy to create a template from an existing page as it is to create a new one.

To save a page as a template, follow these steps:

1. **Open the page that you want to turn into a template the same way that you open any other file in Dreamweaver.**

2. **Choose File⇨Save as Template.**

   The Save As Template dialog box appears.

3. **Use the drop-down menu next to the Site text box to select a site.**

   The menu should list all the sites that you've defined in Dreamweaver.

4. **In the Save As text box, type a name for the template.**

5. **Click the Save button in the top-right corner of the dialog box to save the file as a template.**

6. **Make any changes that you want and choose File⇨Save to save the page. Follow the steps in the earlier section, "Creating templates," to make areas editable.**

   Notice that the file now has the .dwt extension, indicating that it's a template. You can now make changes to this template the same way you edit any other template.

7. **Choose File⇨Close to close the file.**

Making attributes editable in a template

If you want more precise control over your template, you can make specific attributes editable, as well as regions.

To make attributes editable in a template, follow these steps:

1. **Open an existing template or create a new one following the steps in the previous two exercises.**

2. **Select the image or text are you want to alter and choose Modify⇨Templates⇨Make Attribute Editable.**

   The Editable Tag Attributes dialog box opens (shown in Figure 10-4). The image or text that you select as editable becomes an area that can be changed in any page created with the template. Areas that you don't mark as editable are locked and can be changed only if you modify the template itself.

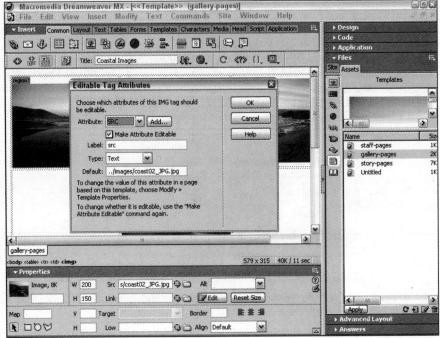

Figure 10-4:
You can
modify any
area of a
template to
make it
editable and
distinguish
between
areas that
can be
altered on a
page and
those that
are locked.

3. **From the Attribute pull-down list, choose the attribute that you want to be editable.**

4. **Click the Make Attribute Editable Box and fill in the options.**

   The attribute options varies depending on whether you selected an image, text, or other element on the page to make an editable region. These options enable you to control not only if an image can be changed, but which attributes of the image tag may be altered when the template is used.

5. **To make the attributes of other images or text areas editable, repeat Steps 6 through 8.**

6. **Save your template and close the file when you're finished.**

Using Templates in Dreamweaver

After you create all of these great templates, you'll want to put them to use. If you want to find out how to use templates in Contribute, see Chapter 3. The following shows you how to use templates in Dreamweaver. You can use templates to create or modify all the pages in your Web site or just use them for specific areas or sections. Using a template to create a new page is similar to creating any other HTML page.

To use a template to create a page, follow these steps:

1. **Choose File⇨New**

2. **Select the Templates tab.**

   The Templates dialog box opens (see Figure 10-5). In this newest version of Dreamweaver, the New from Template dialog box provides access to all the file formats you can create in Dreamweaver.

3. **From the Templates For section on the left, click to select the Template collection you want to use. (Dreamweaver lists all of your templates by site.)**

4. **In the Site section on the right, select any template by double-clicking its name.**

5. **Choose File⇨Save and name the new file as you would any other HTML page.**

6. **You can now edit any of the regions of the page that are editable using Dreamweaver's regular editing features.**

   Note: Dreamweaver's Convert Layers to Tables and Converts Tables to Layers features are not available on pages created with templates.

Figure 10-5:
The New From Template dialog box makes it easy to create a new page based on any template from any site you have set up in Dreamweaver.

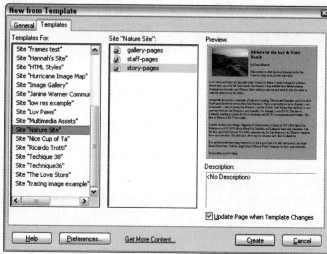

Remember that only the editable regions of the template can be altered when you use a template to create a page. If you want to change a locked region of the page, you have to either remove the template association from the file or open the template and change that area of the file to make it editable by revising the template itself.

You can remove the template association from a file by selecting Modify➪ Templates➪Detach From *templatename*.dwt. This action makes the file fully editable again, but changes you make to the template are not reflected on a detached page. To edit the template itself, choose Modify➪Templates➪Open Attached Template .

You can also apply a template to an existing page. When you apply a template to an existing document, the content in the template is added to the content already in the document. If a template is already applied to the page, Dreamweaver attempts to match editable areas that have the same name in both templates and to insert the contents from the editable regions of the page into the editable regions in the new template. If content in the existing page does not correspond to sections of the template, Dreamweaver asks you where to place the unmatched sections.

You can apply a template to an existing page by using any one of the following techniques:

✔ Choose Modify➪Templates➪Apply Template to Page and then double-click the name of a template to apply it to the page.

✔ Drag the template from the Template panel to the Document window.

✔ Select the template in the Template panel and choose Apply from the pull-down list available through the arrow at the top-right corner of the Template panel.

Making Global Changes with Templates

The greatest advantage of using templates is that you can apply changes to all the pages that use a template all at once. Suppose that you redesign your logo or want to change the positioning of key elements in a section of your site. If you've built those elements into a template, you can make the change and update all the places they are used on the site automatically — a real time saver. You can use the template update commands to update a single page or to update all the places that template has been used in the entire site.

To change a template and update the current page, follow these steps:

1. **Open a document that uses the template that you want to change.**

2. **Choose Modify⇨Templates⇨Open Attached Template.**

   The template opens.

3. **Modify the template as you would edit a new template.**

   For example, to modify the template's page properties, choose Modify⇨Page Properties.

4. **When you're finished making changes to the template, choose Modify⇨Templates⇨Update Template Files (see Figure 10-6).**

   The page you have open changes to reflect the changes you've made to the template.

If you save a template after making changes, the Update Pages dialog box opens automatically, prompting you to choose the page or pages you want to update. Choose Update to update all pages at once, or select one or more pages to update them individually. You can also choose Don't Update if you aren't ready to apply the changes.

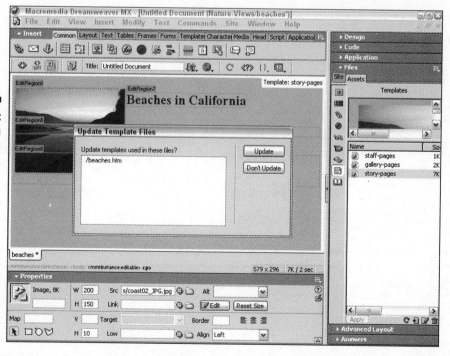

Figure 10-6:
When you alter a template, you can automatically apply those changes to any or all of the pages that are designed with that template.

To change a template and update all the files in your site that use that template at once, follow these steps:

1. **Open an existing template and make the changes that you want to apply.**

2. **Choose Modify⇨Templates⇨Update Pages.**

   The Update Pages dialog box appears.

3. **From the Look In drop-down list, choose one of the following options:**

   • **Entire Site:** Select the site name to update all pages in the selected site to all the corresponding templates.

   • **Files That Use:** Select the template name to update all pages in the current site that use that template.

   Make sure that Templates is selected in the Update option.

4. **Click Start to run the update process.**

   When the update process is completed, the Updated Pages dialog box opens with a report on which pages were altered.

Chapter 11

Testing and Publishing Your Work

· ·

In This Chapter

▶ Understanding Web servers

▶ Testing, testing, testing

▶ Making mistakes go away

▶ Working on multiple Web sites

· ·

Contribute makes publishing your work easy — maybe too easy. With the push of a button, you can publish your pages and make changes to a live Web server, but that also means that with the push of a button, you can make a mistake that can be very public.

If all you want to know how to do is make a few changes to a page and publish it on your server, Chapter 3 covers everything you need to know. But if you want to find out more about how to manage your work and how to develop a review and testing system to make sure your work is ready for prime time before you publish it to your server, then this chapter is for you. If you're interested in finding out a little more about how Web servers work, and what it actually means to publish pages on the Web, I include a little general information on that topic as well to help you better understand how the Internet works.

Testing, Testing, Testing

I don't think it's possible to do too much testing when you work on the Internet. With so many details to pay attention to, so many elements that can get broken, misspelled, or virtually mutilated, it's important to check over your work and have other people to check over it for you.

Before you publish your pages, run through the following Final Check List:

- ✔ Check spelling
- ✔ Preview in a browser
- ✔ Test all of your links
- ✔ Get a friend or colleague to review your work
- ✔ After you send your site to the server, test it again online by visiting the page with a browser and checking the links and formatting

Check spelling

Don't overlook the basics of having an editor review your written work. All writers need good editors because it's impossible to catch all of your own typos, and spell check is not perfect. But spell check is most certainly worth using. So consider this testing step #1 — *always* run spell check over your pages before you publish them. You find a built-in spell checker in Contribute to make this an easy step.

To check spelling in Contribute, choose Format⇨Check Spelling or use the Check Spelling button in the toolbar (the icon is a small check mark with the letters *abc* above it). As you can see in Figure 11-1, Contribute's check spelling feature works much like the spelling checker in a word processing program.

Preview your work in a browser

One of the cool things about the way HTML works is that you can view your pages through a Web browser on your local computer just like you can when they are on the Web. After you've made all of your changes, use Contribute's Preview in Browser option to take a final look at your pages in a program your visitors are likely to be using.

Choose File⇨Preview in Browser, and Contribute creates a temporary version of your page on the server and displays it in whatever browser you have on your computer. After you publish the page, Contribute deletes the temporary version. Although Contribute is designed to work like a browser, sometimes your pages will display differently in a Web browser than they do in Contribute.

And even if they display exactly the same, you may notice things when you are looking at them in a different program because you are more focused on the content rather than the tools you've been using to edit your work.

Test all of your links

Even when you view pages on your local computer, you should still be able to test your links. After you preview your work in a browser, you can follow the links and they should work just like they will when the page is online. To be really sure, make sure you browse to your page again after you've published it to the Web and test your links online as well. Checking your work after it's published also gives you a chance to make sure that all of the related files were uploaded properly and that nothing got broken on the server because it was somehow set up differently from the way your pages were structured on your computer.

Get a little help from your friends

Whenever possible (even if it takes extra effort) try to get someone else to go over your work and help you catch your mistakes. Believe me, if you don't have a friend or colleague do this for you, your readers or site visitors will — and it's a lot more embarrassing when someone finds your mistakes on the live server.

Macromedia knows how important it is to have someone else review your work, so they included the E-mail Review option. This is a great feature that saves a special copy of your work on the server, but in a special URL that no one but the person you send the e-mail to knows to visit. When you use the E-mail Review option, Contribute places a draft copy in a special folder on your server. The temporary version is then removed when you cancel or publish the page.

To use the E-mail Review feature, make sure that you are viewing the page you want to review in Contribute and that you are in Edit mode. Choose File⇨Email Review. Contribute automatically launches your e-mail program and includes the link to the temporary page in the body of the message, as shown in Figure 11-2.

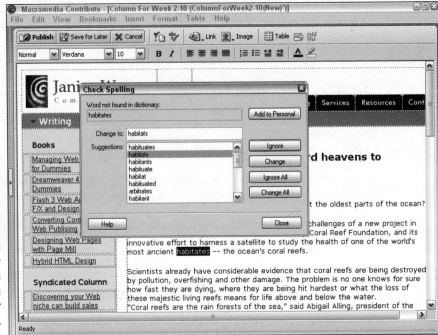

Figure 11-1:
Contribute's
Check
Spelling
feature is an
easy way to
check for
errors
before you
publish your
pages.

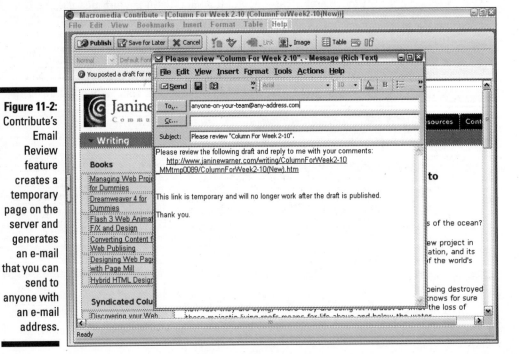

Figure 11-2:
Contribute's
Email
Review
feature
creates a
temporary
page on the
server and
generates
an e-mail
that you can
send to
anyone with
an e-mail
address.

Making Mistakes Go Away with Roll Back

Contribute's most face-saving feature is the Roll Back to Previous Version option, which enables you to "undo" any page you publish by replacing the new page with a specially saved version of the previous one.

Essentially, if you hit the Publish button and then realize you've made a terrible mistake and that it's on the live Web site, this feature lets you quickly put things back the way they were.

Contribute accomplishes this by saving a temporary copy of your pages when you publish them. If you choose Roll Back to Preview Version, Contribute opens the Roll Back Page dialog box, shown in Figure 11-3, and displays any earlier versions available. If you choose a previous version, Contribute deletes the newest version and replaces it with the backup copy.

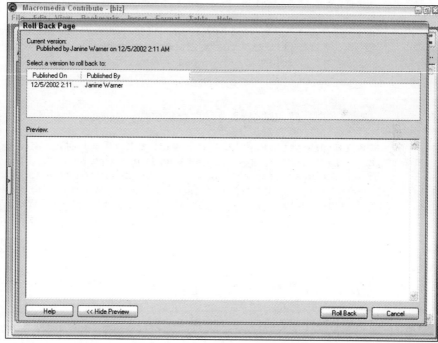

Figure 11-3: The Contribute Roll Back Page dialog box displays previous versions saved as copies in case you ever need them.

Don't rely too heavily on the Roll Back option. This feature gives you the chance to replace your work only with previous copies created in Contribute, so if you're changing a page that was originally created in Dreamweaver or another Web design program, the option may not work at all. Even if the pages were created with Contribute, this feature is not 100 percent reliable and may not work on all of your pages. In addition, your Web site administrator can disable the Roll Back feature (which many do because the backup copies can clutter the server space). If you have trouble making this feature work, and really want to have it as an option, contact your site administrator.

Publishing Your Pages

Just in case you haven't read Chapter 3 or figured this out for yourself, all you have to do to publish your pages is hit the Publish button at the top of the screen. If you don't see a Publish button, you may not be in Edit mode. Start by choosing the Edit button, make your changes, and then you should be able to publish them. If neither of these buttons display in Contribute, then you may not be properly connected to your server. In that case, check the beginning of Chapter 3 and make sure you've properly set up the connection so that you can download, edit, and publish pages to your site.

Saving a draft for later

Just because you can publish your work at the touch of a button doesn't mean you should always put your pages on the live server right away. Sometimes it's better to go to lunch, get a fresh perspective (and a full stomach), and come back and take one more look at your work before you publish it. That's when the Save for Later button is so great. When you choose this option, Contribute saves a copy on your hard drive, closes the file, and stores a reference to it in the Pages panel.

Working on multiple Web sites

Many people work on one Web site, but you find that you are responsible for making changes to multiple sites, you'll appreciate that Contribute enables you to establish connections to multiple sites and then switch between them so that you can quickly move from working on one project to another (see Figure 11-4).

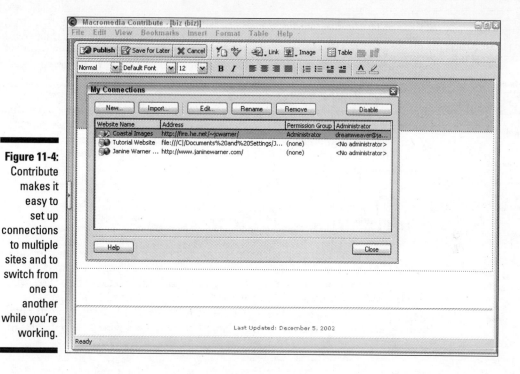

Figure 11-4: Contribute makes it easy to set up connections to multiple sites and to switch from one to another while you're working.

Where Does a Web Site Live?

A schoolteacher once asked me, "When you talk about 'there' on the Internet, where is 'there'?" I pondered that question for weeks, although I knew immediately what she meant. She wondered if some master computer held the entire Internet in one location. Cyberspace is a confusing world to the uninitiated. Come to think of it, it's a confusing world to most of the people who hang out there as well.

I believe it was Lily Tomlin who said, "Wherever you go, there you are." Well, the Internet is like that. There is no one "there." Instead, you find innumerable "theres," each represented by a computer that's connected to another computer to make up a network, which is connected to networks of networks. Essentially, the Internet is a bunch of computers and wires strung together.

But not all computers on the Internet are equal. Some are used by individuals to check e-mail or surf the Web. Other computers host Web sites and store e-mail until you log on to check it. They're often connected through special high-speed phone lines with odd names such as T1 and T3, which afford greater *bandwidth,* meaning that they can transport more information more quickly. They also maintain a connection to the Internet 24 hours a day, seven days a week, so they're always available when you need them. Even more important, they're always there when your customers need them, even if you're catching a tan on the beach.

Contribute makes it so easy and seamless to edit and publish your pages that you don't really need to know much about Web servers or how those pages become available to your visitors, but I always think it's helpful to have a deeper understanding of what you're doing so that you can appreciate the consequences of your actions.

Understanding Web servers

A *Web server* is a computer with a permanent connection to the Internet and special software that enables it to communicate with browsers, also called *clients.* A number of companies, such as Microsoft and Netscape, make software for Web servers as well as the browsers that are used to look at the pages they serve. Each system has its own features and limitations, but all of them do essentially the same thing: "serve" files from a Web site to its visiting audience.

Web servers use the *Hypertext Transfer Protocol* (HTTP) to deliver *HyperText Markup Language* (HTML) and other files to a client, usually a browser. At the low end, a Web server can be set up on almost any desktop computer with a connection to the Internet. If you use a 14.4Kbps or 28.8Kbps modem, the connection is slow, but setting up a Web server doesn't cost much, as long as you have the technical expertise. At the high end of the Web server spectrum, a powerful computer with a fast and dedicated Internet connection and the staff to keep everything working costs many thousands of dollars.

Some servers are designed to handle only one Web site; others handle many sites simultaneously. The latter are generally operated by universities, government organizations, and private companies and are part of the network maintained by the organization.

Internet service providers (ISPs) provide an alternative for smaller businesses and individuals (although many big companies have determined that it's cheaper to use an ISP than to keep all the people on staff needed to keep a Web server running 24/7.) ISPs usually have one or more large servers capable of hosting 100 or more different Web sites each. When you set up your site with an ISP, you essentially rent a small section of the hard drive on a server. ISPs can section off a server and provide you with access to only the part of the server that you're using to manage your Web site, even if many other sites are on the same server.

IS stands for "information services." It's usually used to describe someone who's in charge of all the computers and software used by a company. If you aren't even sure what an IS person does, you definitely don't want to run your own Web server.

Understanding the limits of bandwidth

Bandwidth measures the carrying capacity of a connection on the Internet. Compare it to a garden hose and its capacity to transport water. The larger the diameter of the hose, the more water it can carry. Bandwidth works the same way: The greater the bandwidth, the faster information can be transferred. On the Internet, information is digital data that is measured in kilobytes and megabytes the same way it's measured on your hard drive. The larger the file, the more bandwidth is required to transport it across the Internet.

For example, most short text files (1 to 20 pages) are only a few kilobytes in size so they only take a few seconds to send, even over a 56k modem (the equivalent of a garden hose in this analogy). If you want to send the entire manuscript of *War and Peace* it will take a lot longer, but the kinds of files that take the most bandwidth — the ones that warrant a fire hose or a high-speed connection like a T1 line — are video and animation files, PowerPoint presentations and large color images, which can be many megabytes in size. The more images or other large files on a page the longer it will take to download that page.

To help you compare the differences in bandwidth, visualize them as if they were running water:

- 28.8 modem — garden hose
- DLS or Cable Modem — fire hose
- T1 line — small waterfall
- T3 line — bigger waterfall
- Multiple T3 line — Niagara falls

Part IV

The Administrator's Guide: Setting Up Contribute

The 5th Wave   By Rich Tennant

HAPPY HOLIDAYS
SHAKE FOR SNOW

"Isn't that our administrator? These people always find a creative way to interface."

In this part . . .

This part is for Webmasters, IT staff, and individuals who want to administer their own sites and use Contribute to update them. Although this section is more technical than the first part of the book, you do not need to know how to administer Contribute for use in updating a Web site. This section is not designed to cover all of Dreamweaver's development features — it's designed to serve as a companion to a book such as Dreamweaver MX For Dummies.

Chapter 12

Administering Contribute

*N*o one knows for sure how many times someone has inadvertently erased an important file on a Web site. Pressing yes when the computer tries to verify a mistaken request to delete a file is all too easy, and all too difficult later when you realize that you really needed it and now have no way of recovering the work you've lost. Losing files can be even more problematic when you're working on a Web site with a team of people, especially if a deleted file represents hours of a coworker's — and soon your own — blood, sweat, and tears. Working on any Web site, especially with other people, goes much more smoothly when you can control access to files, and even better, when you can control what can be changed and deleted within those files.

Enter Contribute, Macromedia's powerful new site management utility with features that make setting up different levels of access for Web site contributors an easy task. Fortunately, the team at Macromedia designed Contribute with all the challenges in mind, and made it possible for an administrator to make sure that everyone on a team — even a team of one — works safely and effectively.

This part of the book, The Administrator's Guide, is designed for Web site administrators. If you are working only as a contributor to a Web site, you don't need to worry about this section. You can use Contribute to work on your Web site even if you never use any of the administrative features.

Controlling Workflow on Your Site

Contribute works on the premise that there is a key person (or persons) who is responsible for managing and maintaining a Web site (if you're reading this section, that means that person is you, the administrator). Contribute also assumes that there is a user or group of users who need to update and modify information on the site (all of those people you need to protect from deleting each other's work). Contribute administrators are responsible for setting up connections to the appropriate Web site and defining the actions that users are allowed to perform when they connect and update content.

As a Contribute administrator, you can:

✔ **Control site-specific settings**

- Specify Administrator contact information
- Configure rollbacks — backup-like versioning feature
- Indicate alternate index pages and URLs

✔ **Control Permissions**

- Define user roles by assigning them to groups
- Control folder and file access
- Specify how Contribute generates HTML
- Dictate which styles and fonts a user may use
- Restrict whether users can edit the text or add images to a Web page
- Limit the size of images
- Allow users to create new pages based on templates, or other criteria

Don't worry if you've never done these kinds of administrative tasks or set up access to a Web site for other users before. Contribute makes it remarkably easy to do, and this part of the book is designed to walk you through the process step by step.

Managing Server Access

In order to control the workflow, Contribute installs a file in a specific folder at the root of any Web site you connect to. This file, called the Shared Settings File, enables Contribute to store all the settings you choose when you administer the Web site. Whenever you make a change to one of the user groups or any of the other site settings the change gets stored in this centrally located file. The Shared Settings File enables you to create various groups within a site and to modify the access levels for each of these groups individually without having to send new connection files to the users each time you make a change. For example, you define a group called Editors and give the users the right to add images to pages. Later, you decide that maybe it wasn't a good idea to let them add images. You create another group called Designers, let them add images, and prohibit the Editors group from adding images. Without sending the Editors new connection files, you disabled their access to images, saved yourself some time, and gave the designers something to do.

The Shared Settings File

The Shared Settings File is nothing more than a plain text XML file that holds the settings for the Contribute site connection. When you follow the initial setup steps described later in the "Setting Up a Connection" section, Contribute automatically creates a directory named _mm and places the Share Settings File (an XML text file) within it.

Tempting as it may be for some, do not modify the Shared Settings File manually. Contribute expects the settings file to have a specific format. It is possible to make a change to the file that Contribute does not understand and lose all the settings as a result. Change settings and permissions from within Contribute to avoid headaches.

Using rollback files to back up pages

One of the many features available with Contribute is that of keeping various versions — or backup copies — automatically when editing and publishing Web pages. This feature is especially useful when someone makes a mistake while editing a page and you want to go back and use a previous version. Contribute automatically saves key information within another directory, labeled _baks, created at the root of the Web site.

For the rollback feature to function properly, the _baks directory and any files it contains should not be deleted.

Keeping Your Settings Secure

Because Contribute stores many of the most important files, the setting and record-keeping files, in directories whose names begin with an underscore (for example _mm), making sure that people browsing the Web site can't access these directories by mistake or, even worse, on purpose is very important.

If your Web site is being served by a computer running Microsoft's Internet Information Server *(IIS)*, these folders are probably already secure because IIS is automatically configured to prevent access to folders named in this manner. Many other commercial Web servers are also set up to act this way. Unfortunately, Apache's Web server (one of the world's most popular Web servers) is not among them. If you're using an Apache Web server, you need to set it up yourself to disallow access to any files you want to protect. Because configuring Apache settings is not a part of Contribute's features, consult your Apache Administrator's guide or visit `http://httpd.apache.org` for more information.

Deploying Contribute

In addition to ensuring that all the users who will be using Contribute have it installed on their computers, there are several steps required to administer a Contribute Web site.

The following list highlights the steps necessary to use Contribute to administer a Web site:

- ✔ **Install a copy of Contribute on your computer.** If you have not already done so, go ahead and install a copy of Contribute on your computer. Confirm that everyone who needs to update content on the Web site has a copy of Contribute installed on their computer. Chapter 1 describes this process in detail.

- ✔ **Set up a connection to the Web site that you plan to administer.** Contribute does not limit the number of Web sites that you can connect to and administer. Before you create the connection, you need the following information: the user name you plan to use, your e-mail address, the URL to your Web site, and where the files are stored (either FTP site or local or network drive). This process is described later in this chapter in "Setting Up a Connection."

- ✔ **Figure out who is going to need to update the content on the Web site.** Depending on the design of your Web site and the number of people on your team, you may decide to create one or more groups to specify which users are able to update which sections of the site. See Chapter 13 for more on groups.

- ✔ **Create the administrative user groups and set the appropriate permissions.** After you determine how to organize the work and permissions for the Web site, use Contribute's Administrative tool to set it all up. Chapter 13 explains how Contribute uses groups to set permissions and how to set the groups up.

✔ **Create and send connection files to the users.** When everything is configured and ready to go, you can send the eager new users their own connection files so they can easily get connected and begin to update content on the Web site. See Chapter 14 for more about creating and sharing connection files.

✔ **Make sure that users can connect and update the appropriate Web pages.** Last but not least, make sure that everyone can connect to the Web site and that they can edit what they are supposed to. Chapter 14 details a few common stumbling blocks.

Setting Up a Connection

After you install Contribute on your computer, you are ready to set up a connection. Contribute saves details for all the Web sites that you edit as connections. With Contribute running, you can view the available connections by choosing Edit⇨My Connections on Contribute's menu.

Before you begin setting up the connection, save yourself a little time by gathering the information it asks you for:

✔ Your name as you want it to be displayed to other Contribute users.

✔ The e-mail address Contribute displays to users.

Contribute uses your name and e-mail address to identify users and the pages they are updating, which prevents headaches by not allowing more than one user to edit a page at one time.

✔ The URL used to browse the Web site being connected to.

The URL is the Web address (www.somesite.com) that is used to connect to the Web site on the Internet or the local intranet.

✔ Either the network path to the Web site files or the FTP site used to access the files.

You can use Contribute to edit a site on your local network, local computer, or a remote FTP site. If more than one person will be working with the Web site, you probably want to use either a local network path or an FTP site and not the local computer's hard drive.

If you choose a network path, you need the server name and directory name for the location of the files. For an FTP site, you need the name of the FTP server, the FTP login name, and the FTP password.

Armed with all of this information, you are ready to create a new connection.

Using the Connection Wizard

To make a new connection in Contribute, follow these steps:

1. **If Contribute is not already running, go ahead and start Contribute.**

2. **On Contribute's menu bar, choose Edit⟿My Connections to bring up the My Connections dialog box, as shown in Figure 12-1.**

   My Connections serves as the central point where you can add, import, change, or remove connections to Web sites.

3. **Choose the New button to start the Connection Wizard.**

4. **Press Next on the Connection Wizard and enter the requested information, as shown in Figure 12-2.**

   The Connection Wizard displays a message letting you know that you can double-click a connection file at this point to automatically enter the settings. Because you are the administrator creating a new connection at this time, your only option is to press Next to continue.

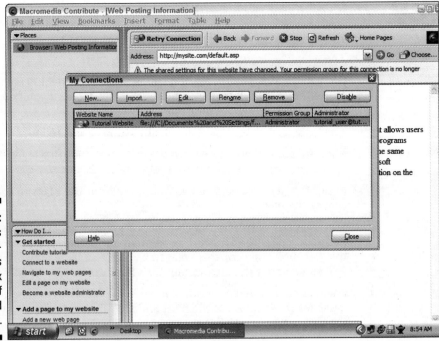

Figure 12-1:
Contribute's
My Con-
nections
dialog box
shows all of
the defined
connections.

Figure 12-2:
The initial
Connection
Wizard
screen.

5. **Enter your name and e-mail address and press Next.**

6. **Enter your Web sites URL in the space provided and press Next.**

7. **Select either FTP or Local/Network as the method to connect to your Web server (see Figure 12-3) and continue with the appropriate step.**

   If your Web site files are accessible on a local network or drive, choose Local/Network and continue with Step 8; if you need to access your files using file transfer protocol (FTP), choose FTP and go to Step 9.

Figure 12-3:
Web server
file
locations.

8. **If you choose Local/Network, enter the path and press Next.**

   You can type the path where the files are located or you can click Browse and navigate to find the folder where the Web site files are stored.

Choose Open and then Select in the file browsing dialog to automatically enter the path.

9. **If your Web server files are located on an FTP server, enter the login and server information and press Next.**

   Enter the name of your FTP server in the first box (for example: ftp.myserver.com); in the FTP login field, enter the user name you use to login to the FTP server; and in the Password field, enter your FTP password. If your FTP server requires that Contribute connects to it using passive FTP — Contribute manages the FTP connection, rather than the server — then you may press the Advanced button to bring up the Advanced Connection Settings dialog box (see Figure 12-4). Then check the box next to "Use passive FTP to connect to the server."

Figure 12-4:
Using the
Advanced
Connection
Settings
dialog box,
you can tell
Contribute
to use
passive FTP
and whether
to use the
global
firewall
settings
when using
this
connection

If you are behind a firewall, you can also configure the connection settings by pressing the Firewall Settings button and reading the section "Working around firewalls" in this chapter. If you opened the Advanced Connection Settings dialog box, press OK to close it.

When you finish entering all the information, press next.

Be patient. Contribute may seem to hang as it takes a few seconds to check the connection to the FTP site and make sure it can log in. This is normal.

10. Choose "Yes, I want to be the administrator" and then type in a password and press Next.

The password you use here is especially important because the administrator's access level has the power to prevent other users from modifying the administrative settings of this connection from Contribute. Use something that is hard to guess but easy to remember. Write the password down and keep it somewhere safe for future reference.

As with all passwords, it should be at least eight characters long and include both letters and numbers. Write the password down and keep it somewhere safe for future reference.

11. Press Done.

Congratulations! You created a new Web site connection and assigned yourself as the site administrator. Contribute adds the connection you created to the list on the My Connections dialog box.

Working around firewalls

When working with the Internet, eventually you run into the term *firewall*. A firewall is similar to a security guard posted at a gate (your Internet Connection) and checking all traffic in and out of a gated community (your network or computer). A firewall is just a device or software that filters the information that can pass through the Internet connection and into your private network or computer. The firewall checks every bit of information trying to get through and decides according to its configuration whether or not it should allow the information to pass.

If there is a firewall between you and the FTP server that hosts your Web site, Contribute needs to be configured before it will work correctly.

There are two ways to get to the same firewall settings dialog box for Contribute. Step 9 in the "Using the Connection Wizard" section covered the first of these. Don't worry if you didn't press the Advanced button while setting up the FTP connection for your site. You can also get to Contribute's firewall settings by choosing Edit⇨Preferences on Contribute's main screen and then choosing Firewall in the list of categories on the Preferences dialog box.

No matter how you get to the firewall category, this is a global application setting for Contribute. You cannot choose different firewalls for different connections. The only thing you can specify is whether or not an FTP connection will use the settings in the Firewall preferences category.

When the Firewall preferences category is highlighted in the Preferences dialog box, type the name or IP address of the firewall in the Firewall Host text box and the port in the Firewall Port text box, as shown in Figure 12-5. If you are not sure what the firewall host and port are, ask your network administrator.

Figure 12-5:
Contribute
uses the
same
firewall
settings
for all
connections
configured
to use a
firewall

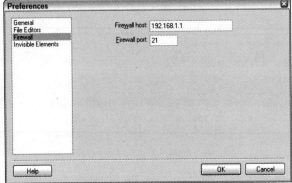

Setting Up and Accessing Administrator Settings

Contribute allows site connections to be created and used without setting up an administrator. Earlier in this chapter, I show you how to setup a connection from scratch in the "Using the Connection Wizard" section. During that process, Contribute asks if you want to be the administrator for the site. If you chose "No, I don't want to be the administrator," all is not lost. When you first choose to administer a connection, Contribute asks you if you want to be the administrator if none has been specified for the site (see Step 2 in this section).

The name of the site I will be administering is "My Site - mysite.com/" and you can do the same for any site you like. This is how you get to the Administer Website dialog box:

1. **Choose Edit⇨Administer Websites⇨My Site - mysite.com/, as shown in Figure 12-6.**

   My Site - mysite.com/ is the name of the site that I am setting an administrator for. You can choose any site to add an administrator.

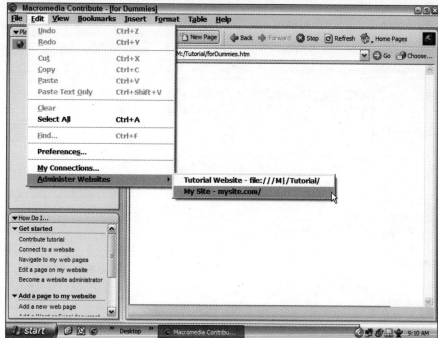

Figure 12-6:
Choosing
which
site to
administer.

2. **If there is no administrator for the site, Contribute asks you if you want to be the administrator with a message like that in Figure 12-7; otherwise, it asks you for the Administrator's password to gain access to the settings.**

   If Contribute asks you for the Administrator Password, enter it into the box, press OK, and go to Step 4.

   If not, Contribute tells you that there is no administrator for the Web site and asks you "Do you want to be the administrator?" Press Yes.

3. **Type a password that is hard to guess but easy to remember in both the "New password" and "Confirm new password" boxes in the Administrator Password dialog box; then press OK (see Figure 12-8).**

   The password you choose ensures that no one else can administer the Web site using Contribute. The password you choose should be easy to remember but hard to guess. As with all passwords, it should be at least eight characters long and include both letters and numbers.

Figure 12-7:
The Administrator Password dialog box, in which You must enter the administrator password each time you access the administrative settings.

Figure 12-8:
Setting the administrator password: Contribute asks you for this password each time you administer the Web site.

4. **The Administer Website dialog box appears as shown in Figure 12-9.**

The Administer Website dialog box is the central place where all administrative settings can be configured. The following section, "Configuring Site Settings," covers setting up Sitewide Settings.

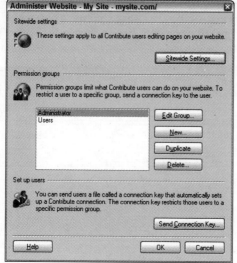

Figure 12-9:
Administer
Website
dialog box:
The place
where all
adminis-
trative
settings are
configured.

Configuring Site Settings

There are various tasks that can be performed when administering a
Contribute Web site. The following two sections detail the Sitewide settings,
which include

✔ Supplying Administrator e-mail address and password

✔ Setting rollback — or backup — options

✔ More advanced settings, such as choosing the default Web pages and
additional server names for the site

Sitewide settings apply to *all* users that connect to the Web site using
Contribute. Other administrative tasks like working with Permission Groups
and creating and sending connection files deal with specific users and groups
and are discussed in Chapters 13 and 14, respectively.

Controlling Administrator E-mail Address and Password

Contribute users use the Administrator contact e-mail address to contact the
administrator if they have any problems. You can use your e-mail address or
that of someone else (like your company's helpdesk) who will help end users
with their questions.

1. **If you don't already have the Administer Website dialog box open, please refer to the prior section "Setting Up and Accessing Administrator Settings" to open the dialog shown in Figure 12-9; then continue with Step 2.**

2. **Click the Sitewide Settings button to open the settings screen, as shown in Figure 12-10.**

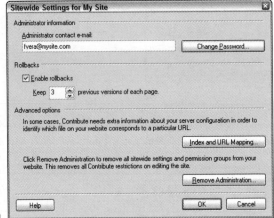

Figure 12-10:
The Site-
wide Set-
tings dialog
box.

3. **Type in the e-mail address under "Administrator contact e-mail."**

4. **To change the administrator's password click the Change Password button.**

   Figure 12-11 shows the Change Administrator Password. Type your old password in the corresponding box and then the new password in both of the other boxes and press OK.

Figure 12-11:
Change
Adminis-
trator
password.

The password you choose ensures that no one else can administer the Web site using Contribute. The password you choose should be easy to remember but hard to guess. As with all passwords, it should be at least eight characters long and include both letters and numbers

If you forget the administrator password, you can reset it, but most of the sites settings will need to be reconfigured. Chapter 14 shows you how to reset the site.

Understanding and Enabling Rollback

Imagine using Contribute to edit a Web page and add some text. You press Publish and suddenly you realize that you inadvertently erased three paragraphs describing the mating habits of sea anemones. You know nothing about this topic and are up in arms about what to do. Fortunately, rollback was enabled for this site and all you had to do is go to File➪Roll Back to Previous Version and choose the version before you erased all that information about sea anemones.

Rollback is like a backup. In and of itself, it does not remove the need to back up a Web site onto some sort of removable storage like a CD-ROM. It does, however, prevent accidents like the one involving those poor sea anemones. By default, Contribute automatically enables rollback for each site and saves up to three versions of each Web page. It saves the backed-up versions in a folder called _baks in the root of the Web site. You can choose to disable rollback for a specific site or you can change the number of previous versions that Contribute will save.

Although you can tell Contribute to save up to 99 versions of each page, this requires a significant amount of disk space. A Web site where 10 separate pages are edited daily will have 990 separate copies after 99 days.

In order to configure rollback options:

1. **If you don't already have the Administer Website dialog box open, please refer to the prior section "Setting Up and Accessing Administrator Settings" to open the dialog box shown in Figure 12-9; then continue with Step 2.**

2. **Click the Sitewide Settings button to open the settings screen (refer to Figure 12-10).**

3. **Make sure that the box next to "Enable rollbacks" is checked if you want rollbacks.**

4. **Type a number between 1 and 99 in the box provided.**

   Contribute lets you enter 0 for the number, but automatically changes it to 1 when you press OK.

5. **Press OK to save your settings.**

Managing Advanced Site Settings

Contribute automatically tries to figure out all the possible Web server configurations when you connect to a site. Depending on how the Web server is configured and the intricacy of the Web site, it may not be able to do so and may require additional advanced settings regarding index files and additional web site addresses.

In order to revise these settings in the following two sections, you need to open the Advanced Sitewide Settings dialog box:

1. **If you don't already have the Administer Website dialog box open, please refer to the earlier section "Setting Up and Accessing Administrator Settings" to open the dialog box shown in Figure 12-9; then continue with Step 2.**

2. **Click the Sitewide Settings button to open the settings screen (refer to Figure 12-10).**

3. **Press the Index and URL Mapping button under Advanced Options to open the Advanced Sitewide Settings screen, as shown in Figure 12-12.**

   From this dialog box, you can edit the list of index files (main site pages) and which addresses can be used to access your site.

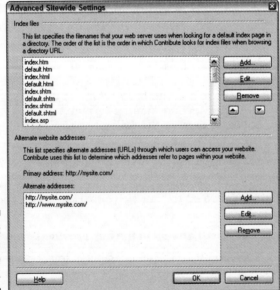

Figure 12-12:
Advanced
Sitewide
Settings.

Changing the main site page

The main site page — or index page — for a site is the default page that is seen by someone when they visit your site but don't specify what page to display. For example if the visitor typed www.somesite.com, the actual page displayed may be a file called index.htm. In this case, the actual URL that the person visited was www.somesite.com/index.htm. Which page, or pages, are displayed by default varies for web servers. Additionally, some Web servers are set up to look for various index pages in a specific order. For example, if index.htm is not found, the Web server may look for index.html. If it doesn't find that one, it may look for default.asp. It may continue through a list of files to look for. Contribute ships with a list of common index page names like index.htm, default.htm, and default.cfm, to name a few.

If the index page for your server is listed in the Index files list on the Advanced Sitewide Settings dialog box, then you can skip this section.

You can modify, delete, add, and change the order of the pages Contribute treats as index pages. I show you how by walking you through adding a fictional index file, changing the order, and finally deleting it:

1. **Open the Advanced Sitewide Settings window (refer to Figure 12-12) according to the steps in the previous section if it isn't already open.**

2. **Click the Add button on the top right of the window in the Index files section.**

3. **Type main.shtml in the Add or Edit Filename box and press OK.**

   Contribute adds the name at the end of the index files list and highlights it, as shown in Figure 12-13.

Figure 12-13:
Contribute adds "main.shtml" to the end of the list

4. **If Contribute did not highlight main.shtml, find main.shtml in the list and select it.**

5. **You can change the order in which Contribute looks for this file by pressing the up and down arrow (right below the top Remove button).**

6. **Delete main.shtml by selecting it in the list and pressing Remove.**

Directing multiple domain names

Web servers can be configured to serve the same page even though it was accessed using a different name. A Web visitor can visit www.mysite.com or they can visit www.somesite.com and the same Web server shows the visitor the same file. Contribute allows the administrator to specify all the possible names used to visit the web site.

If Contribute users access the Web site using a different name, directory path, or port number, then you must tell Contribute about all of these differences. You don't need to tell Contribute about all of the various possibilities when a visitor views the site, only the different ways Contribute users may use to access it.

In order to specify these alternate Web site addresses:

1. **Open the Advanced Sitewide Settings window (refer to Figure 12-12) according to the steps in the previous section if it isn't already open.**

2. **For each alternate address, click Add in the Alternate addresses section of the Advanced Sitewide Settings screen.**

   Type the full alternate URL in the Add or Edit Alternate Address dialog box.

Chapter 13

Controlling Access: Managing Groups

· ·

· ·

*O*ne of the biggest challenges when multiple people are collaborating on a Web site is managing who can do what when they work. Macromedia recognizes this and makes controlling access straightforward using Contribute. You'll find various ways to manage permissions with this little program, and Contribute uses one of the more flexible techniques. Instead of allowing or disallowing specific users to perform a specific task, Contribute allows the setting of permissions through groups. This system of assigning access levels presents the administrator with a precise level of control over which operations a specific group of people can perform and makes it especially simple to make changes that apply to various people all at once.

If you're just flipping through this book or you thought you'd jump ahead, be aware that this part is only for the Webmaster or site administrator. Unless you have to manage the technical back end of your Web site, you don't have to worry about all of this stuff. If you're just going to be updating pages — adding images and text and stuff like that — you shouldn't have to read this techie chapter at all. Jump ahead to the Part of Tens section toward the end of the book to find some quick tips, or look up the specific task you want to do in the index and go right to that section.

Understanding Permissions

Access control and permissions is nothing new to computers and Web sites. Operating systems such as Windows XP, Unix, and Linux have permissions based on both users and groups. The simplest way to organize the permissions is to define privileges for predetermined groups and then assign users to each group according to the necessary level of access. For example, you have a folder named `marketing_data` that has files that John and Sue need to view but Samantha and James need to modify. You could create a group called *Viewers*, grant that group read-only access to the folder by limiting them to editing data within specific folders and leaving the list empty, and assign John and Sue to that group. Subsequently, you may create a group called *Modifiers*, grant that group read-write permission to `marketing data`, and associate James and Samantha with that permission group. Anyone in the *Viewers* group can read files in `marketing_data` but not change them. The users in the *Modifiers* group can both view and change the files in the folder.

Contribute uses groups to control access to a Web site. By creating groups and assigning people to those groups, you can control the following actions:

- ✔ Which files users can edit.
- ✔ Whether users can delete files.
- ✔ Access to specific portions of a page.
- ✔ Permissions for assigning styles (formatting attributes) to text.
- ✔ Which users can create files or images.

Contribute creates two permission groups by default. They are the Administrator and User groups. After considering your needs, you may decide that the default groups will work for you. If not, the following section details the steps I followed to create the permission groups for "My Site."

Table 13-1 describes most of the configurable group settings and permissions available in Contribute.

Table 13-1	Group Settings and Permissions	
Category	*Contribute Setting*	*Function*
General	Group home page	Identifies the main page URL for the group. When the site was originally configured, the site's home page was specified (`http://mysite.com/default.asp`). It may be more appropriate, for example, for the Marketing group to use `http://mysite.com/marketing/default.asp` as the home page.
Folder/File Access	Folder access	Defines whether users can edit the files in any folder or only those in folders you specify.

Category	Contribute Setting	Function
	File deletion	Controls the ability to delete files, and controls whether rollback (backup) versions are erased when the original is wiped out.
Editing	Non-template pages	For pages not protected by Dreamweaver templates, you can specify the ability to either edit only text and formatting on a page, or specify unrestricted editing with optional protection of underlying script and form HTML tags.
	Paragraph spacing	Controls whether pressing the Enter key creates either a one-line or a two-line gap between paragraphs.
	Other editing options	Specifies whether multiple spaces are allowed between words, whether accessibility options to make pages more manageable to readers with disabilities are enforced, whether bold and italic tags will be created according to the current HTML specification, and which character sequence to use for line breaks.
Styles and Fonts	Styles	Controls access to text formatting options.
	Fonts	Specifies whether users can change the font and size of text and, if they can, how the HTML is generated and what unit of measurement to use.
New Pages	Allow a user to (Creation Methods)	Controls whether users can create new blank pages, create pages based on sample Contribute pages or on existing pages on the Web site (all of them or specific ones), or create pages using all available or user-defined Dreamweaver templates.
New Images	Maximum file size	Specifies whether users can create new image files of any size or whether a limit (in kilobytes) exists. Note: You can prevent the creation of new images by specifying a size of zero kilobytes.

Creating Permission Groups

Before working with Contribute's permission groups, you should take a moment and consider the design of your site and the responsibilities of the individuals who work on it. I will demonstrate the process of defining groups by using my fictional, news Web site `http://mysite.com`. This fictional site is organized into a few different sections and directories. The folder named `marketing` holds all of the marketing and advertising information. The `news` and `archive` folders house current and old technology articles, respectively. Finally, the `images` directory possesses all of the associated artwork for use on the site. I have several imaginary people (whom I don't talk to — really!) and one real one (me) who work on the Web site, and I grouped them into the following categories for various reasons:

- ✔ **Administrator:** I happen to be the only one to fall in this group, although that will not always be the case.

- ✔ **Marketing:** These individuals only need to edit and create pages in the marketing section of the Web site. They do not edit or add images to pages, nor do they format the text that they enter. Additionally, marketing users create pages based only on the `marketing.asp` Dreamweaver template.

- ✔ **News Authors:** News authors are responsible for creating and modifying news articles in the `news` directory. Either they create standard articles that talk about some exciting topic, or they create feature articles that speak about broader subjects and link to various supporting standard articles. News Authors use predefined styles to format their writings and can insert existing artwork from the `images` folder. In addition, news authors are responsible for moving old articles to the `archive` folder once a month.

- ✔ **Designers:** This group formats pages and creates the images used on the site. Unfortunately, this overzealous group tends to create exceedingly large images; therefore, limits will be set on the size of images that they create.

In order to create a permission group, the site must be set up for administration. Chapter 12's section, "Setting Up and Accessing Administrator Settings," covers this in detail.

The name of the site that I will create permission groups for is My Site - mysite.com/. You can follow along with any site you prefer. Using the groups I detailed for `mysite.com`, the following steps demonstrate how to create new groups, copy existing ones, and delete unnecessary ones:

1. **Click Edit⊳Administer Websites⊳"My Site - mysite.com/" on the Contribute main menu, as shown in Figure 13-1.**

   I am editing permissions for My Site - mysite.com. Follow along with any site you choose.

2. **Enter the administrative password and click OK to open the Administer Website dialog box, as shown in Figure 13-2.**

   Don't fret if you forgot your password. The section "What to do if you forget the administrator password" in Chapter 14 will help you.

3. **To create the Marketing group, select the default group called Users.**

4. **Click the Duplicate button to open the Permission Group Name dialog box, as shown in Figure 13-3.**

5. **Type** Marketing **in the box and click OK.**

   To create the News Authors group, repeat Steps 3 to 5.

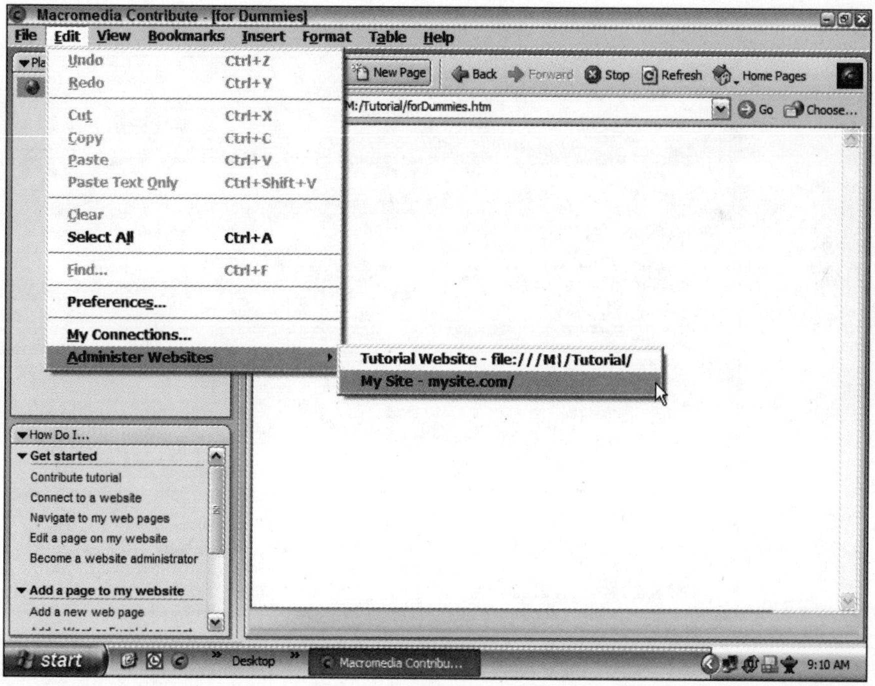

Figure 13-1: Click Edit⊳ Administer Websites to view the list of Web sites you can manage.

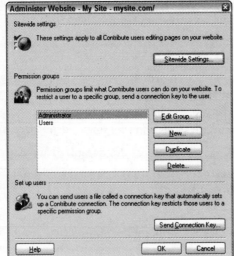

Figure 13-2:
After you
enter your
adminis-
trative pass-
word, the
Administer
Website
dialog box
opens.

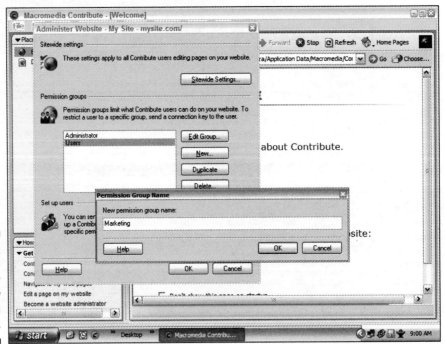

Figure 13-3:
Contribute
asks for
the new
permission
group name.

6. **Create the Designers group by clicking the New... button on the Administer Website dialog box.**

7. **Type** Designers **in the Permission Group dialog box and click OK.**

8. **Delete the unnecessary Users group by selecting it from the list, clicking the Delete... button, and choosing Yes on the confirmation box shown in Figure 13-4.**

Figure 13-4:
Contribute
verifies that
you want to
delete a
permission
group.

Contribute

⚠ Are you sure you want to delete permission group "Users"?

[Yes]   [No]

Because I defined four groups for my site (Administrator, Marketing, News Authors, and Designers), I do not need the default Users group.

You don't have to delete unused groups if you don't want to. I delete them so that I know that only the groups in the list are the ones that are used on this site.

Managing site permissions

Creating the groups for mysite.com is the first step. Now you define each of the individual permissions for each group. In order to administer the group permissions, you need to have the Administer Website dialog box open.

If you don't already have the Administer Website dialog box open, you can follow these steps to open it:

1. **Click Edit▷Administer Websites▷"My Site - mysite.com/" on the Contribute main menu.**

    I am working with the fictional site called My Site - mysite.com/. You can work with any site you choose.

2. **Enter the administrative password to open the Administer Website dialog box.**

Refer to Figure 13-4 to see the Administer Website dialog box with the groups that I discussed in the previous section, "Creating Permission Groups."

Defining general settings

General group settings include a brief description for the group and the home page that Contribute user sees when they connect to the Web site. The main home page for My Site is http://mysite.com/default.asp, and this is fine for the Designers and the Administrator. The Marketing and News Authors, however, work with specific sections on the site, and it makes sense to set their startup page differently.

Table 13-2 shows the description and initial group home page for each of the groups discussed in the section "Creating Permission Groups."

Table 13-2 Home page and description for your permission groups		
Group	**Home page**	**Description**
Administrator	http://mysite.com/ default.asp	Members of this permission group are administrators of this Web site.
Marketing	http://mysite.com/ marketing/default.asp	Members of this permission group work on the marketing section of this Web site.
News Authors	http://mysite.com/ news/default.asp	Members of this permission group work on the news section of this Web site.
Designers	http://mysite.com/ default.asp	Members of this permission group are designers of this Web site.

If the Administer Website dialog box is not open, open it by following steps 1 and 2 in the "Managing site permissions" section.

The steps for setting the group description and home page are the same for each group. The following list shows you how to set them for the Marketing group, and you can repeat these steps for all of the other groups:

1. **Select Marketing from the list of groups in the Administer Website dialog box.**

2. **Click Edit Group... to open the Permission Group dialog box.**

3. **Select General from the list of categories on the Permission Group dialog box, as shown in Figure 13-5.**

4. **Type the Marketing group description in the Group description box.**

5. **Enter the URL** `http://mysite.com/marketing/default.asp` **in the Group home page box.**

   You can also click the Choose button to browse to the file you want to use as the group home page, as shown in Figure 13-6, and then click OK.

6. **Click OK in the Permission Group dialog box to return to the Administer Website dialog box.**

7. **Click OK in the Administer Website dialog box to save your settings.**

   Contribute does not save the settings configured in the Permission Group dialog box until you click OK in the Administer Website dialog box. Contribute will discard all of the settings if you click Cancel.

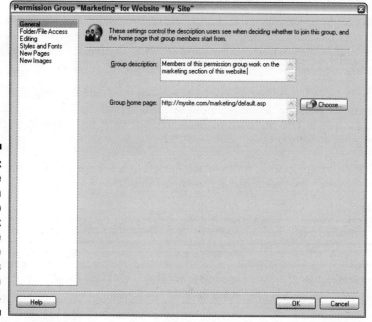

Figure 13-5:
The Permission Group dialog box lists the configurable categories for each group.

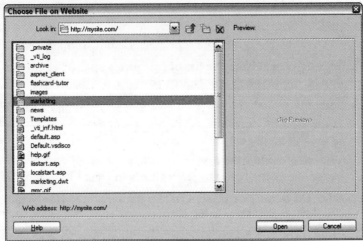

Figure 13-6:
This dialog
box lets you
choose a
file to use as
the group
home page.

Controlling folder access and Web page deletion

You set in which folders a user can edit files through Contribute's Folder/File Access permission category. You also control whether members of the group can delete files in these folders and whether Contribute will delete any rollback (backup) versions when the user erases the original.

Carefully think about configuring the deletion of rollback files. Checking the "Remove rollback versions on delete" option makes a file deletion final. For `mysite.com`, I do not want to erase rollback versions, just in case there is an accidental deletion.

The groups discussed in "Creating Permission Groups" require the folder access and deletion settings shown in Table 13-3.

Table 13-3 Folder Access and Deletion Settings for Your Groups

Group	Folder access	File deletion
Administrator	Allowed to edit files in any folder.	Permitted to delete files.
Marketing	Can edit files under only `http://mysite.com/marketing/`.	Not allowed to delete files.

Group	Folder access	File deletion
News Authors	Allowed to edit files in `http://mysite.com/news/` and `http://mysite.com/archive/`.	Permitted to delete files.
Designers	Allowed to edit files in any folder.	Permitted to delete files.

Like the general settings, the steps for configuring folder access are the same for each group. The following list shows you how to set folder access for the News Authors group:

1. **If the Administer Website dialog box is not open, open it by following steps 1 and 2 in "Managing site permissions."**

2. **Select News Authors from the list of groups in the Administer Website dialog box.**

3. **Click the Edit Group... button to open the Permission Group dialog box.**

4. **Choose Folder/File Access in the list of categories to show the associated settings.**

5. **Click the radio button next to "Only allow editing within these folders."**

   News Authors can edit files only in specific folders. You need to select this option before you can limit the folders that they are allowed to work with.

6. **Click the Add Folder... button to browse for the folder that they can work in.**

7. **Browse into the folder that the group can work in and click Select Folder to choose the folder and return to the Permission Group dialog box.**

   Because the News Authors can edit files in `http://mysite.com/news/` and `http://mysite.com/archive/`, repeat steps 6 and 7 once for each folder.

8. **Check the box next to "Allow users to delete files they have permission to edit."**

   News Authors need to republish old news stories from the `news` folder in the `archive` folder. After they do this, they delete the original in the `news` folder.

9. **Make sure that the check box next to "Remove rollback versions on delete" is not checked.**

    I decided that old rollback versions will not be deleted as a safeguard; it is entirely possible — and probable — that someone might delete the wrong file by mistake at some point.

    Figure 13-7 shows the Permission Group dialog box with all of the Folder/File Access settings configured.

10. **Click OK to return to the Administer Website screen.**

11. **Click OK to save your settings.**

    The settings configured on the Permission Group screen are not saved until you click OK in the Administer Website dialog box.

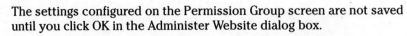

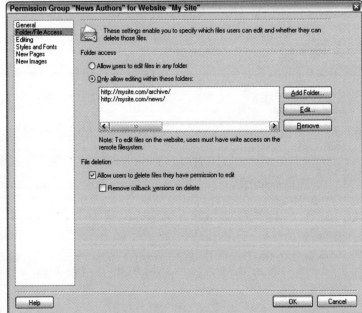

Figure 13-7: The Folder/ File Access category settings for the fictional News Authors group.

Setting Page-Level Permissions

Page-level permissions fall under the Contribute's *Editing* and *Styles and Fonts* permission categories. Contribute lets you specify how users interact with the pages they edit. You can control whether users can only edit text on a page, how Contribute handles paragraph spacing and line breaks, and various other HTML and formatting features.

Managing non-Dreamweaver templates

The *Non-template pages* section of the Editing category controls what kind of changes a user makes to pages not based on Dreamweaver templates. Dreamweaver templates are created using Macromedia's Dreamweaver and are discussed in Chapter 10.

The following list describes the Non-template pages options and what they control:

- **Allow unrestricted editing:** Allows the user to edit any text or tables and insert images on the page.

- **Protect scripts and forms:** When checked, users cannot change script tags, server-side include statements, code tags (such as those for ASP, JSP, PHP, or ColdFusion), form tags, and form elements.

  Only disable script and form protection for experienced users. Normally, only web developers should edit these tags outside of Contribute.

- **Only allow text editing and formatting:** Specifies that individuals can only edit text, modify styles, and create bulleted or numbered lists. They are not able to add or edit links, images, or tables, and they are not able to delete server instructions or plug-in content.

Controlling how Contribute generates HTML

The two remaining Editing permission category sections involve how Contribute treats HTML and whether accessibility options, for visitors with disabilities, are enforced.

In the Paragraph Spacing section of the editing category, you have two options: "One line, as in standard word processors" or "Two lines, as in web page editors." These options control how much space is created between paragraphs when a user presses Enter or Return. The first option uses Cascading Style Sheet attributes to force a new paragraph to start immediately after the preceding paragraph — much like most word processors. The "two line" option uses standard HTML paragraph tags and results in a space between paragraphs. See Figure13-8 for an example.

The following list describes the Other Editing Options section of the Editing category:

- **Allow multiple consecutive spaces:** Specifies whether users can type multiple spaces between words. If selected, Contribute uses   in the underlying HTML to force this feature.

- **Enforce accessibility options:** "Accessibility options" refers to making HTML more accessible to readers with disabilities. For example, images can have alternative text associated with them in the event that the reader of the page has visual disabilities. Enabling this option makes Contribute prompt the user to enter alternative information for disabled users.

- **Use `<strong>` and `<em>` in place of `<b>` and `<i>`:** According to the most recent HTML specification released by the World Wide Web Consortium (http://www.w3c.com), `<b>` tags — used for making text bold — should be replaced by `<strong>` tags. Italic tags, `<i>`, should be replaced by `<em>` tags. Checking this box forces Contribute to adhere to this specification.

- **Line break type:** When a user types at a computer and presses the Enter or Return key, the resulting character sequence is called a line break code. Depending on the operating system, it could be a one- or two-character combination. You probably do not need to change the default setting.

Setting font and style permissions

The Styles and Fonts permission category controls whether the user can apply style formatting to text, change font type and size, and change how the resulting HTML is created.

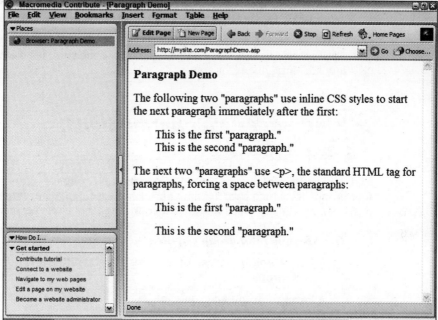

Figure 13-8:
This demon-
strates the
difference
between
paragraph
spacing
options.

The following list describes the Styles and Fonts category options:

- **Allow users to apply styles:** When this option is selected, individuals can modify heading and paragraph styles using the Contribute toolbar or menu commands (one of the next two options must also be enabled for this to be true). If this option is deselected, the user cannot apply new paragraph styles, and any associated buttons and menu commands will not be displayed.

- **Include HTML paragraph and heading styles in the Style menu:** This tells Contribute that the standard HTML paragraph (<p>) and heading (<h1>,<h2>,...,<h6>) tags are available.

- **Include CSS styles in the Style menu:** This option indicates that any Cascading Style Sheet (CSS) styles defined for the page will appear in the style menu.

- **Allow users to apply fonts and sizes:** This enables the font and style menus on Contribute's toolbar. If this option is not selected, Contribute will use the default fonts specified in the pages HTML source code.

✔ **HTML tags or Inline CSS styles:** This controls whether font settings will generate CSS style attributes or standard `<font>` HTML tags in the page's HTML source.

✔ **Apply styles using:** This controls the unit of measure used when sizing fonts (points, pixels, or ems).

Setting page-level permissions: An example

Earlier in this chapter — in "Creating Permission Groups" — I described the four groups for which I am defining permission groups. According to their descriptions, these groups require the following Page Level permissions.

✔ **The Administrator group requires these permissions:**

- **Non-template pages:** Allow unrestricted editing and no script and form protection.

- **Paragraph spacing:** One line.

- **Other editing options:** Allow multiple spaces, enforce accessibility options, and use `<strong>` and `<em>`.

✔ **The Marketing group requires these permissions:**

- **Non-template pages:** Only allow text editing and formatting.

- **Paragraph spacing:** One line.

- **Other editing options:** Disallow multiple spaces, enable enforced accessibility options, and use `<strong>` and `<em>`.

✔ **The News Authors group requires these permissions:**

- **Non-template pages:** Allow unrestricted editing and enable script and form protection.

- **Paragraph spacing:** One line.

- **Other editing options:** Restrict multiple spaces, enable enforcement of accessibility options, and use `<strong>` and `<em>`.

✔ **The Designers group requires these permissions:**

- **Non-template pages:** Allow unrestricted editing and enable script and form protection.

- **Paragraph spacing:** One line.

- **Other editing options:** Allow multiple spaces, enforce accessibility options, and use `<strong>` and `<em>`.

The steps for configuring the Editing category settings are the same for each group. The following steps show how to do it for the Designers group:

1. **If the Administer Website dialog box is not open, open it by following steps 1 and 2 in "Managing site permissions."**

2. **Select Designers from the list of groups in the Administer Website dialog box.**

3. **Click the Edit Group... button to open the Permission Group dialog box.**

4. **Choose Editing in the list of categories to show the associated settings.**

5. **Click "Allow unrestricted editing" in the Non-template pages section to enable the option.**

6. **Check the box next to "Protect scripts and forms."**

7. **In the Paragraph spacing section, select the "One line, as in standard word processors" setting.**

8. **Check the box for "Allow multiple consecutive spaces."**

9. **Check the "Enforce accessibility options" setting.**

10. **Click in the box next to "Use `<strong>` and `<em>` in place of `<b>` and `<I>`" to enable it.**

    You can compare your settings to the ones shown in Figure 13-9.

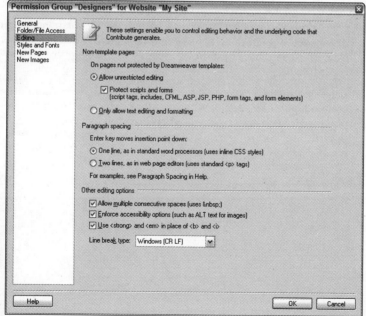

Figure 13-9:
This shows the Editing category settings for the fictional Designers group.

11. **Click OK to return to the Administer Website dialog box.**

12. **Click OK to save your settings.**

Permission settings are not saved until you click OK in the Administer Website dialog box.

Specifying File Creation Privileges

Contribute allows you to specify if and how users are able to create new Web pages and images. You can dictate whether users can create new, create blank pages, and create duplicate pages by copying the current page, and you can specify what Dreamweaver templates users are able to see and use.

Setting permissions for new pages

The New Pages category allows you to define the following options:

- ✔ **Create a blank page:** Allows the user to create blank new pages when selected.

- ✔ **Use built in sample pages:** The user may use sample Contribute pages as a base when creating new pages if this option is enabled.

- ✔ **Create a new page by copying any page on the Web site:** If checked, any page on the Web site can be copied to create a new page.

- ✔ **Create a new page by copying a page from this list:** Users can create new pages only from selected existing pages. The new pages will show up in the Templates folder of the New Page dialog box, as shown in Figure 13-10.

- ✔ **Use Dreamweaver templates:** If "Use Dreamweaver Templates" is enabled, you can specify whether all or selected Dreamweaver templates will be visible to users when creating new Web pages. The two options are "Show users all templates" and "Only show users these templates.

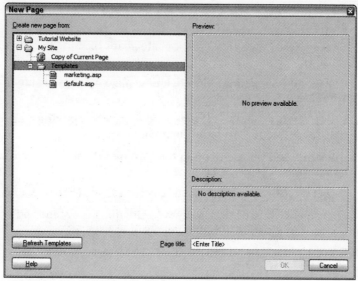

The following list describes the New Page settings for the groups discussed in the earlier section, "Creating Permission Groups."

- ✔ **Administrator and Designers:** All options except "Create a new page by copying pages from this list" are enabled. Administrators can also use any available Dreamweaver template.

- ✔ **Marketing:** Users in the marketing group can only create files by using the marketing.asp Dreamweaver template.

- ✔ **News Authors:** News Authors can create a new page by copying any page on the site. Additionally, the pages article.asp and feature.asp are placed in the "Create pages by copying a page in this list" box so that they can quickly find them under the Templates folder when they create a new file.

To set the New Page options for the News Authors group, follow these steps:

1. **If the Administer Website dialog box is not open, open it by following steps 1 and 2 in "Managing site permissions."**

2. **Select News Authors from the list of groups in the Administer Website dialog box.**

3. Click the Edit Group... button to open the Permission Group dialog box.

4. Choose New Pages in the list of categories to show the associated settings.

5. Check the box next to "Create a new page by copying any page on the Web site."

6. Check the box next to "Create a new page by copying a page on this list" to enable the Add and Remove buttons.

7. Click the Add button to open the Choose File on Website dialog box, as shown in Figure 13-11.

8. Select the file `http://mysite.com/news/article.asp` and click OK.

   I'm using files that exist on my Web site for these steps and you can choose any existing files that you want to use.

9. Repeat steps 7 and 8 for the file `http://mysite.com/news/feature.asp`.

10. Make sure the remaining options are unchecked, as shown in Figure 13-12.

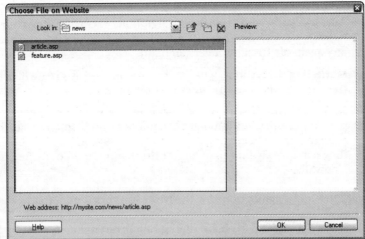

Figure 13-11:
Choose File
on Web site
window.

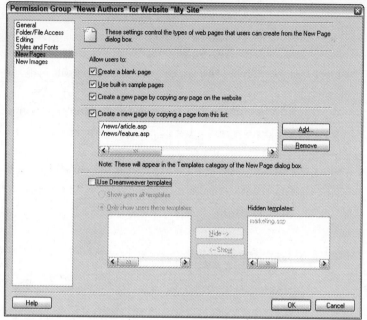

Figure 13-12:
The New
Pages
settings
window.

"Create a blank page," "Use built in sample pages," and "Use Dreamweaver templates" should not be checked.

11. **Click OK to return to the Administer Website dialog box.**

12. **Click OK to save your settings.**

Configuring new image privileges

The New Images permission category enables you to specify the maximum file size of new images added by individuals.

The following are the new image permissions for the groups discussed in "Creating Permission Groups."

✔ **Administrator:** Unlimited file size.

✔ **Marketing:** Limited to zero kilobytes (disables new image creation).

✔ **News Authors:** Limited to zero kilobytes.

✔ **Designers:** Limited to 35 kilobytes.

To set the permissions for the Designers group, follow these steps:

1. **If the Administer Website dialog box is not open, open it by following steps 1 and 2 in "Managing site permissions."**

2. **Select Designers from the list of groups in the Administer Website dialog box.**

3. **Click the Edit Group... button to open the Permission Group dialog box.**

4. **Choose New Images in the list of categories to show the associated settings.**

5. **Select "limited to" and type 35 in the text box, as shown in Figure 13-13.**

6. **Click OK to return to the Administer Website dialog box.**

7. **Click OK to save your settings.**

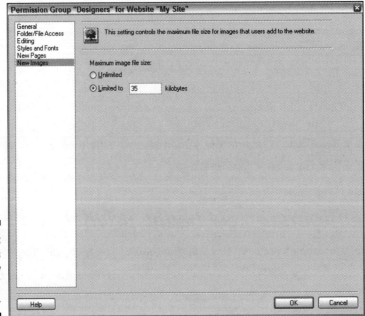

Figure 13-13:
Contribute's
"New
Images"
settings.

Chapter 14

Collaborating and Troubleshooting

- -

In This Chapter

▶ Sending a site connection

▶ Reviewing Contribute pages

▶ Working offline

▶ Restoring a deleted page

▶ Improving application performance

- -

The reason that an administrator configures Contribute is so that users can ultimately create, edit, and publish Web pages. The last two chapters covered how to create a Web site connection and how to set up permissions for the users who use them. This chapter concludes the administrative part of this book and shows you how to share site connections with new users, how Contribute makes it easy for users to review each others work, and how to make everyone's life a little less aggravating by working through some of Contribute's more common issues.

Sharing Site Connections with New Users

Contribute keeps track of the Web sites you work with and saves them as a list of connections. Before you can share a site connection with new users, you must first create the site connection and set up group permissions. Chapter's 12 and 13 show you how to do this. Now that everything is ready to go, you want to send the soon-to-be "contributors" their connection keys. A connection key is an XML file with the extension .stc, including pertinent connection information. Connection settings, login information, and passwords are encrypted — using a password or phrase of your choice — and saved in one of the fields in this file.

Exporting a Web connection

Before exporting a Web connection, consider the password or phrase that you will tell Contribute to use to encrypt any sensitive information. You do not want to use any private passwords like those for your e-mail or FTP logins because you need to share this password with the users before they can import the connection settings.

To export a Web connection, follow these steps:

1. **Click Edit⇨Administer Websites⇨My Site - mysite.com/ on Contribute's menu, as shown in Figure 14-1.**

   I am working with the my fictional site called My Site - mysite.com/. You can work with any site you choose.

2. **Enter the administrative password to open the Administer Website dialog box.**

   Figure 14-2 shows the Administer Website dialog box for my site.

3. **Click the Send Connection Key button near the bottom of the dialog box to open the Export Wizard dialog box.**

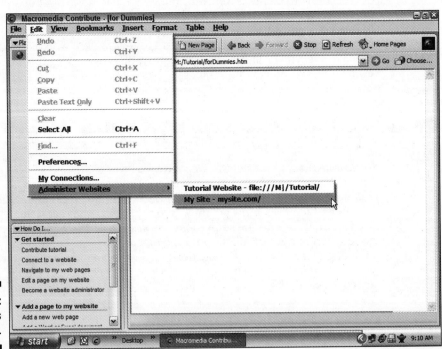

Figure 14-1:
Contribute's
menu.

Figure 14-2:
The
Administer
Website
dialog box.

4. **Select Yes or No when Contribute asks if you would like to send your current connection settings, as shown in Figure 14-3, and continue with the appropriate step.**

   Contribute gives you three options when exporting a connection:

   • You can send your current connection settings by choosing Yes.

   • If you choose Yes and you connect to your site via FTP, you may also send your FTP login and password information by checking the box next to "Include my FTP login and password."

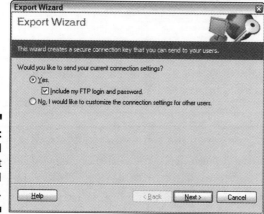

Figure 14-3:
The initial
Export
Wizard
dialog box.

Contribute encrypts any of the connection information sent to users. They will not be able to see the login information even if they open the connection file with a text editor. If you do not include your login information, you will have to tell the new users by some other means (for example, e-mail or phone call).

- You may alternatively decide to customize the connection method by choosing No.

If you decide to send your current connection settings, proceed to step 6; otherwise, continue with step 5.

5. After choosing No on the initial Export Wizard dialog box, fill in the appropriate connection information and click Next.

You can select either FTP or Local/Network from the list that asks, "How do you connect to your Web server?" In my case, I use FTP as my connection method, and Contribute shows me the screen in Figure 14-4.

Figure 14-4:
Export
Wizard:
Connection
Information.

Export Wizard

Export Wizard
Connection Information

Customize the server connection settings for this connection key.

How do your users connect to your web server?

| FTP | ▾ | Advanced... |

What is the name of your FTP server?

| mysite.com | (Example: ftp.mysite.com)

What is the FTP login?

| fvera |

What is the FTP password?

| •••••• |

| Help | | < Back | Next > | Cancel |

If you are connecting through FTP, you may specify whether Contribute connects using passive FTP (Contribute manages the FTP connection, rather than the server) or alternative firewall settings by clicking the Advanced button, filling in the appropriate information (as shown in Figure 14-5), and clicking OK.

6. Select the group for users of the connection key, and click Next.

Contribute lists all of the groups defined for the site, as shown in Figure 14-6. Select the group to which the new users belong, and click Next.

7. Choose either Send in E-mail or Save to Local Machine.

Contribute gives you the option of exporting the connection key directly to your default e-mail program or as a file on your computer.

Figure 14-5:
Advanced
Connection
Settings.

(figure: Advanced Connection Settings dialog box)
Advanced Connection Settings
☑ Use passive FTP to connect to the server
Select this option if your server supports passive FTP and Contribute cannot connect using standard FTP.
☑ Use firewall settings when connecting
Select this option if the recipient is behind a firewall, then enter the firewall's host and port information.
Firewall host: 192.168.1.1|
Firewall port: 21
Help   OK   Cancel

Figure 14-6:
Export
Wizard:
Group
Information.

(figure: Export Wizard dialog box)
Export Wizard
Export Wizard
Group Information
Specify the group for users of this connection key.
Select a group:
Administrator
Marketing
News Authors
Designers
Group description:
Members of this permission group work on the marketing section of this website.
Help   < Back   Next >   Cancel

If you use Web-based e-mail such as MSN Hotmail or Yahoo! Mail as your default e-mail provider, choose Save to Local Machine. Contribute may not be able to send the file through Web-based e-mail.

Contribute doesn't let you choose where to save the connection key file until you click Done on the final summary screen.

8. **Enter a password or phrase in the two text boxes, as shown in Figure 14-7, and click Next to go to the Summary screen.**

Contribute uses the phrase you type in these two boxes to encrypt the settings in the connection file. You may type in a single word or a whole phrase. Remember to send the password phrase to the users who will import the Web site connection. Without this phrase, a new user cannot import the connection settings.

For additional security, do not send the encryption password in the same e-mail as the connection key. Send the password in another e-mail or tell users in person.

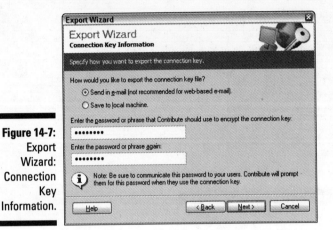

Figure 14-7:
Export
Wizard:
Connection
Key
Information.

9. **Look over the settings on the summary screen and click Done.**

When you click Done, Contribute will do one of two things:

- If you chose to send the connection key in an e-mail, Contribute opens a new e-mail window with an attached connection key file. Contribute waits until you either send the e-mail or close the window before you can click on any of its windows.

- If you wanted to save the connection key as a file on your local machine, a file dialog box opens so that you can choose where to save your file. Choose the folder you want to save the file in, type in a new name, and click Save.

Testing Contribute Pages

After you — or fellow "contributors" — edit or create a Web page, you should check that the page looks and behaves as you expect. Frequently, a Web page looks one way in an editor and looks another way in a Web browser. Contribute allows you to view the page you are editing in your default Web browser by clicking File⇨Preview in Browser in Contribute's menu bar. In order to preview the Web page, Contribute saves a copy of the page in a temporary folder — that is deleted after clicking Publish or Cancel — and instructs your browser to go the corresponding URL. While previewing the page in the browser, make sure everything looks as you expect and click on all of the links to verify that they lead to the expected pages.

When you are satisfied with the results, you may publish the page by clicking the Publish button on the editor.

Reviewing other people's work

It is possible that you are not the only one working on a Web site. If this is the case, you may have to let others see your work before you get the go-ahead to publish the page. Contribute allows you to save a temporary page and create an e-mail with the temporary URL so that others can look at it and let you know what they think. You can do this as many times as necessary until the Web page meets everyone's approval. When you publish a page that has been under review, Contribute automatically erases the temporary copy and saves the edited file.

In order to start the e-mail review process, click File⇨E-mail Review in Contribute's menu. Contribute creates a new e-mail message with a link to the temporary URL. All you need to do is enter the e-mail addresses of the reviewers.

Under certain circumstances, Contribute may not be able to find or start your default e-mail program to create the review message. If this is the case, you can do the following:

1. **Create a new message using your e-mail software.**

2. **Write a message letting people know that you want them to review this draft and asking them to reply to you with their comments, but do not send your message yet.**

3. **In Contribute, click the words Click Here just above the editor window, as shown in Figure 14-8.**

   Contribute opens your default Web browser with the temporary review file's URL.

Figure 14-8:
Contribute
lets you
know that a
draft is set
for review.

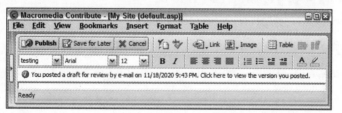

4. **On your Web browser, copy the URL in the address bar and paste it into your e-mail message.**

5. **Send your e-mail.**

After everyone replies, you can go back to the file by clicking on the page's name in the Page sidebar panel. Then you can continue to edit the file, publish the file, or cancel your changes.

Understanding the most common problems

Macromedia did a good job of making Contribute straightforward to use. Editing Web pages never seemed so easy. In spite of this, you may run into a few common pitfalls or challenges while working with Contribute. This section covers some of the most common challenges that people face when using Contribute.

Working offline

Contribute allows you to work on your Web site even if you are not connected to a network — or the Internet. This is called "working offline." You may choose to work offline if you normally connect to the Internet using your phone line. This way, the phone line is available while you work with Contribute. You may also decide to work offline when using Contribute on a laptop that you are disconnecting from your office network. This allows you to continue editing any drafts that you already started to work with, and it even allows you to create new pages.

When working offline, Contribute allows you to do the following:

- Work on previously created drafts.
- Create new pages for your web site.
- Delete any new pages you created while working offline.

Keep in mind that you cannot access pages on the Web site while working offline.

Before you work offline, make sure you edit and save for later any existing Web pages you need to change. Contribute places a shortcut to each draft you save on the Pages panel of the sidebar, as shown in Figure 14-9.

One common problem is that the Publish or Cancel buttons are unavailable or disabled while working with a draft. If you are working offline, you may only save drafts for later. You may only cancel drafts that you create while working in offline mode.

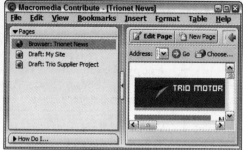

Figure 14-9:
Contribute
helps you
keep track
of drafts by
placing
them in the
Pages
panel.

Another common problem is that the Edit⇨My Connections menu item and
all of the sites under Edit⇨Administer Websites are disabled. Contribute
enables these items only when working online.

You can tell if you are working offline by going to Contribute's menu, clicking
File, searching for the menu item that says Work Offline and looking for a
checkmark next to that item, as shown in Figure 14-10. If the checkmark is
there, you are working offline. To switch between online and offline modes,
click the checkbox next to Working Offline to toggle the checkmark.

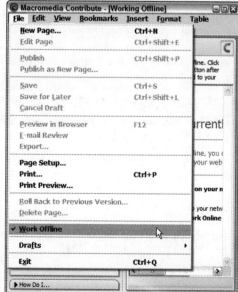

Figure 14-10:
Working
with
Contribute
in offline
mode.

Restoring a deleted Web page

Contribute allows you to enable a backup feature called *rollback*. With this feature enabled, a Web page can be "rolled back" to a previous version if any mistakes are made. Contribute keeps a copy of each folder's edited Web pages in a subfolder called _baks. Chapter 12's section "Understanding and Enabling Rollback" discusses rollbacks in more detail.

What if a user accidentally deletes a Web page? If rollbacks are enabled, and if the group to which the user belongs is not configured to "remove rollback versions on delete" (see Chapter 13 for more details), you can restore a deleted page.

If you disabled rollbacks for the Web site and configured the user's group settings to erase rollback versions of a page upon its deletion, you cannot restore a deleted page unless an alternative backup system is in place.

In order to restore a deleted Web page, follow these steps:

1. **Browse to the deleted page.**

   Click on a link on an existing page that brings you to the address of the deleted page, or type the URL of the deleted page in Contribute's Address bar. This causes the Web server to respond with an HTTP 404, page not found error page.

   Some Web servers are set up to redirect you to another page instead of displaying a page not found error. If this is the case, you can manually copy the rollback file from the _baks folder to the appropriate location using an FTP client.

2. **Click File⇨Roll Back to Previous Version, as shown in Figure 14-11.**

3. **In the Roll Back Page dialog box, select the previous version you want from the list of pages, and click Roll Back.**

   The Roll Back Page dialog box shows you a list of previous versions and an optional preview of the currently selected version, as shown in Figure 14-12.

Improving Contribute's start-up time and performance

Upon startup, Contribute connects to each configured Web site in the My Connections dialog box and stays connected until Contribute is closed. If you have many Web site connections defined but are only working on a couple of them, you can improve Contribute's performance by disabling all connections except those you need to work on.

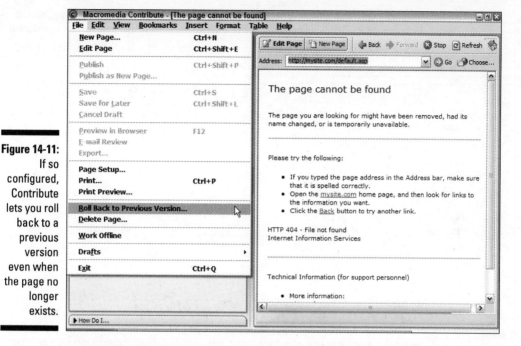

Figure 14-11:
If so configured, Contribute lets you roll back to a previous version even when the page no longer exists.

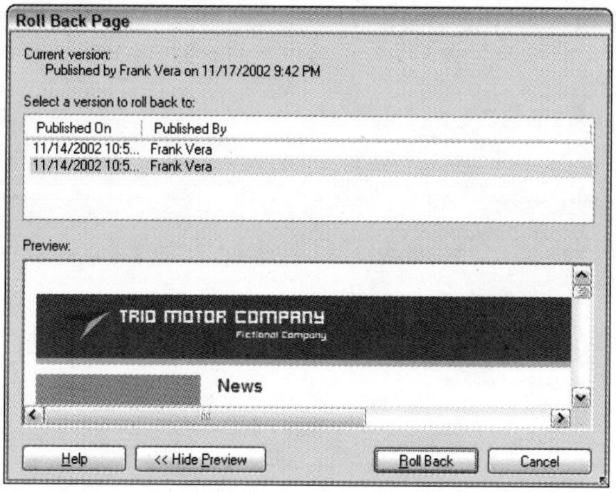

Figure 14-12:
The Roll Back Page dialog box displays up to 99 previous versions.

In order to disable or enable a connection, follow these steps:

1. **Click Edit⇨My Connections on Contribute's menu to open the My Connections dialog box.**

2. **Select the Web site that you want to enable or disable from the list, and click the top right button labeled either Enable or Disable.**

Contribute displays an icon for each of the defined connections, which looks like a little computer with a globe just behind and to the right of it. A disabled connection has a red, diagonal slash (/) superimposed on this icon, as shown in Figure 14-13.

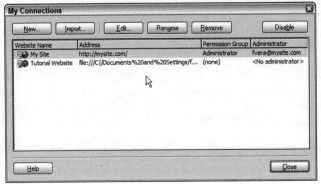

Figure 14-13: The My Connections dialog box with My Site enabled and Tutorial Site disabled.

Unlocking a file in Contribute

Contribute keeps track of which user has a page open for editing by creating a lock file with that user's information. A lock file is just a text file with the same name as the edited file with an additional .lck extension. Normally, this file is used to display a message letting a user know that someone else is working with the file, as shown in Figure 14-14.

Figure 14-14: Contribute lets you know when someone else is editing a page.

Under most circumstances, it should not be necessary to allow another user to edit a locked page. In the following instances, however, this may be the case:

- ✔ When an unavailable user leaves a file in a locked state.
- ✔ When someone using Dreamweaver MX checks out the page and inadvertently leaves the page locked.
- ✔ When some unforeseen system error prevents a user from checking in a page that he or she finished editing.

To delete a lock file, follow these steps:

1. **Browse to the page you want to unlock.**

2. **In the address bar, append the** `.lck` **extension to the filename and press Enter.**

   For example, if the URL for the locked file is `http://mysite.com/default.asp`, make sure you type in `http://mysite.com/default.asp.lck`.

3. **Select File⇨Delete Page while viewing the File Placeholder page.**

   When you browse to a file that Contribute cannot open, it displays the File Placeholder page, as shown in Figure 14-15.

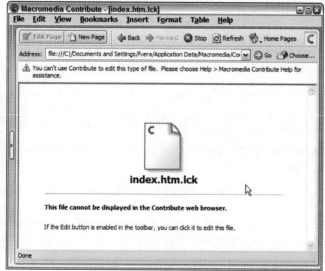

Figure 14-15: Contribute cannot open a locked file, so it displays the File Placeholder page instead.

   If Contribute's group permissions for the user do not allow them to delete files, this menu item is disabled. For details about delete permissions, see Chapter 13.

4. **Click Yes on both confirmation dialog boxes to delete the file.**

   Contribute verifies that you are sure that you want to delete the file, and then it warns you that the file you are trying to delete is a special file. You can cancel the unlocking procedure by clicking No on either of these dialog boxes.

Forgetting the administrator password

If you work with computers, logins, and passwords long enough you are bound to run into one of the most unnerving of challenges: forgetting your password. If you happen to forget your administrator password for one of your defined connections, you can reset the password by deleting the shared settings file on the Web site and creating a new one.

To help you not to forget your password, write it down and put it somewhere safe. When you reset a site's password, you will need to reassign all of the site's group permissions. See Chapter 13 for more information about groups and permission settings.

Here are the steps to reset the administrator password:

1. **Open your Web site's root folder, and then open the contained _mm folder.**

   A Web browser cannot usually do this. You will have to use either FTP, SSH, telnet, or a similar software client to connect to the Web site.

2. **Delete** `contribute.xml` **in the _mm folder.**

   The Web site's shared settings file is `contribute.xml`. Deleting this file resets the Web site permissions and shared settings.

3. **In Contribute, click Edit⇨My Connection to open the My Connection dialog box.**

4. **Select the Web site whose shared settings file you deleted and click the Edit button.**

5. **Verify your site's settings by clicking Next until you see the Administrator Information screen, as shown in Figure 14-16.**

6. **Select "Yes, I want to be the administrator."**

7. **Enter your password in both textboxes, and click Next.**

   Your password should be at least eight characters long and include both letters and numbers. Write the password down and keep it somewhere safe for future reference.

8. **Review your settings, and click Done.**

   Contribute ask you whether you want to change the administrator settings after you click Done. Remember that all previous administrator settings were lost when the shared settings file was deleted. For more information about group permissions, refer to Chapter 13.

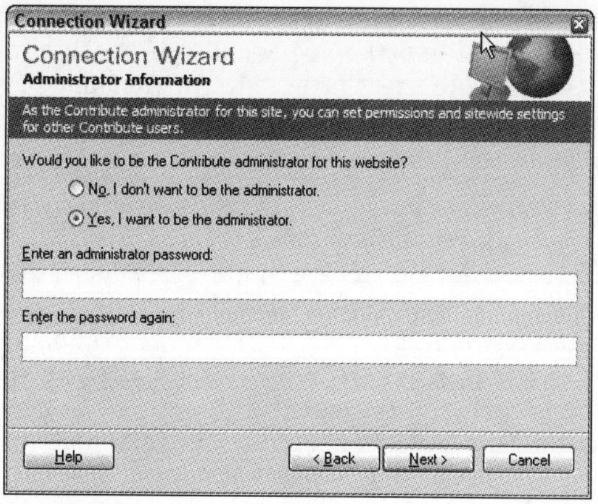

Connection Wizard

Connection Wizard
Administrator Information

Figure 14-16:
The
Connection
Wizard's
Administra-
tor Informa-
tion screen.

Working with dynamic pages

Although I do not discuss specific problems with dynamic pages, you should be aware of some things to avoid problems. A dynamic page is a Web page where the Web server executes embedded code, such as ASP code, and generates part of a page or the entire page on the fly. Macromedia designed Contribute to edit HTML content on Web sites. Contribute users cannot add or edit dynamic tags in Web pages. It is up to the administrator to protect dynamic pages as necessary.

Protecting dynamic pages is done, for the most part, through group permission settings. Chapter 13 discusses how to set the various restrictions associated with dynamic pages.

When protecting dynamic pages, you have two basic options:

✔ Disable users from editing dynamic pages.

✔ Enable editing of static sections of dynamic pages.

Disabling users from editing dynamic pages

In order to prevent users from making changes to dynamic pages, use the following techniques:

✔ **Disable access to specific folders:** Using the techniques described in Chapter 13, you can limit folder access. Place dynamic pages in one folder and editable pages in another. Excluding the folder containing dynamic pages from the list of folders that the group can edit effectively prevents the users from editing a dynamic page.

✔ **Set dynamic page file permissions to read-only:** Using FTP or some other file access tool, set the dynamic page file permission to read-only to lock the file. If Contribute users browse to the dynamic page and click Edit, they will get a message stating that the page is read-only and they cannot edit it.

According to the folks at Macromedia, you *must* disable rollbacks for the entire Web site for this method to work — see Chapter 12 for more information about rollbacks. An alternative method is to base the dynamic pages on Dreamweaver templates (discussed in the next section and in Chapter 10) without any editable regions. This way, when an editor tries to make changes to the page, Contribute does not allow them to alter your dynamic code. This requires an extra step in creating templates for these pages, but it means you can keep the rollback function operating, which I consider a great feature in Contribute because it let's you save backups automatically when "contributors" make changes to page.

Editing static sections of dynamic pages

If users need to make changes to sections of dynamic pages, you may use the following techniques:

✔ **Enable the "protect scripts and forms" group setting or the "only allow text editing and formatting" group setting:**

By default, Contribute protects server-side code from deletion. This prevents the deletion of common dynamic Web tags. The "Setting page level permissions: An example" section in Chapter 13 shows you how to set these permissions.

✔ **Use Dreamweaver templates for greater control over which sections are editable:**

Contribute allows you to specify Dreamweaver templates as the starting point for creating new files. A Dreamweaver template is a basic Web page used as a "stencil" for creating new Web pages. With a Dreamweaver template, you can mark specific regions of the page as editable while locking out the rest of the page. Chapter 10 covers the creation of templates in more detail; Chapter 13 explains how to disable a user from using anything but a template as a new page.

Part V
The Part of Tens

The 5th Wave   By Rich Tennant

"Come on Walt—time to freshen the company Web page."

In this part . . .

The Part of Tens features ten timesaving techniques to help you get the most out of Contribute; ten great design and interface tips to keep in mind as you build your Web site; ten tips for managing a team of designers; and finally, ten great sites that were designed with Dreamweaver and Contribute. (Keeping track of all of those Contributors can get complicated.)

Chapter 15

Ten Timesaving Contribute Tips

*E*ven the best programs get better when you know how to make the most of them. As I put this book together, I collected tips and tricks I thought were especially helpful if you're in a hurry or trying to work more efficiently. This chapter is designed to feature them in a handy list you can use a quick reference.

Importing a Connection Key

If you're working with a good Web site administrator, he or she should send you a Connection key, usually via e-mail, which you can easily import into Contribute to take care of all the connection setup automatically. If you haven't been sent a connection key and you're having trouble connecting to your Web server, make sure you get in touch with your site administrator.

Using Sample Pages

Macromedia included a variety of sample page designs that you can use to create new pages that already include some formatting. In the Sample Web Pages folder, available in the New Page dialog box every time you create a new page, you find many great starter pages designed to make it quick and easy to create common page styles, such as calendar pages that come preformatted with boxes for days of the month, and resume pages that make it easy to format the sections common on a professional resume. To use these pre-designed pages, simply select the design you want as you are creating a new page and Contribute bases the new page on that design.

Creating a New Page from a Template

Of all the different ways that you can create a new page with Contribute, the ability to use templates designed especially for your Web site in Dreamweaver is the most powerful. Templates enable you to leverage the strength and design skills of your designers and make their work available so that other team members can create new pages more easily.

A template can include all the main design elements of page, such as the logo, navigation bar, and so on, and then include spaces where you can easily add photo new photos or text. Macromedia makes templates even more powerful by including a feature in Dreamweaver that "locks" any part of the design, even when it is used in Contribute. So although you may be able to easily change a photo, you may not be able to change the navigation bar and logo area at all. This enables your professional designers to create template pages that are easy to update, while protecting important sections of the page that they know should not be changed — especially by accident. When you are working with a team of people with different skill levels and experience in Web design, the ability to lock certain sections of a template can save you lots of time, grief and frustration by preventing mistakes.

E-Mail Review

The Email Review option is designed to facilitate your sharing your work with other members of your team before it goes live on the site. When you select this option a copy of your page is saved on the server at a special address, which is then included in an e-mail message that you can send to anyone who you want to look over your work. (You find more information about the Email Review feature in Chapter 11.)

Adding Keywords and Descriptions

The Keywords and Description option launches a dialog box where you can enter information you want to make available to search engines. This information is stored in the Meta data of your page (if you don't know what Meta data means, it's information stored at the top of the HTML document, but it doesn't show up on the page that viewer's see.) Keywords and description text are read by most search engines and used to rank your placement when visitors search for keywords. This is an easy step to forget because you don't actually see this text displayed on your page (it's all behind the scenes). That's what makes Contribute's Keywords and Description option so helpful and it's really easy to use, just choose Format⇨Keywords and Description and fill out the two text boxes with a brief description of your site and a list of keywords you want to match if someone searches for you.

Adding Content from Microsoft Word and Excel

The Insert Microsoft Word and Excel Documents feature enables you to insert the entire contents of a Word or Excel document by simply opening the page within Contribute. The biggest advantage of this feature is that Contribute automatically formats the content to be as close to the original document as possible when it inserts the text and any other elements on your Web page. That means you don't have to recreate the formatting, a definite time saver. To use this feature, open the page you where you want to add the content, or create a new page, and place your cursor where you want the content to be inserted. Then choose Insert⇨Microsoft Word Document or Insert⇨Microsoft Excel Document and browse to find and select the file you want to add to your page.

Working on Multiple Web Sites

Many people on work on one Web site, but if you find that you are responsible for making changes to multiple sites, you'll appreciate that Contribute enables you to establish connections to multiple sites and then switch between them so that you can quickly move from working on one project to another. Choose Edit⇨My Connections to open the My Connections dialog box where you can set up and manage each connection.

Tabling Your Designs

HTML tables offer one of the easiest ways to create complex Web designs. Fortunately, Contribute makes it easy to create tables in its visual design area. Simply choose Insert⇨Table or choose the table icon in the toolbar to insert a table of any size and number of rows and columns. Then click and drag to change the dimensions of cells and use the merge and split cells buttons in the toolbar to make the table accommodate different designs. Remember you can set the border to 0 on a table, making it invisible when the page is displayed and use the cells to arrange text and images on your pages. You find more information about working with tables in Chapter 7.

Designing in a Flash

Flash rocks! Macromedia's vector-based design and animation program, Flash, is one of the hottest programs on the Web today because it makes creating fast-loading images and animations that dynamically adjust to fit any screen size. Now that the Flash plug-in is built into most current browsers, Flash has become a standard, and Contribute makes it easy to add Flash files to your Web pages. Choose Insert Flash Movie to launch the Open dialog box and then navigate around your hard drive until you find the Flash file you want to add to your page.

Making Fireworks with Your Images

If you have little or no experience with creating and editing images, you may find it easier to use Fireworks, an image program Macromedia created especially for Web design, than Adobe Photoshop, the most commonly use image program available. Although both tools do a great job of converting images into GIF and JPEG formats for the Web, Fireworks includes a great wizard that makes it really easy to do the conversion, even if you've never used a graphics program before. You can download a fully-functional 30-day trial version of Fireworks from the download section of www.macromedia.com.

Bonus Tips to Keep You Going

Don't stop just because you've come almost to the end of this book. Here are a few additional tips and resources that will help you get even more out of Contribute.

✔ Do the tutorials that accompany Contribute.

✔ Visit the Macromedia site and check out the Contribute section at www.macromedia.com/desdev/contribute. Also visit the Contribute Web forum to share your experience and/or read messages from other Contribute users at webforums.macromedia.com/contribute.

Chapter 16

Ten Keys to Managing a Team of "Contributors"

*O*ne of the most common mistakes new Web designers make is plunging into developing a site without thinking through all of their goals, priorities, budget, and design options. The instinct is to simply start creating pages, throw them all into one big directory, and then string stuff together with links. Then, when they finally test it out on their audience, they're often surprised when users say the site is hard to navigate and users can't find the pages they want to use. Do yourself a favor and save yourself some grief by planning ahead and spending some time with the entire team before you throw them into the Web soup with all the other ingredients.

Preparing for Contributors

One of the first things I recommend is that you hold a brainstorming session with a few people who understand the goals you have for your Web site and who the various players are who will be contributing. The purpose of this session is to come up with the features and elements that Contributors should work on, as well as potential challenges and areas you may need to watch out for.

A good brainstorming session is a nonjudgmental free-for-all — a chance for everyone involved to make all the suggestions that they can think of, whether realistic or not. Not discrediting ideas at the brainstorming stage is important. Often an unrealistic idea can lead to a great idea that no one may have thought of otherwise. And if you stifle one person's creative ideas too quickly, that person may feel less inclined to voice other ideas in the future.

After the brainstorming session, you should have a long list of possible features to develop into your site and other issues of interest or concern. Now the challenge is to edit that list down to the best and most realistic ideas and to plan your course of development to ensure everything works well together as the site grows and develops.

Creating a Manager's Check List

Before you let other people start working on your Web site, make sure you're clear on the basics. Some of the following you may have already done, but if you haven't got a good answer to every one of the following questions, now is a good time to sit down with your boss, your staff, or your team, and make sure you're all clear on them:

- ✔ What do you want to accomplish with your Web site? (What are your goals and objectives?)
- ✔ Who is your target audience?
- ✔ Who will be working on your site? How many developers do you have to manage?
- ✔ How will you create or collect the text and images you'll need for your site?
- ✔ Who will be responsible for interactive features, such as a feedback form or chat room?
- ✔ What kind of navigation system will you have for your site (that is, how can you make it easy for visitors to move from one area of your Web site to another, especially if different departments or groups have different designs)?
- ✔ How will you accommodate growth and future development?

What Do You Call Your Web Pages?

Contribute lets you name your files any name that works on your operating system, even long names with spaces, like this is the most embarrassing photo from the Christmas party.htm. Be aware, however, that your Web server may use a different operating system that's more restrictive. Many of the servers on the Web are run on UNIX machines, which are not only case-sensitive, but they also don't allow spaces or special characters, except for the underscore (_). So coming up with names that work and that you — and everyone else on your site development team — can remember can be difficult. For example, `staff stuff.htm` is not a good file name because it has a space in it, but `staff_stuff.htm` is fine, because the underscore will work on any server, and you still have a break between the words to make them easier to read.

Keeping track of the information on the pages in your Web site is much easier if you develop a naming structure that makes sense to everyone working on the project. For example, say your Web site has a news section that includes articles about the best gossip and rumors in your office (okay, maybe you wouldn't want all that on the Web, but let me use it as an example).

If you're working on the gossip section, a simple name like office-affair.html and busted.html may make sense to you this week because you're familiar with who is the topic of conversation around the water cooler. But six months from now, if you're looking to confirm the last affair, just to compare it to the latest one, you may not remember that you called it hot_stuff.html. Adding dates to the end of filenames can help you identify the files that you may need months — or even years — down the road. Remember that you can't use spaces, but you can use the underscore. So a good filename would be, `hot_stuff_10_2003.html` or `affair_10_2003.html` because they dates should help you at least remember when these incidents occurred.

Another option is to create a folder for each new update and name it with a date. For example, a folder named `gossip10_2003` could contain all the stories from the October, 2003. Then you can put `hot_stuff.html` and any other stories from that issue in the `gossip10_2003` folder, and you can find them by date as well as by filename. (This works really well for newsletters, calendar updates, and other content that's more likely to go up on your Web site.)

Whatever the content you manage on your site, talk to other people who will also be doing updates and create a system that makes sense to everyone and is easy to explain if a new person joins the team. Whatever you do, don't name files randomly and throw them all in one directory. You should also consider documenting your naming system.

Never Say You're Under Construction

All good Web sites are under construction; it's the nature of the Web. But build your site in such a way that you can add pages when they're ready instead of putting up placeholders. Don't greet your viewers with a guy in a yellow hat who seems to say, "You clicked this link for no good reason. Come back another day, and maybe we'll have something for you to see." Instead of creating "Under Construction" placeholders, create directory structures that make adding new pages later easy. You can let readers know that new things are coming by putting notices on pages that already have content — a message like "Come here next Thursday for a link to something even cooler" is a great idea. But never make users click a link and wait for a page to load only to find that nothing but a guy with a hard hat is waiting for them.

Managing Your Site's Internal Structure

Managing the structure of a Web site has two sides: the side that users see, which depends on how you set up links and the interface design, and the behind-the-scenes side that depends on how you organize files and folders.

Before you open your Web site to other contributors, spend some time thinking about the behind-the-scenes side and all the management issues involved in keeping track of the files that make up your site. By *files,* I mean all the images, HTML pages, animations, sound files, and anything else you put in your Web site. As you create pages for your Web site, it's best to organize them in separate folders or directories and to organize images and other elements that correspond to those pages in a way that makes it easy to find them later.

Keeping track of all the files and folders on a site when you're working on it by yourself is hard enough, but if you're going to have other people helping you update the site, it's even more important to make sure that you have organized files and folders in a way that makes sense and is easy to manage. Fortunately, Dreamweaver includes site management tools that make it easy for you to move files and folders around while Dreamweaver automatically fixes links that relate to them. However, these site management features don't exist in Contribute, so you'll need to do this kind of site organization in Dreamweaver or in another Web design program, such as Adobe GoLive.

Contribute uses a browse function to identify the page a user wants to work on, so they open pages much like users of a site would — by following the links on pages. Therefore, the behind the scenes site management is most important to the site administrator and/or designer. If that's you, spending some time organizing these files so you can find them quickly if you do need to fix or replace something can save you some serious grief later.

If you're still not sure what I'm getting at with this tip, consider this. Before you build in new sections or pages, think about where you're likely to add content in the future. Think about creating logical sections of a site that anticipate growth. For example, you may start with one page that lists all of your staff; however, after they see how cool it is, each staff member may want to develop his or her own page. In that case, you may want a separate folder dedicated to staff pages. If you're providing information for your sales team, you may find that you want a separate section for each product. As you add new sections, such as the ones I mention here, create new subdirectories or subfolders to store their respective files. Creating subdirectories also makes it easier to manage a site that's built by multiple people. If each subsection has a separate folder, then each developer can better manage his or her own section without affecting the other sections of the site.

Organizing Images and Handling Links

Before I go on, I want to make a few points about organizing images in a Web site. I've heard many HTML teachers and consultants suggest that you place all of your images in a single folder at the top level of the directory structure and call it Images or Graphics. You may also find that some HTML authoring tools require you to keep all of your images in one folder.

The advantage of keeping all of your images in one folder is that the path to all of your images can be the same, and you only have to go one place to look for them. However, the problem with using just one folder is that if all of your images are in one place, you're likely to end up with a long list of image files, making it easy to lose track of which image is which if you want to change or remove one later.

If you have images that link throughout the site — a logo, for example — you may want to create an *images* folder at the top level of your directory structure for those images so they are easy to find from any folder in the site. However, if you have lots of images that relate to subsections of your site, a good alternative is to store your images in multiple *image* folders within the subfolders that hold the HTML files where those images appear. For example, keep all of your pets photos for your pet pages in an *images* folder within a subfolder called *pets*.

Dreamweaver makes no distinction between a folder called images and a folder by any other name, so you can call these folders whatever you like, including my personal favorite: embarrassing_pictures.

Finding and Fixing Broken Links

If you're trying to rein in a chaotic Web site, or if you fear that it may have broken links, don't forget that Dreamweaver has a Check Links feature. You can't use this in Contribute, but if you do suspect serious problems with broken links, switching over to Dreamweaver to find and fix them is well worth the effort. If you don't have Dreamweaver or don't know how to use it yourself, this is an example of a time when it's worth asking the Webmaster or administrator for help because Dreamweaver does this so much better than Contribute.

You can use Check Links to verify the links in a single file or an entire Web site, and you can even automatically fix all the referring links at once. Here's an example of what Check Links can do. Assume that someone on your team (because you would never do such a thing yourself) has changed the name of a file from cool.htm to stupid.htm without using the Dreamweaver automatic link update process to fix the corresponding links. Maybe this person changed the name using another program or simply changed the name in the Finder on the Mac or in the Explorer in Windows. Changing the filename was easy, but what this person may not have realized is that if he or she didn't change the links to the file when the file was renamed, the links are now broken.

If only one page links to the file your clueless teammate changed, fixing it isn't such a big deal. As long as you remember what file the page links from, you can simply open that page and use the Property Inspector to reset the link the same way you would create a link in the first place.

But many times, a single page in a Web site is referred to by links on many other pages. When that's the case, fixing all the link references can be time-consuming, and it's all too easy to forget some of them. That's why Check Links is so helpful. First, it serves as a diagnostic tool that identifies broken links throughout the site (so you don't have to second-guess where someone may have changed a filename or moved a file). Then it serves as a global fix-it tool. You can use the Check Links dialog box to identify the page a broken link should go to, and then you can have Dreamweaver automatically fix all links referring to that page. The following section walks you through the process.

Periodically Check Over the Entire Site

If you have several people adding and editing pages on a Web site, it's a good idea to check over their work once in a while. But manually testing every page and looking for all the details that could be wrong is a tedious waste of your time. This is another place where the more advanced power of Dreamweaver is worth harnessing, even if you have to learn how to use it.

Dreamweaver has a great set of testing tools in its Site Reporting arena. You can create a variety of reports, and even customize them, to identify problems with external links, redundant and empty tags, untitled documents and missing Alt text. These are all easy things to miss — especially when you're working on a tight deadline — and these little details can cause real problems for your viewers if you leave them unfixed. Check Dreamweaver's help files to find out how to use Site Reporting or pick up a copy of *Dreamweaver MX For Dummies* to find lots of great tips about making the most of these error-correcting features.

Assigning Clear Deadlines

Everyone complains about deadlines, but the truth is, almost nothing ever gets finished without one. The trick is to set realistic deadlines and the convince everyone they are real and have to be met. This gets harder on the Web than it is in print because with print deadlines you usually have a real time limit that is associated with the process of getting whatever your creating printed and distributed. Newspapers, for example, have deadlines that make it possible to schedule and efficiently use the giant printing presses that are required to publish them and the complex delivery system of trucks and kids with paper routes that get them to reader's doorsteps in the morning. Missing a deadline in a newspaper can cost hundreds of thousands of dollars in overtime and lost sales so people who work in newspapers take deadlines really seriously.

On the Web, there are no expensive printing presses and no teenage paper boys or girls who are likely to be late for school if the newspaper is printed late. But the phenomena is still true. If you don't assign a real deadline to a project, it doesn't usually get done. If you're going to ask someone to update a section of the site or build in new information, make sure you tell them when it has to be finished, and ideally, coordinate that time with something tangible, like an upcoming conference or even a meeting where it will be unveiled and shown to the boss and/or the rest of the staff.

Trust me, setting deadlines makes all the difference, just make sure you set realistic ones. If you set deadlines that really are impossible to make, then they get missed and no one dies, and it becomes harder and harder to keep people respecting deadlines the next time.

Here's the formula that seems to work best. Assign a clearly defined task, set a deadline that is perceived as reasonable to all parties, attach some outside force to the deadline, such as a review meeting, and then make sure you check in with the person the task is assigned to well before the deadline to make sure all is going well and provide any necessary review and assistance.

Creating Contingency Plans

Okay, so that deadline tip that comes just before this one was written for an ideal world, but even if the deadlines you face seem impossible, they often still get made if the rest of those elements are in place. But just in case they don't, you want to have some contingency plans in place.

On a well-managed Web project, you'll have contingency plans not just for missed deadlines, but for a long list of things that can go wrong. For example, a contingency plan for broken links may involve having someone assigned to fixing broken links as soon as they are discovered no matter where they are on the site. This person should know enough about using Dreamweaver to take advantage of its advanced features. He or she will also have to access to the Web server and the ability to get into the site to fix it. Look for your sharpest, fastest team member for this job. Broken links are so embarrassing, you'll want them fixed right away.

As for missed deadlines, having other team members standing by to jump in and help at the last minute can save a project that's gone off course. And finally, make sure that more than one person on the team knows how to manage the Web server or contact your service provider. All the great effort you put into building and maintaining a Web site will be useless if you don't also make sure that the site stays up and running all the time.

Chapter 17

Ten Intuitive Interface Tips

The world of Web design has many rules. While most of these rules are designed to remedy most common mistakes, they also serve as guidelines to those who are new to the business and reminders to those who may have swayed off course through the years.

The best designs, however, are usually created by people who know the rules so well, they can push the limits in ways that make them exceptional. Rules are made to be broken (or at least bent), some say. I say they serve as guidelines. If you break a rule, you should have good reason. If you don't, you're probably better off following the rule.

The following ten tips are designed to help make sure you know the basic rules, the ones worth following. The rest is up to you.

Make It Easy to Get Around

Creating a clear and intuitive navigational system is one of the most important elements in creating a Web site. Nothing is likely to frustrate your visitors more than not being able to find what they're looking for. Make sure that visitors can easily get to all the main sections of your site from every page in the site.

You can best do this by creating a set of links to each of the main sections and placing it at the top or side of every page. I call this set of links a *navigation row* or *navigation bar,* and it's a common feature on most well-designed sites. If the pages are very long, consider including a navigation bar, or footer, at the bottom of the page as well. Often the navigation bar at the bottom of the page is just a list of text links. The bottom of the page is also an ideal place to include basic contact information. A set of graphical icons can make this navigational element an attractive part of your design. Your goal is to make sure that viewers don't have to use the Back button in their browsers to move around your site.

White Space Is Not Wasted Space

Often one of the best design features you can add to a page is nothing at all (also known as *white space*). Understand that white space, in this case, is not always white; it's simply space that you haven't crammed full of text or images. It can be any color, but it's usually most effective if it's the color or pattern of your background. White space gives the eye a rest, something readers need even more when they've been staring at a computer monitor for any length of time. You can use white space to separate one type of information from another and to focus the viewer's attention where you want it most. Some of the most beautiful and compelling designs on the Web use only a few well-thought-out elements against lots of white space.

Design for Your Audience

No matter how technically sophisticated a Web site is or how great the writing, most people notice the design first. Make sure that you leave plenty of time and budget to develop an appropriate and attractive design for your Web site. The right design is one that best suits your audience — that may or may not mean lots of fancy graphics and animations.

Think about who you want to attract to your Web site before you develop the design. A gaming Web site geared toward teenagers should look very different from a Web site with gardening tips or an online banking site for adults. Review other sites designed for your target market. Consider your audience's time constraints and attention span, and, most importantly, consider your audience's goals. If you design your site to provide information to busy businesspeople, you want fast-loading pages with few graphics and little or no animation. If you design your site for entertainment, your audience may be willing to wait a little longer for animation and other interactive features.

Back It Up

Make sure you have a system in place to back up your Web site. Always keep a copy of all the files that are on your server in a separate location and update it regularly to make sure you have the latest version of your site backed up at all times. Even the best Internet Service Providers sometimes have technical problems, so you should keep a backup of your site where you have easy access to it and can get it back online quickly if something ever does happen to delete any or all the files you have on the server.

Also keep a backup of your original source files, such as Photoshop images. For example, when you develop images for the Web, you usually start in a program like Photoshop or Fireworks, creating a high-resolution image that may include layers and other elements. Before the image goes on your Web site, those layers get flattened and the image gets compressed or reduced and converted into a GIF or JPEG. If you ever want to go back and alter that image in the future, you'll want the original source file before it was compressed and the layers were flattened. Whether you create your own images or your hire a professional designer, make sure you develop a system for saving all these original elements when they are created.

Be Consistent

As you lay out your Web page, keep related items physically close to one another. You want your viewers to instantly understand which pieces of information are related. Give elements of similar importance the same weight on a page. Distinguish different kinds of information by their design, location, and prominence. This kind of organization makes following information visually much easier for your viewers.

Make sure that all similar elements follow the same design parameters, such as type style, banner size, and page background color. If you use too many different elements on a page or within the same Web site, you quickly have a very "busy" design and may confuse your viewers. Defining a set of colors, shapes, or other elements that you use throughout the site is a good way to ensure a consistent style. Choose two or three fonts for your Web site and use those consistently as well. Using too many fonts makes your pages less appealing and harder to read.

Small and Fast

Despite all the promises that unlimited bandwidth was coming soon, the biggest problem on the Internet is still speed. Making sure that your pages download quickly makes your viewers more likely to keep clicking. You may create the best design ever to grace the Web, but if it takes too long to appear on your viewers' screens, no one will wait around long enough to compliment your design talents.

If your page designs take a long time to download, here are a few likely reasons and suggestions for how to make them load faster: First, take a look at multimedia elements and consider reducing the size or at least offering users the option to skip large multimedia files, such as Flash introductions. You especially don't want to make users wait too long for the first page of your site. If you suspect that static images are the problem, consider compression methods and use a program such as Fireworks or ImageReady that are designed for optimizing images for the Web. Finally, use Dreamweaver's code cleanup feature to get rid of extra tags that can contribute to a heavier page. To use this, choose Commands➪Clean Up HTML.

Accessible Designs

As you design your site, keep in mind that viewers come to your pages with a variety of computers, operating systems, and monitors. Ensure that your site is accessible to all your potential viewers by testing your pages on a variety of systems. If you want to attract a large audience to your site, you need to ensure that it looks good on a broad range of systems. A design that looks great in Navigator 4.0 and higher may be unreadable in Internet Explorer 3.0. And many people still use old browsers because they haven't bothered — or don't know how — to download new versions.

Accessible design on the Web also includes pages that can be read (actually, converted to synthesized speech) by special browsers used by the blind. Using the ALT attribute in your image tags is a simple way to ensure that all visitors can get the information they need. The ALT attribute specifies a text alternative that is displayed if the image doesn't appear. It's inserted into an image tag like this:

```
<IMG SRC="CAT.GIF" ALT="A picture of a black and white cat.">
```

In Contribute, you never have to look at the HTML code, and you can easily add Alt text in the Image Properties dialog box. Simply double-click any image to open the Image Properties dialog box and then enter the Alt text in the Description (Alt text) text box.

Follow the Three Clicks Rule

The Three Clicks Rule states that no important piece of information should ever be more than three clicks away from anywhere else on your Web site. The most important information should be even closer at hand. Some information, such as contact information, should never be more than one click away. Make it easy for viewers to find information by creating a site map (as I explain in the next section) and a *navigation bar* — a set of links to all the main sections on your site.

Map It Out

As your site gets larger, providing easy access to all the information on your Web site may get harder and harder. A great solution is to provide a *site map,* which is a page that includes links to almost every other page in the site. The site map can become a busy page and usually appears best in outline form. This page should be highly functional — it doesn't matter if it looks pretty. Don't put lots of graphics on this page; it should load quickly and provide easy access to anything that your visitors need.

Late-Breaking News

One of the greatest challenges of any Web site is the ability to post new information quickly, especially under pressure or in times of crisis. Don't wait for an emergency to find out if you're prepared to update your Web site quickly, and don't think that because you manage a Web site for a business or a non-profit group, you don't have to worry about being able to send breaking news to the Internet.

With a little planning and key systems set up in advance, you can be prepared for events that require timely updates — whether it's an international crises or an embarrassing event that makes your CEO cringe and demand that the "real" story be told as soon as possible.

Here are a few steps you can take to be prepared for timely updates on your site:

1. **Make sure you can send new information to your Web site quickly.**

   Many Web sites are designed with testing systems that safeguard against careless mistakes, but these systems can add hours, or even days, to the time it takes to add new information to your Web site. Work with your technical staff or consultants to make sure you can update your site quickly if necessary. This may require creating a new section that can be updated independently from the rest of the site or being able to override the regular update system.

2. **Identify key staff to be trained to update the site.**

   With Contribute, you don't need to have much technical experience to make simple updates to a site, but your staff will need some instruction and regular reminders. Make sure you also develop a schedule for retraining to ensure that no one forgets emergency procedures. Your most serious emergency could happen tomorrow or may not happen for years to come — you never know, so it pays to be prepared.

Part VI
Appendixes

The 5th Wave   By Rich Tennant

SCHOOL OF ENTOMOLOGY

PEARSON BUG EXTERMINATOR

"You'd better come out here — I've got someone who wants to run a banner ad on our Web site."

In this part . . .

*P*art VI is designed to keep answering your questions, even after you've finished the book (or even while you're in the middle of reading it). Appendix A is a comprehensive glossary with all the terms and acronyms you're likely to see while you're working on the Web. Often, vocabulary is the biggest hurdle for new designers, so being able to figure out what they're talking about is important. In Appendix B, you find a collection of Web sites designed with Dreamweaver and Contribute.

Appendix A

Glossary

● ●

*R*efer to this glossary anytime you get lost in techspeak. Visit www. webopedia.com if you're online and you need a definition fast or you can't find what you're looking for here. Also check out About.com's Internet for Beginners channel to learn more about terms like *Internet, intranet,* and *extranet.* Look for it at www.about.com.

absolute link (or absolute URL): An HTML hyperlink that you set by using the complete URL, starting with the machine name or domain name on which the file is located. For example: <A HREF="http://www.domain_name.com/ directory/ filename.html">. See also *relative link*.

absolute positioning: An HTML feature that enables you to specify the precise location of an element in relation to the window.

Acrobat: Adobe's software suite for creating portable electronic documents (PDFs).

Active Server Pages (ASP): A server technology that comes, at no additional cost, built into Windows 2000 and can be easily installed into Windows 98 and NT as well. Used in conjunction with Microsoft IIS or Personal Web Server, ASP is not a standalone programming language, as much of the code you'll write for ASP pages are in VB Script or JavaScript.

ActiveX: A set of technologies created by Microsoft that enables software components to interact with one another in a networked environment regardless of the computer language in which they were created.

add-on: An accessory or utility program that extends the capabilities of an application. See also *plug-in*.

anchor: The destination of a hyperlink used for jump links. See also *absolute link* and *relative link*.

animated GIF: Part of the GIF89a specification that enables you to store multiple still frames in the same graphics file, which, upon loading, appear in a specified sequence to create movielike motion. Created with programs such as GIF Builder. See also *animation*.

animation: A series of images that, when displayed one after the other, creates the effect of movement.

anti-aliasing: A process that gives the illusion of smoothing the jagged edges of a graphic by intermixing pixels of the adjoining colors along the edges of the graphic.

Applet: A small application created with the Java programming language.

application (or program): Any program (such as a word processor, spreadsheet, database, or desktop publishing program) that performs functions for a user.

application server: Helps the Web server to process specially marked Web pages. When one of these pages is requested by the browser, the Web server hands the page off to the application server which processes it, often inserting dynamic content into a template, before sending the page to the browser.

ASCII (American Standard Code for Information Exchange): Pronounced "ask-ee." The original 128-character set, or a file containing only those characters and no special formatting.

attachment: An electronic file (such as text or a graphic) that's sent along with an e-mail message.

attribute: A part of the HTML specification that modifies the behavior of a tag as well as the text, graphic, or other element that the tag describes.

AVI (Audio/Video/Interactive): A Windows-native animation format that's similar to *QuickTime*.

background: A solid color, image, or textured pattern that appears behind the text and graphics on a Web page.

bandwidth: The amount of data that can be sent through a communications channel. Represents the Internet's carrying capacity. Some kinds of information, such as graphics, take up more bandwidth than others, such as text.

banner: An advertisement on a Web page; usually a commercial advertisement that links to the advertiser's site. Banner ads are usually composed of bitmapped GIF graphics and animated GIFs.

batch processing: Performing the same function on many files or documents at the same time.

baud: A measure of the speed at which data is transmitted. Baud rate indicates the number of bits of data transmitted in one second. One baud is equal to one bit per second. Common modems today have baud rates of 14,400, 28,800, 33,600, or 56,000 kilobits per second (Kbps).

beta version: The last stages of development of a computer program before it's ready to be sold to the public. The beta version of the program is released to a select group of users for testing for errors, commonly called bugs.

bit (for *binary digit*): The smallest piece of information a computer uses. Bits can be combined in various ways to represent different kinds of information. Eight bits form a byte.

bitmapped image: A graphic formed by an array of dots (pixels) on a screen.

bookmark: A way to save a Web site's URL for easy access later. Also known as favorites.

bps (bits per second): A measure of how fast data is transmitted. See also *baud*.

browse: To look over a collection of information casually, especially in an effort to find something of interest, as in browsing through folders (directories) or browsing the World Wide Web.

browser: A program, such as Netscape Navigator or Microsoft Internet Explorer, that's used along with an Internet connection to view pages on the World Wide Web.

bulletin board system (BBS): An electronic messaging system, such as an online discussion area, that you dial into directly to read and contribute messages.

byte: A measurement of computer storage. Usually equals eight bits.

C, C++: Programming languages preferred by many professional programmers.

cache: Pronounced "cash." A special section of RAM or disk memory that's set aside to store frequently accessed information. *Cache* is also used as a verb to refer to the act of storing such information. Many Web browsers cache information on your computer to help download Web pages more quickly.

Cascading Style Sheets (CSS): Part of the HTML specification used for defining style properties (such as font, color, and spacing) and using them to control the appearance of elements. Cascading Style Sheets enable you to make global formatting changes by redefining and applying styles, similar to the way styles are used in word-processing and desktop-publishing programs.

CGI (Common Gateway Interface) script: A program that provides greater levels of interactivity than basic HTML by passing information from browsers to servers via forms or queries. Many Web sites use CGI scripts to perform functions, such as online discussion areas and shopping systems. These scripts are written in sophisticated programming languages like Perl, C, and C++.

chat: Real-time written discussion that takes place on the Internet.

clear GIF: An invisible GIF. It can be any size but is usually only a few pixels square. Clear GIFs are used to create white space on a Web page for better placement of text by changing the height and width attributes of an image tag.

client: The Internet is a client/server arrangement. The client (usually a Web browser) is the end-user side, which usually resides on a personal computer and communicates with a Web server. See also *server*.

close tag (or end tag): An HTML tag that designates the end of a formatting section, usually the same as the opening tag but with a forward slash mark. For example, the close `<CENTER>` tag is `</CENTER>`.

compressed file: A data file that has been modified to consume less space, often by using a program such as *Zip* or StuffIt. Prior to use, a compressed file must be decompressed.

contact link: Information that makes it easy for Web site visitors to contact the people behind the Web site. It could link to the site developer's e-mail address, to an e-mail form, or to a page of e-mail addresses for key contacts.

cookie: Information stored on your hard drive by a program on a Web site that you visit. This information can be used to track your preferences and activities as you use the site and if you return to it later. Cookie technology enables a Web site to greet you by name, remember your password, and provide custom information. Cookies have become controversial because some people view them as an invasion of privacy. Most of the latest browsers enable you to prevent cookies from being stored on your computer.

cross-platform: Having versions for more than one operating system, such as UNIX, Macintosh, and Windows 98. Can also refer to applications, such as those created in Java, that run across multiple, incompatible computer systems with little or no modification.

CSS value or CSS attribute: Specifies the parameter for a Cascading Style Sheet (CSS) property.

cyberspace: The entire world of online information and services. Coined by William Gibson is his novel *Neuromancer.*

data binding: The process of automatically placing or connecting data in an HTML element from a data source.

database: A collection of information compiled in one or more *tables* with *fields* organized in columns, and *records* in rows.

database program: Enables the collection of data in an organized format, permitting manipulation of the data in a variety of ways. Examples include FileMaker Pro, Access, FoxPro, and dBase.

default: A condition set automatically in a program when no explicit selection has been made. In HTML, the value assigned to an attribute when none is supplied.

desktop: In a graphical environment, a term assigned to the always-open file folder that you first see when your computer finishes booting up. In Windows 95 and 98, the physical path to the desktop is c:/windows/desktop. Desktops are traditionally decorated with background images.

desktop publishing program: An application, such as PageMaker or QuarkXPress, that's used for typeset publications like newsletters and magazines.

dialog box: An on-screen message area that conveys or requests information.

digital format: The form of something, such as an image or a sound, when it's stored as computer data.

digital subscriber line (DSL): A high-speed Internet access option that works over standard copper telephone wires like the ones already installed in most homes. With DSL, data can be delivered at a rate of 1.5 mbps (around 30 times faster than through a 56Kbps modem).

dingbats: Ornamental characters such as bullets, stars, and flowers used to decorate a page.

Director movie: An animation, presentation, or interactive title created in Macromedia Director, the most widely used program for creating multimedia.

directory (or subdirectory): A list of computer files contained on a disk or drive. May be nested to facilitate the organization of data. Directories are called folders on Macintosh or Windows 95 and later systems. See also *nested*.

dithering: A method employed to simulate natural shading in an image with a limited color range. Shades are represented with combinations of colored dots (pixels) on the screen in various patterns. Often used to give the appearance of smoother transitions between shades.

document source: The HTML code behind a page displayed on the World Wide Web. You can view this information for almost every Web page.

domain name: A unique identifier that assigns a name to a specific IP address. IP addresses are long, hard-to-remember numbers. A computer on the Internet is perfectly happy to take you to the Web site of 204.71.200.67 if you ask for it by IP address, but www.yahoo.com is much easier for you to remember.

DOS (Disk Operating System): The underlying control system for many personal computers. Usually refers to MS-DOS, the original operating system for IBM-compatible computers. Today, most people use the Windows operating system rather than DOS.

download: To move information from a remote computer to your computer. For example, when you download images from a Web site, you copy them from the server to your computer to display or save them.

dpi (dots per inch): A measure of image resolution that counts the dots in a linear inch. The higher the dpi, the better the resolution (and the larger the file size). A 600-dpi printer gives you more detailed printouts than a 300-dpi printer. When you design images for print, the general rule is the higher the resolution, the better because you get better quality when you enlarge them or print them out. When you design images for the Web, however, you want the lowest resolution possible because that's how you get the smallest file size and the fastest download time. Most images created for the Web are 72 dpi because they're designed to be displayed by computer monitors and monitors don't display more than 72 dots per inch so anything more than that would be wasted, and the file size would be larger than necessary for the Web.

dynamic: Marked by continuous activity or change.

dynamic HTML (DHTML): A part of the HTML specification that adds the capability to change style or positioning properties with a scripting language. DHTML includes Cascading Style Sheets, layers, timelines, and behaviors. See also *scripting language*.

dynamic styles: The capability to change the style attributes or values of any element when a page is loaded or an action is otherwise triggered.

element: A component of a hierarchical structure (for example, in a Web site). Also, any shape that can be individually manipulated in a graphic. In this usage, the term *element* is synonymous with *object*.

e-mail (electronic mail): A system that enables one computer user to send messages to other users over a *network*.

e-mail address: A domain-based address used for sending e-mail to a specified destination. Within company systems and commercial service providers such as America Online, the e-mail address is often just the name the person has chosen as an address. On the greater Internet, e-mail addresses must include an @ sign and an extension, such as .com or .org. Example: editor@janinewarner.com

embed: To place a command directly in a program. Also, an HTML tag used to link objects and elements that require plug-ins for viewing. See also *plug-in*.

encrypt: To convert data into a format that can't be read without a key or password. Encryption is the most common system used to transfer information over the Internet privately.

end tag: See *close tag*.

end user: A person who uses a computer program or device to perform a function, such as word processing.

environment: The hardware and/or operating system for applications (DOS, Macintosh, or Windows).

Ethernet: One of the most widely used standards on a LAN (local area network). Ethernet was cooperatively developed by Xerox Corporation, DEC, and Intel in the 1970s and enables relatively fast data transfer rates — up to 1,000 megabits per second. If you connect your computer to the network at your office, you likely use an Ethernet card to do so.

event: A user-initiated happening, such as an icon that changes at a mouse click. Elements on Web sites often are designed to respond to events.

extension (or filename extension): *1.* Tags or attributes that are introduced by a browser company such as Netscape or Microsoft but are not part of the current HTML specifications, usually supported only by that browser. *2.* The latter portion of a filename on a DOS or UNIX machine, such as .doc for Microsoft Word documents and .gif for Graphics Interchange Format. Macintosh filenames don't require extensions. However, all files that are to be displayed by a browser must include extensions.

external style sheet: A Cascading Style Sheet file that's a separate text file that contains style definitions and can be linked to any of the HTML files on a Web site.

extranet: A sort of mix between an Intranet and Internet Web site. Think of this as an extension of a company's intranet that enables users with special privileges to access the intranet from outside the company. Extranets are commonly used to provide outside sales staff access to internal information and to facilitate communication and business with special clients and suppliers.

FAQ (Frequently Asked Questions): A list of questions and answers with basic information about a Web site or other resource. The FAQ concept originated as a method for Internet users to find answers to common questions online.

favorites: A way to save a Web site's URL for easy access later. Also known as bookmarks.

Fetch: The most popular FTP Macintosh program for transferring files between client and server.

filename: The name of a document (or file) on a computer, such as a word-processing document or a graphics file.

first-generation browsers: Early versions of browsers that predate the capability to recognize plug-ins, tables, animated GIFs, background colors, or background images.

Flash: One of the most popular animation programs on the Web, Macromedia Flash uses vector-based technology to create fast-loading animations that can incorporate sound, video, and still images. To view Flash files on the Web requires a plug-in, but because Flash is so popular, the vast majority of users of the Web already have the plug-in and the ability to view these files.

folder: A container of files held on a disk or drive. Computer files are often stored in folders, which can be nested (in subfolders) to facilitate the organization of data. Called directories on DOS or UNIX systems and on early versions of Microsoft Windows. See also *directory* and *nested*.

font: A complete collection of letters, punctuation marks, numbers, and special characters with a consistent and identifiable typeface, weightand size. Sometimes used to refer to typefaces or font families.

font family: A set of fonts in several sizes and weights that share the same typeface.

frames: A Netscape HTML extension, now supported by Microsoft Internet Explorer, that enables more than one HTML document to be displayed on a Web page. Creates distinct sections of a page that can be scrolled and that can contain links that alter the contents of other sections, or frames, on the same Web page.

FTP (File Transfer Protocol): A system for copying files to and from servers elsewhere on a network, such as the Internet.

GIF (Graphics Interchange Format): A bitmapped image format that uses compression to reduce file sizes. The format was pioneered by CompuServe for storing and transmitting graphics over remote networks. It's currently the most universally accepted graphics file format on the World Wide Web.

GIF87a: The original specification for the Graphics Interchange Format standard. See also *animated GIF*.

GIF89a: An enhanced specification that gives GIF the capability to display any color as transparent and to store and display multiple files as an animation. See also *animated GIF*.

graphic: A representation of an image on a two-dimensional surface.

graphical environment: An environment that includes the use of graphics in addition to text.

graphical user interface (GUI): An interface that uses graphical metaphors to run a computer program or operating system. These interfaces, such as the ones used on Windows and Macintosh computers, replaced text-based operating systems such as DOS.

home page: The first page that appears when you access a Web site. Also called the title page or front page. On a small site (for example, a personal site), the home page may be the only page. On a larger site (a business's, for instance), it's the main page and includes links to other pages within the site.

host: A computer that enables users to communicate by using application programs such as e-mail, Telnet, and FTP. Any computer capable of connecting to others on the Internet is a host. This term generally refers to Web servers.

HTML (HyperText Markup Language): The programming language used to create Web pages and other files for distribution over the Internet. HTML is a subset of SGML (Standard Generalized Markup Language). See also *hypertext*.

HTML authoring tool: A program designed to edit or convert HTML documents.

HTML converter: A program that changes documents from various programs into HTML documents.

HTML editor: A program you use to alter or create HTML pages.

HTTP (HyperText Transfer Protocol): The protocol that makes the transfer of information between a Web browser and a Web server possible.

hyperlink (or link): A programmed connection between locations in the same file (Web site) or two different files. See also *hypertext*.

hypertext: A word or series of words with related HTML programming linking the word(s) to another location. You click on these words to skip from one document to the next or from one area of a document to another area of the same document.

icon: A small image meant to convey a message that takes less time to read and is more universally understood than words are.

image map: A set of coordinates to designate distinct areas of a GIF or JPEG image by using square, circular, or polygon shapes. These areas can be linked to any URL so that a user reaches different destinations by selecting different sections of the image.

inline image: An image that can be given a specific location on a Web page in context with text and other multimedia elements. Inline images can be viewed by a Web browser and don't require a plug-in or a separate window for viewing.

interface: The place where independent and often unrelated systems meet and act on or communicate with one another. See also *graphical user interface (GUI)*.

interlacing: A process that enables an image to load in several stages. Creates the illusion that graphics (and therefore whole pages) load more quickly and gives the reader a chance to see a fuzzy but recognizable image quickly enough to know whether to wait or move on.

Internet: Note the capital *I. An internet* is a network; *the Internet* is an international collection of interconnected networks. The Internet is the largest internet in the world.

intranet: A private Web site that's set up and maintained within a corporation or organization. Unlike Internet sites, intranet sites are restricted to a particular audience, usually the employees of a company.

IP (Internet Protocol): Enables information to be passed from one network (set of computers) to another by using a unique string of numbers (as an address) for each network. See *protocol.*

Internet service provider (ISP): A national or local company that sells access to the Internet. Well-known examples in the United States include America Online and AT&T WorldNet.

Java: A programming language invented by Sun Microsystems that can be used on any computer platform. This versatility makes Java popular because it enables programmers to create one program that will work on many different computers, such as Macintosh or Windows. Programs written in other languages, such as C or C++, require different versions for each platform. Java is especially popular on the Web because it can be run on any computer connected to the Internet. See also *applet*.

JavaScript: A scripting language that enables interactive features on Web sites. JavaScript can interact with code written in HTML and shares some of the features of Java but it is not an sophisticated programming language, such as Java or C++.

JavaServerPages (JSP): JSP is from Sun Microsystems. Its dynamic code is based on Java, which makes it possible to run the pages from non-Microsoft Web servers. JSP can be used on Macromedia JRun Server and IBM WebSphere. Using JSP, you can create and keep the dynamic code separated from the HTML pages (by using Java Beans) or you can embed the JSP code into the page.

JPEG (Joint Photographic Experts Group): A file format commonly used on the Web for full-color, continuous-tone images (such as photographs).

JScript: Microsoft's implementation of JavaScript in Internet Explorer. See also *JavaScript*.

jump link: A hyperlink that connects to an anchor in a specific part of a page. Jump links can be used to link text from one part of a page to another or from one page to a particular place on another page. See also *anchor*.

kilobits per second (Kbps): A measurement of communication speed (of modems, for example).

kilobyte (K): 1,024 bytes of data. See also *byte*.

link: See *hyperlink*.

load: To transfer program instructions or data from a disk or drive to a computer's random-access memory (RAM).

loop: A set of program instructions that execute repeatedly until a condition is satisfied. Animations are often designed to loop so that the images that comprise the animation repeat.

lossy compression: So called because not all detail is preserved when a file is compressed (some loss occurs).

macro: A stored list of commands to perform tedious and often-repeated tasks. Macros often are used in Microsoft Word to automate common tasks.

markup language: Special characters embedded within a text file to instruct a program how to handle or display the file's contents. HTML is a markup language.

megabyte (MB): 1,024 kilobytes, or 1,048,576 bytes. See also *byte*.

menu: A list of options that a program or Web site presents to a user.

menu bar: In graphical programs (and many desktop applications), menus representing the program's most common functions are often positioned for easy access in a horizontal bar across the top of the window. On a Web site, the menu bar is often a collection of graphic or text links that provide access to all the main pages of the site.

metacharacter: A character within a text file that signals the need for special handling. In HTML, metacharacters are angle brackets (<>), ampersands (&), pound signs (#), and semicolons (;).

Microsoft Internet Explorer: One of the two most widely used graphical Web browsers. (Netscape Navigator is the other.) See also *browser*.

Microsoft Office viewer: A program that enables users to view Word, Excel, and PowerPoint documents on the Internet in their native form without converting them to HTML.

MIDI (Musical Instrument Device Interface): Pronounced "middy." A protocol for the exchange of information between computers and musical synthesizers. After being placed in computer-represented form, all the aspects of the digitized sound can be edited and altered.

MIME (Multipurpose Internet Mail Extensions): An extension to Internet e-mail that enables the transfer of nontextual data, such as graphics, audio, and video.

modem (for *modulator-demodulator*): A device that converts electrical pulses from a computer to signals suitable for transmission over a telephone line.

Moiré: Pronounced "mwah-ray." An optical illusion perceived as flickering that sometimes occurs when high-contrast line patterns are placed too close together.

Mosaic: The first graphical Web browser. Evolved into the browser that we now call Netscape.

Mozilla: An early name for Netscape products that derived from "Mosaic meets Godzilla." The word and associated image often appear in Netscape products and references to them. Mozilla is also the name of a new open-source browser based on Netscape's technology. Check out www.Mozilla.org for downloads and news.

multimedia: The presentation of information on a computer using video sequences, animation, sound (either as background or synchronized to a video or animation), and vector illustrations.

nanosecond: One-billionth of a second.

netiquette: Internet etiquette. The written and unwritten rules for behavior on the Net.

nested: One structure occurring within another. HTML tags often are nested by placing one formatting tag inside another.

Netscape Navigator: One of the two most widely used graphical Web browsers. (Microsoft Internet Explorer is the other.) See also *browser*.

network: A system of computers or other devices interconnected by cables, telephone wires, or other means to share data or other information.

network administrator: See *system administrator*.

node: An individual connection point in a network.

PDF (Portable Document File): A file that carries all font and layout specifications with it, regardless of the platform on which it's viewed. The best solution for putting documents on the Web when they must be as close as possible to their print counterparts. Generally requires a viewer such as Adobe Acrobat.

PERL (Practical Extraction and Reporting Language): A language developed for UNIX systems that's frequently used for writing *CGI* scripts for the Web.

PHP: An increasingly popular scripting language based on C, Perl and Java, that is well suited for Web development. A good thing about PHP is that you can get more functionality with it right out of the box than you can with ASP.

pixel (for picture element): The smallest dot that a computer can display on-screen. Images created for the Web and spacing attributes in HTML tags are commonly measured in pixels.

plain text: A text format that doesn't include formatting codes designating the layout and appearance of text.

platform: A computer hardware and software standard, such as Windows, IBM PC-compatible, or Macintosh personal computer.

plug-in: An accessory or utility program that extends the capabilities of an application, such as Real Audio Player.

program: See *application*.

progressive JPEG: Like interlaced GIF, progressive JPEG enables an image to load in stages of increasingly higher resolution.

properties: Characteristics of an object, often called *attributes*, that define its state, appearance, or value.

protocol: A set of rules for how programs on a network interact. These rules generally include requirements for formatting data and error checking.

query: A method by which data is requested from a server. You enter a query to search a database.

QuickTime: Apple Computer's standard for integrating video and sound into application programs. QuickTime files are often used on the Web for full-motion video.

RAM (random access memory): Computer memory that stores the ongoing work of any operating systems and applications running at the moment. Think of a computer's RAM as short-term memory and its hard drive as long-term memory.

raster image: The horizontal pattern of lines, made up of pixels, that forms an image on a computer screen. See also *bitmapped image*.

raw code: Used to refer to the HTML programming behind a Web page. Can also be used to refer to any kind of programming code.

RealAudio: A sound technology developed by Progressive Networks to enable streaming sound play on Web pages.

relative link (URL): A link set by using a path within a Web site directory structure that doesn't include the domain name. For example: `<a HREF="/resources/file_name.html">`. Contrast with *absolute link*.

render: Describes the action when a browser converts HTML code into viewable graphics and text. Also means to convert an outline of an image into a detailed version. Used when working with three-dimensional images.

resolution: The number of picture elements per unit in an image. Resolution on a printer is described in dots per inch (dpi). Resolution on a monitor is described in pixels horizontally and lines vertically.

ROM (read-only memory): Storage capacity that can be read but not deleted or altered. For example, you can't save data to or delete information from a standard CD-ROM; you can only read it or copy information off of it.

router: A device that reads the destination address on information sent over a network and sends the information to the next step in its route.

sans serif: A typeface category in which the individual characters have no cross-strokes at the ends of the main strokes.

scripting language: A computer language, such as JavaScript, ASP, or VBScript. Because they can run within a Web browser they are often used to add interactive features to a Web site.

scrolling: Moving a window horizontally or vertically to make the information that extends beyond the viewing area visible.

search engine: *1.* A Web site that contains searchable databases or search programs capable of retrieving other Web pages based on user queries. *2.* A program created to search the contents of a Web site for information related to a specific topic or keyword that a user supplies.

serif: A typeface category in which the individual characters have cross-strokes at the ends of the main strokes.

server (or Web server): A computer connected to the Internet that "serves" files by sending them to another computer. The Internet is a client/server arrangement. The server is on a remote computer and responds to requests from the client. See also *client*.

SGML (Standard Generalized Markup Language): A sequence of characters organized physically as a set of entities and logically into a hierarchy of elements. A document definition, specification, and creation mechanism that makes platform and display differences across multiple computers irrelevant to the delivery and rendering of documents.

shareware: Copyrighted software that can be freely shared with others provided that certain restrictions regarding distribution, as specified by the author, are followed. These restrictions often involve paying a fee to the author for continued use after a free trial period.

Shockwave: A Macromedia product for viewing Director files, Flash movies, and FreeHand files. Shockwave plug-ins exist for both Macintosh and Windows systems.

special characters: Typed characters, such as ~ and &, and foreign characters, such as letters with accents. On Web pages, these characters must be created as HTML entities or by using special character tags. With the exception of the underline (or underscore) character, these characters should not be used in filenames for pages that will appear on the Web. See also *character tags*.

splash screen: An opening screen that appears when you start a program or first access some Web sites. Many splash screens on the Web are created in Macromedia Flash and usually include some kind of animation. Splash screens have fallen from grace, however, because many people think they are a waste of time and energy to create and to watch. If you do feel compelled to start your site with a splash screen at least provide a skip button so users can go right into the site if they prefer.

start tag: In HTML programming, identifies the start of an HTML element. Can include attributes. See also *close tag*.

streaming: A technology that enables sound, video, or other data to begin playing as soon as enough material has downloaded so that the file can play as the rest downloads.

string: A series of related text or formatting characters.

subdirectory (or subfolder): A directory (also known as a folder) that resides inside another directory (or folder). See also *directory*.

surfing: The act of moving from one place to another on the Web with no apparent plan or pattern — following any "wave" (or link) that looks good.

synchronize: To arrange events so that they happen simultaneously.

syntax: Rules that govern the use of code in programming languages.

system (or network) administrator: The person or group responsible for configuring and maintaining a network or Web server.

T1 line: A high-speed, dedicated connection to the Internet. Transmits a digital signal at 1.544 megabits per second.

T3 line: A very high-speed, dedicated connection to the Internet. Transmits a digital signal at 44.746 megabits per second.

table tags: In HTML, tags that use columns and rows (much like a spreadsheet) to organize text and/or graphics in relation to one another on a Web page.

tag: The formal name for an element of HTML, usually enclosed in angle brackets (<>).

TCP/IP (Transmission Control Protocol/Internet Protocol): A suite of protocols and services used to manage network communications and applications over the Internet.

third-party: An accessory, such as a plug-in or programming code, manufactured by a separate vendor and designed to work with a given brand of computer equipment or application.

tool: *1.* An icon or palette item in a graphical program that performs specific functions when selected. *2.* A useful software program.

transparent GIF (tGIF): Generally, a GIF that appears as a graphic that "floats" over the background of a Web page because the image's background is transparent. Transparency can be set to any single color section, making it appear as if that area of the image has disappeared.

typeface: The distinctive design of a set of type. Grouped into two categories: serif and sans serif.

UNIX: Pronounced "you-nicks." An operating system written in the C programming language for a variety of computers, from PCs to mainframes. Many Web servers use the UNIX operating system.

upload: To move information from your computer to a remote computer, as in uploading Web site files to a server.

URL (Uniform Resource Locator): Pronounced "U-R-L" or "earl." Server and path information that locates a document on the Internet. Example: http://www.domain_name.com

user: A person who visits a Web site.

utility software: Software used to maintain and improve a computer system's efficiency.

vector graphics: Images whose shapes are described by geometric formulas. Vector files are resolution independent, meaning that they're always drawn at the best possible resolution of the device generating them. Because even a fairly complex geometric shape can be described in a few lines of text as a formula, vector graphics tend to be much smaller than typical bitmap images, which have to be described by using several bits of data for each pixel in the image.

viewer: *1.* A special program launched by a browser to display elements, such as sound files or video, that the browser can't display. *2.* A person who visits a Web site.

viewing window: A defined area of the computer screen through which portions of text or other information can be seen. See also *window*.

virtual reality: An artificial environment experienced through sensory stimuli (as sights and sounds) provided by a computer and in which your actions partially determine what happens in the environment.

Visual Basic Scripting Edition (VBScript): The Microsoft scripting language designed to compete with JavaScript. It's basically a stripped-down version of Visual Basic, a program used to create Windows applications.

VRML (Virtual Reality Modeling Language): A language that enables the creation of three-dimensional models and walk-through spaces that provide a more real-life experience. Graphics can be mapped to the surfaces of three-dimensional models, and links can be attached to surfaces. Links can display a media type, take users to another model or another part of the current model, or perform any of the functions of any Web hyperlink.

Web designer (or developer): A professional or hobbyist who creates Web pages.

Web page: One file in a collection of files that make up a Web site. Usually used to describe the first page that appears on a Web site. See also *home page*.

Web server: See *server*.

Web site: A specific location on the Internet, housed on a Web server and accessible through a URL. Consists of one or more Web pages.

Webmaster: One of many titles used to describe people who design Web sites. (I've always preferred Electronic Goddess.)

window: A frame on a computer screen that displays information, such as a document or application.

Windows: Microsoft's operating system (available in Versions 3.1, 95, 98, 2000, ME, NT, and XP)

Windows Media: Microsoft's answer to Real and QuickTime technologies. There are various Windows Media formats, such as ASF and WMA, which are the most widely used copyright-protected video and music formats capable of video (like Real and QuickTime) and CD-quality music like MP3.

wizard: A special mini-program within a software product that leads you step-by-step through a task.

World Wide Web (WWW): All Web servers available on the Internet.

World Wide Web Consortium (W3C): An industry group that seeks to promote standards for the evolution of the Web and interoperability among Web products by producing specifications and reference software.

WYSIWYG (What You See Is What You Get): Pronounced "wizzy-wig." Describes HTML authoring tools and other programs that attempt to show on-screen what the final document will look like.

zip: A compression method used on Windows and DOS computers. WinZip is a popular compression program that creates zip files, which store data in a compressed format so that it requires less space on a hard drive and can be transferred more quickly over a network, such as the Internet. Uses the .zip file extension.

zipped archive: A file that consists of compressed files.

zone: The right-most part of a Web address, which tells you what type of institution the name is related to. Examples include the familiar .com (commercial), .edu (educational), .net (network operations), .gov (U.S. government), or .mil (U.S. military). Most countries also have a country code, such as .us (United States), .uk (United Kingdom), and .au (Australia).

zoom: To enlarge a document view so that it fills the screen, or to make it smaller so that more of the document can be seen.

Appendix B

Great Sites Designed with Dreamweaver and Contribute

In This Chapter

▶ Hot Latin Tracks showcases music library online

▶ Filmmaker combines the power of Flash and Dreamweaver

▶ ModernMethod shows its stuff with interactivity

▶ . . . and a couple more to look at, too

As the clear choice of many professional Web designers, Dreamweaver deserves credit for providing the development power behind many of the most popular sites on the Web. Taking the time to review some of these sites, and appreciate how they were created, is an ideal way to pick up good ideas for your own Web project.

Many of the sites featured in this chapter take advantage of the latest Web technologies, integrating Dynamic HTML, Flash, and more to create vivid animations and powerful interactivity.

All of the sites in this chapter are also great candidates for Contribute because they lend themselves to development by multiple people and Macromedia's careful attention to integration means that any site designed in Dreamweaver can easily be edited with Contribute.

The sites featured in this chapter provide an excellent overview of what you can do with Dreamweaver — and they're all great examples of what's possible on the Web today. Review the descriptions of these sites to find out what tools they used and then spend some time online, visiting each site to appreciate the full impact of their design, navigation, and other features.

Latin Music Library Is Online Resource

www.HotLatinTracks.com

The Hot Latin Tracks music library, shown in Figure B-1, uses its Web site to showcase an exceptional variety of authentic Latin music and make it easy for clients to sample music from a wide range of Latin styles including Salsa, Flamenco, and Latin Rock.

The site features work by a long list of composers, arrangers, instrumentalists, vocalists, engineers and music editors. But they'll tell you right away, they're not Web designers, so they hired a professional Web design company to build the site and use Contribute to update pages and add new titles and sound files.

The music at Hot Latin Tracks is often used in commercials, television shows and films. If you don't find the music you want in the library, they'll be happy to compose something specially for you.

Figure B-1:
Hot Latin
Tracks
(www.
hotlatin
tracks.
com)
showcases
a Latin
music
library
featuring a
wide range
of styles,
including
Tango,
Salsa, and
Mambo.

Presenting Film and Photography

www.mashat.com

When F.M. Mashat, a photographer and filmmaker, decided to take his work online, he wanted more than just a static Web site. He wanted to create a site that had the look and feel of a major motion picture, yet still loaded quickly and was easy to navigate. He also had the challenge of presenting both of his talents — film and photography — in one site (see the opening page in Figure B-2).

He found just what he was looking for in Francisco Rivera, a multi-talented Web designer, who drew on his experience with animation and the entertainment industry to help Mashat create a dynamic, almost cinematic site. (To find out more about Rivera, visit his site at www.balam.net.) This entire project was done in Flash, using Dreamweaver to pull it all together. The biggest challenges were keeping the image and film clips small enough that they would load quickly. In the case of the film clips, they opted to create three versions of each clip: one for very low bandwidth connections (and limited quality), another for faster modems, and finally one for visitors with high-speed connections that made the film look as good as possible on the Web.

Figure B-2:
FM Mashat's site (www.mashat.com) captures the work of a filmmaker and photographer with almost cinematic presentation.

A site such as this one that is designed by a professional developer is ideally suited to Contribute because the client, in this case the photographer, can use Contribute to make simple updates to the Web site himself rather than having to go back to his consultant every time.

Modern Web Design

www.modernmethod.com

The ModernMethod Web site shown in Figure B-3 is essentially a self-promotional piece designed in Corel PhotoPaint and Flash and then pieced together with Dreamweaver.

Yanier Gonzalez, creative director, says, "Using Dreamweaver and other products from the Macromedia line makes creating big sites bearable. We use the Image Map and JavaScript Behavior tools extensively to allow our designers to get more done in less time and free our programmers to work on the hard stuff."

ModernMethod is now starting to give Contribute to their clients to make it easy for them to update and revise their own sites when they want to make small changes and save the staff at ModernMethod for the more complex projects and significant changes to the site.

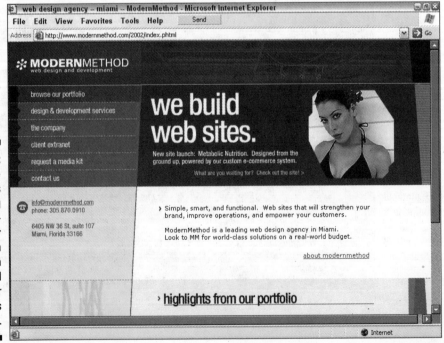

Figure B-3:
Modern-Method has been using Dreamweaver for years on their own sites as well as their client's sites.

Learning to Say It Better

www.sayitbetter.com

When Kare Anderson put her talents to work online, she was one of the first authors and professional speakers to take advantage of this new medium. Kare's Say It Better Web site (see Figure B-4) is packed with tips about communication, negotiation, and joint marketing. It's not only a great marketing tool for her business, it's also a great resource for your and a real-life example of the ways small and medium-sized businesses are making valuable information available to their visitors, and attracting repeat customers as a result.

If you're an independent consultant or a small-business owner, follow Kare's example and offer more than just your bio, customer list, or portfolio online. Kare's site features a wealth of joint-marketing and communication tips, as well as references to other speakers and consultants. She's gone a step further with her e-mail newsletter — a relatively inexpensive service that keeps visitor's informed and more likely to come back.

Figure B-4: Kare Anderson's Say it Better Web site is packed with great marketing and communications tips and resources.

Kare employs a professional editor to update her site (Malinda McCain of `www.sharewords.com/copyedit`), but she's now considering using Contribute to do some of the updates herself. Even though her editor uses Microsoft FrontPage to work on the site, Kare can still use Macromedia Contribute for her own updates.

Yours Truly

`http://www.janinewarner.com`

I would love to take credit for the design of my own Web site (see Figure B-5), but the truth is that my talented co-author, Ivonne Berkowitz, developed my site using Dreamweaver's great features to create a complex design that is simple to update and maintain. (I can handle all the technical development on my site, but Ivonne is a much better designer.)

The subtle animation she created on the front page made it possible for me to include quotes from two different sources, and the roll-over effects make the navigation buttons come alive. I use Dreamweaver to make regular additions to the site and handle site management when I want to add new sections or make more significant changes.

Figure B-5:
My own
Web site at
`www.`
`janine`
`warner.`
`com` was, of
course, built
with Dream-
weaver.

Just for the record, I really do think Dreamweaver is the best Web design program on the market, and I can't imagine using anything else on my own site. Now that I have Contribute as an additional resource, I'm looking forward to being able to use my assistant, who's not a professional Web designer, to help me make regular updates to my site, such as adding in my newspaper columns as they are published.

Index

FOR DUMMIES

The easy way to get more done and have more fun

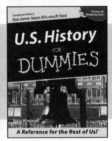

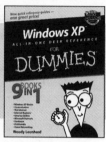